BURT
LANCASTER

BURT LANCASTER

MINTY CLINCH

STEIN AND DAY/*Publishers*/New York

First published in the United States of America in 1985
Copyright © 1984 by Minty Clinch
All rights reserved, Stein and Day, Incorporated
Printed in the United States of America

STEIN AND DAY/*Publishers*
Scarborough House
Briarcliff Manor, N.Y. 10510

Library of Congress Cataloging in Publication Data

Clinch, Minty.
  Burt Lancaster.

  Filmography: p.
  Bibliography: p.
  Includes index.
  1. Lancaster, Burt, 1913-   2. Moving-picture
actors and actresses—United States—Biography.
I. Title.
PN2287.L246C55   1985   791.43′028′0924 [B]   84-40625
ISBN 0-8128-3016-4

CONTENTS

ILLUSTRATIONS

one
LADY LUCK

Burt Lancaster was born under a lucky star. It rose unspectacularly enough on Friday, 2 November 1913, when a poor but respectable couple celebrated the birth of their fourth child. It was a healthy blond-haired, blue-eyed boy whom they, in due course, christened Burton Stephen.

The Lancaster family apartment was at 209 East 106th Street in Manhattan's East Harlem. In those days the predominantly Italian neighbourhood was working class, rather than the crime-infested ghetto it has become today. However there was nothing in this drab urban background to suggest that one day the infant would make himself more millions than the solid citizens could imagine in their wildest dreams, nor that he would break all the rules at the very start of his screen career by setting up a production company that flouted Hollywood's entrenched studio system. Nor could the olive-skinned children he fought in the streets have foreseen that young 'Dutch' Lancaster would use his looks to create a box-office legend, then search the international cinema for parts that would prove he could act as well.

Even seventy years later, there are few clues in Lancaster's childhood as to the strangely ambivalent man he would become. There is no record of the temper that would be the scourge of Hollywood during his early days in the industry, nor of the social conscience that would inspire him to fly, at his own expense, from a film location in Paris to Washington for a single day to march in support of Dr Martin Luther King. He was no great enthusiast as a child actor, performing at school under duress because it earned plus marks towards the total he needed to be sent to summer camp. That, for an ordinary street-smart kid like Burt in the early twenties, was the great annual escape for which any sacrifice was worthwhile.

Burt's father, James H. Lancaster, generally known as Jim, worked downtown in the Madison Square Garden branch of the New York City Post Office in the safe, if uninspiring occupation of clerk. His performance was solidly responsible rather than spectacular, and he rose steadily to become supervisor, the highest position his blind alley could offer, at which point he earned forty-eight dollars a week.

It doesn't sound much, but it was enough to keep his wife and four children – Jane, the eldest and the only girl, William, James and Burton – from going hungry. As the landlord's daughter, their mother inherited the house in which they lived. It was divided into flats, with communal lavatories on each floor, but the proprietors had no great advantages over their tenants, as Burt recalled many years later from the depths of an armchair in a luxury Beverly Hills restaurant.

'Like our neighbours, we Lancasters just squeaked by, yet it was a rich life because there was a great deal of love and affection in our home. My mother was a strong-willed, formidable character – a woman who insisted on honesty, truth and loyalty. My father was a gentle, kind, warm sort of a man. We lived well. I wore my brothers' hand-me-down clothes, true, but when you're young, that just doesn't matter. So I was lucky. We had all the food we needed on the table – in those days food was cheap. My mother would send me to the corner shop and I'd get the greens thrown in for nothing. At the butcher's, it was the same story. The sweetbreads and the hearts were given to you.'

Although the family liked to believe they were descended from the aristocratic English House of Lancaster, the evidence points towards a more immediate Irish heritage. Both parents were outstandingly good looking and their most famous son recalls that even when his mother was in her forties, guys whistled appreciatively at her in the street. The Lancasters liked to keep open house as far as their means allowed and to join in the open-air street life so beloved by the Italian community. Down-and-outs, instinctively scenting a soft touch, would knock on the door of the flat. When Mrs Lancaster saw them, she'd bawl them out, then she'd relent and feed them.

She'd even talk broken English to her neighbours, many of them newly arrived in the turn-of-the-century wave of immigration from Europe, so that they wouldn't feel at a disadvantage. On warm summer evenings, Jim would sit on the front step and sing Irish songs in a soft clear voice, and his hot-blooded Mediterranean audience would respond enthusiastically. Burt's first taste of show business came when he joined his father on one such occasion. Jim stopped in mid-song, but continued with the accompaniment, leaving the boy on his own. 'That way I rated the applause,' Burt recalled. 'It was my first applause and I thoroughly enjoyed it.'

The new generation of flaxen-haired Lancasters stood out among their Latin contemporaries but, to this day, Burt isn't sure why the Italians, believing him to be German when he was in fact Anglo-Irish, persisted in calling him 'Dutch'. Typical perversity, he assumed, but it didn't stop him joining their gangs, nor from hurling insults at the opposition. That was the way of East Harlem youth in a rough and abrasive but non-criminal environment.

Any temptation to join the minority on the wrong side of the law that Burt and his brothers may have felt was ruthlessly stamped out by their mother. She didn't hesitate to use her strong right arm to impose her stern humanitarian integrity on her sons. 'Ma was such a determined lady and she instilled concepts as strong as an orthodox religion. However poor you were, you never lied, you never stole and you always stuck by a promise. I've always remembered her rules because she made sure I would. If I didn't honour them, I could expect – and got – a cuff that hurt.'

Burt also remembers the long cold Harlem winters when he had to keep on the move so as not to freeze. The Lancasters may have had enough to eat, but their clothing was never quite sufficient to cope with the climate. The children used the streets as their playground, and enjoyed the exhilaration of the running battles that occupied out-of-school hours. They fought enthusiastically for their rights, gang against gang, avenging insults with fists or sticks and stones, but never with weapons.

'You had to fight to assert yourself in those days in East Harlem, but it was a wonderful place to live because we always shared and took pot luck. I hoped for a better world for my children to grow up in, but then I realised that money had nothing to do with it. When we lived in Bel Air and I had to make a baseball field for them in the garden, I used to tell them how lucky I'd been to be able to walk out of my home and there were parks nearby, schools, backyards and roofs to play on.'

Burt was a small child, expected by his parents to become the runt of the family, and he rapidly developed the quick reactions and fleetness of foot he needed to compensate in a crisis. From the age of seven, his burning ambition was to be like Douglas Fairbanks, to which end he would haunt the Atlas Theatre in his neighbourhood from opening time

3

at eleven in the morning. Twelve hours later, he'd still be there, transfixed by *The Mark of Zorro*, having quite forgotten about mealtimes in between. At this point, one of his brothers would be sent to bring him home, using whatever show of force might be necessary. That however was only the beginning of the chaos the would-be acrobat could create.

'He'd go around the house jumping over everything in sight, trying to imitate Fairbanks' feats,' Jim Lancaster wrote in an article about his son in *Photoplay* in January 1953. 'He was a great movie fan, but it never occurred to me that he'd eventually become an athlete. He was a dreamer when he was a little kid. He could be off in his own world for hours, and he wouldn't hear a thing you'd say to him. He grew up into an essentially serious-minded guy, inclined to get intense about ideas and situations.'

The more cerebral side of Burt Lancaster was initially manifested by a consuming passion for books which he assuaged at the neighbourhood public library throughout his days at P.S. 83 and De Witt Clinton High School. In other respects, he was an undistinguished student, though he showed enough promise at the despised pursuit of acting at the age of eleven for his teacher to send a theatrical agent round to his parents' apartment to ask if they'd allow him to study on a scholarship. The play he'd been spotted in was called *Three Pills in a Bottle*, and Burt played a small boy in a wheelchair who was dying of leukaemia.

'It was sissy stuff. I never wanted to be an actor and I'd been so embarrassed about doing that play. There was no way I was going to have anything to do with that scholarship.'

Nor did he, concentrating instead on singing and athletics. Music apparently was less sissy than acting, and Burt fostered an ambition to be an opera singer by performing regularly in the church choir. Not surprisingly, his Italian neighbourhood was full of would-be opera stars, both amateur and professional, and sneaking into the local Town Hall during performances was a way of life for Burt. His strategy was to wait outside until the interval, then walk in brazenly without paying and find a seat, and it never failed him. His fascination with opera has lasted until the present day, but his potential as a singer ended abruptly when his voice broke.

'I lost it and I've spent the rest of my life searching for it,' he commented wryly. Nor was his aptitude for the piano any more striking. 'Ordinarily it's comparatively simple for me to learn anything in which I'm sufficiently interested but learning to play a piano – brother, that really stumped me. I practised for three months once – hard – and I can manoeuvre my way through a few simple arrangements. Student stuff. But someday I'd like to be a real musician.'

His skill at athletics proved much more enduring. When he was thirteen, he began to grow rapidly, eventually outstripping his brothers to become the tallest member of the family at six foot two inches. He had a lithe muscular build to match his physique and a natural aptitude for a range of ball games. His talents on the field were developed at the Union Settlement House on 104th Street, which he credits, along with the public library, for the fact that he avoided juvenile delinquency during his teenage years. When he became famous, he paid off this debt by sending large annual donations to keep the Settlement House afloat, and on occasion, visited it in person.

It was basically a youth club and sports centre where adolescents could play games, do gymnastics and generally fill their free time more profitably and less dangerously than by hanging out in gangs in the streets. That was okay for pre-teenage children, but adolescents who went out looking for trouble were apt to find it, and lawlessness could quickly become a bad habit.

Instead Burt used his new-found height and strength to become something of a star at basketball, a talent he developed at high school to the level at which he won an athletics scholarship to New York University. Meanwhile he had met his lifelong henchman, Nick Cravat, at the Settlement House. Although the dark pint-sized Nick and the golden giant that Lancaster had become had nothing in common at this time but an abiding love of acrobatics, it was enough to form the basis of the most enduring friendship in Lancaster's career, one that would carry him through his years of poverty in the Depression and last into old age.

The two youths started out together in stunt gymnastics, then trained under Curley Brent, an Australian ex-circus performer whom Burt spotted one day working out on the horizontal bars. When the veteran saw the admiration in the watcher's eyes, he offered to teach him and so great was the pupil's enthusiasm that the lessons soon became daily. At this point, Burt had to consider whether to opt for a circus career or take up his place at college, a decision he made with characteristic common sense inspired by his indomitable mother.

'The whole community took pride in kids that got on. My brothers went to New York University. So did I. I think it was a much more stable world in those days. When I was growing up, people in East Harlem helped each other. It was a community so people cared. Now

5

they're more interested in getting what they can than in taking pride in what they do.'

Lancaster began his university course in the autumn of 1929, aged seventeen. He played basketball, baseball and football and took part in boxing, track and gymnastics with a view to qualifying as an athletics coach and physical education teacher. Unfashionably among his brawny peers, he wanted to study as well but the college was chronically understaffed and classes often had between a hundred and fifty and two hundred students. The teachers delivered their lectures over a loud-speaker system and questions were forbidden which made the tedium unendurable, at least to Burt. By 1931, he'd had enough. 'I walked out of class one day and I never went back.'

Returning to the Settlement House, he resumed instruction under Curley Brent and persuaded Nick Cravat to join him in a double acrobatic act. Although Lancaster was two years younger than his diminutive partner, he was always the leader, the one who made and implemented the decisions. The pattern was set during their first profes-sional engagements for which they billed themselves as Lang and Cra-vat. Once they'd reached the necessary standard, they scraped up ninety dollars to buy a decrepit car, and drove it, somewhat apprehen-sively, to Petersburg, Virginia, where the Kay Brothers Circus was looking for a bar act.

Their audition was a nightmare of falls, bruises and ripped tights, and the fledgling act was lucky to get hired for three dollars a week, plus board. For this meagre wage, the pair were expected to set up the tents, ride in the parades and fill in on any odd jobs that nobody else would do. As it was the depths of the Depression, Lang and Cravat were operating in a buyer's market and considered themselves lucky to be employed at all so they did whatever they were asked without complain-ing. By the end of the first month, they were gratified to learn that they'd developed their act sufficiently to be rewarded with a two dollar a week rise.

They stayed with the Kay Brothers for thirty-weeks in all, then moved on to a succession of small-time tent shows, carnivals and vaudeville, becoming an expert bar act as the engagements came and went. On occasion, they toured for a while with the big-time Ringling Brothers Circus, then returned to the nightclub circuit where they earned a not very munificent fifteen dollars a show.

It was a nomadic life, full of colour and camaraderie, and it provided Lancaster with a kaleidoscopic view of the underbelly of America. He

6

saw the rawest side of show business where those like himself, who lived dangerously, competed with freaks and clowns for audience time and slim pickings. He had little control over his own destiny as he travelled ever onwards in pursuit of work and wages to keep body and soul together, but he developed the survivor's instincts that were to serve him so well when he went into films.

In 1935, he attempted to settle down, as least so far as his personal life was concerned, by marrying June Ernst, a circus aerialist whom he admired for being 'the only woman in America who could do horizontal bar tricks'. As a basis for a stable marriage, it wasn't anywhere near enough and the couple were divorced the next year. However, Lancaster acquired a more enduring benefit from the liaison in the shape of his mother-in-law, an accomplished trapeze artist, with whom he worked for the next few years.

It was in the late thirties that Burt decided to take another look at the despised profession of acting. He returned to Manhattan and joined the Federal Theater Project, the theatrical branch of the Work Projects Administration that had been set up by Franklin Roosevelt as part of his acclaimed 'New Deal' to find occupations for the unemployed. Lancaster studied under those who had learned their trade from Richard Boleslawski, the Polish-born film director who had interpreted the Stanislavsky method of acting in his book, *Six Lessons of Dramatic Art*. This was the direct forerunner of the Method school of acting that became so popular after World War II.

Burt learned to good effect, but he wasn't yet ready to commit himself to a theatrical career. Instead he returned to the thrills of the big top in a circus in St Louis, although nearly a decade on the road had netted him nothing financially and precious little in terms of career prospects. At this moment in time, fate intervened when he ripped open the forefinger of his right hand during rehearsal and it became so badly infected that the doctors advised him that leaving the show was the only alternative to amputation.

Discouraged, he went to Chicago and put up with circus friends, the Smiletas, while he looked for his first regular job. Unqualified for anything but the fringes of show business, he was obliged to accept a position as lingerie salesman at Marshall Field's department store and it wasn't long before the ladies of the Windy City were responding enthusiastically to his sales pitch. He claims it came naturally to him, something there is no reason to doubt because he later won his only Oscar for a similar con job in *Elmer Gantry*. Perhaps his lady-killing was

7

a little too lethal for the conservative store, but he was rapidly moved on to gents' haberdashery, and then to furniture.

The boredom of the work and the restrictions of the regular hours were anathema to a man who was accustomed to the freedom of circus life, and to the delighted surprise of the other assistants, he relieved the monotony with a few acrobatic stunts across the fitted carpeting. The management was less amused and before six months had passed, he was out on his ear. Later he worked as a fireman, an engineer in a meat-packing company and a serviceman for home refrigerators. He also spent several weeks as a singing waiter in a dingy night spot in New Jersey, the only time his putative operatic skills were plied for commercial gain, before finding a more suitable niche in the Community Concerts Bureau run by CBS in New York City.

They needed a personable, silver-tongued salesman to travel around the country promoting the Bureau's new shows before they arrived in town. Who better than Burt Lancaster, with his wide toothy smile and his spectacular physique? Delighted by its musical associations, he accepted the job and was duly trained for it, but had no time to dig himself in before the draft letter dropped through his mail box in July 1942.

It was at this point in his life that his lucky star began to gain ascendancy. He might, after all, have had to fight in a global war. He might even have been killed. Instead, when he reported to Fort Riley, he learned that his time in the circus had qualified him to become an entertainer in the Special Service Division of the Fifth Army. Nearly a year later he landed in North Africa and followed the troops through the Sicilian and Italian campaigns into Austria. As part of a revue called *Stars and Gripes*, he wrote sketches, directed and occasionally performed them in and around the battle zones for twenty-six largely enjoyable months.

He served as a private with occasional promotions to NCO, usually followed almost immediately by demotion to the ranks. His mild insubordination was triggered by two kinds of officer: those who thought they could stage better revues than he could and those who were rash enough to imply that he was onto a soft option in the Special Services. Though there were elements of truth in both premises, Lancaster was never one to take insults lying down and a fracas invariably ensued.

However he showed leadership of another, probably more useful, kind and displayed the propensity for bucking the system that was to prove so invaluable in his future career, when it came to supplies.

8

'During the war, when I was a Sergeant stationed in the desert near Casablanca,' he recalled, 'the food was pretty terrible. One day when our company was on guard duty at a ration dump nearby, I instructed the boys to take a truck in and load it with hams, bacon, peaches – everything. Our operation was in broad daylight, so straightforward that the lieutenant in charge thought it was legitimate and didn't stop us. We ate like kings for weeks. I could have been court-martialled.'

But he wasn't. Instead he acquired two assets that supported him over the next twenty years or so, and one that remained with him for much longer. The first was Norma Anderson, a USO entertainer, who saw him on stage in Italy and arranged for an introduction that would lead to marriage. The second was a certain insight into military bearing that became the bottom line of his early acting career. In the immediate aftermath of war, plays and films about tough sergeants in combat stations around the globe were standard fare and one who was always ready and able to play them was Burton Stephen Lancaster. The third was an enduring love of Italy that would inspire him to go international in the sixties and seventies: making films for Visconti and Bertolucci and dividing his time between Rome and Los Angeles.

Come the late summer of 1945 and the declaration of peace, Lancaster found himself demobbed and unemployed in New York, a position from which it was far easier to appreciate the reality of Norma Anderson than those nebulous future advantages on the stage military or cultural front. Accordingly, he turned his footsteps towards the office of a radio producer, Ray Knight, where Norma was working as a secretary, with a view to taking her out to lunch. On the way up in the elevator, he was surprised to see a stranger watching him closely, and even more surprised to receive a phone call in Norma's office a few minutes after he'd kissed her hello.

Would he be interested, the stranger enquired, in playing a leading role on Broadway? The caller was Jack Mahor, an associate of Irving Jacobs, the show's producer, and the part was the first of many tough sergeants. Mahor thought Lancaster looked just right for it and sent him hotfoot to the Warwick Hotel to audition. With little expectation of being chosen, Burt bluffed his way through the interview and was astonished to learn that he had an alter ego: Sergeant Joseph Mooney, in Harry Brown's play, *A Sound of Hunting*, about American GIs on the Italian Front at Cassino during World War II. (When the play was filmed in 1952 by Columbia, as *Eight Iron Men*, Lee Marvin took the Lancaster role.)

Directed by Anthony Brown, the show opened some weeks later on 21 November 1945 at the Lyceum Theatre to reasonable reviews and lousy business, probably because it presented the bitterness of war to audiences who were only too aware of it, but preferred to forget. Burton Lancaster, as he was billed, shared the limelight with Sam Levene, Frank Lovejoy, William Beal and Stacy Harris for the twenty-three nights the show lasted. 'Acting on stage is nowhere near as frightening as performing as a circus acrobat,' was Burt's verdict. 'I wasn't nervous at all. I said to myself, "What can happen to me? I can miss a line, but I can't get hurt."'

Nor was he, even by the New York critics who can be so adept at assassinating a fledgling career. *PM* found his performance 'attractive', while Robert Garland of the *New York Journal-American*, wrote, 'Burton Lancaster, as Mooney, is the non-com every private prays for.' Others were equally enthusiastic about the physical presence and commanding personality of the beautiful blond hulk, and Hollywood's talent scouts were quick to take the hint and pass it on. Within weeks, seven firm offers from major studios were winging their way from the West Coast to Manhattan and Lancaster, now thirty-two, was on his way west.

two
JACKPOT

In 1946 Hollywood wasn't quite living up to its reputation as the fleshpot of the universe. Food rationing had killed the extravaganza circuit stone dead and Humphrey Bogart, Ray Milland and Dick Powell were going to work by motor bike to beat oil rationing. Certainly actors were coming home from the war, or whatever peripheral theatre of it their talents had led them to, but the industry hadn't re-stocked itself in five years. The studios, sitting firmly on the contracts of an ageing galaxy of stars, many of whom had tried but failed to buck the system in the thirties, saw no reason for change, let alone revolution.

Television had been invented, but it wasn't yet a force in the average home, and the tycoons saw a few years leeway before they needed to face up to its reality. In this at least they were right. Audiences, starved of entertainment during the war when propaganda films of the direst simplicity had been the prescribed diet, were anxious to get themselves in front of a screen, any screen so long as it had images of old favourites and new glamour on it. Gable, Grant, Fonda, Stewart, Bogart, Cagney, Cooper and Co. were employable and employed, but they couldn't hope to fill all the heroes' roles in an expanding market.

By the early fifties, the time would be ripe for another kind of star, personifying the restless rebelliousness of the emerging beat generation. Marlon Brando and James Dean were the leaders of the louche cult, universally identified with by the youth of the day because of their curl-lipped aggression and their non-conformist charisma. They would be the new anti-heroes, their scowls the antithesis of the flashing smiles that had made Hollywood rich. But before they swept all before them, there was still time for a sandwich generation of clean-cut hunks to establish themselves. The fastest off the starting blocks was Burt Lancaster.

When Hollywood columnist, Sheilah Graham, first saw him on the set of *The Killers*, his first film, she was overwhelmed. 'Masculinity was oozing from every pore,' she wrote. 'He was thirty-two but looked twenty-two, and what a physique! I could see the muscles rippling up and down beneath his open thirt. It is a pleasure being with a future star at the beginning. He is always so friendly, so eager to please. He makes a hit and it is a different man.'

Her words were prophetic, for Lancaster had a lot going for him. Apart from being so spectacularly well-equipped physically, his foot-loose years in the big top had given him a shrewd idea of the safeguards he needed to find security and rich rewards in his new domain. Better still, he was prepared to take expert advice on how to acquire them. The man he chose to give it was Harold Hecht, an agent to whom he was introduced by Sam Levene, his lead actor in *A Sound of Hunting*. Hecht was the son of a New York iron contractor, and some seven years older than his prospective client. He'd been a student under Richard Boleslawski in the early twenties at the American Laboratory Theatre. In the thirties, he'd assisted the Polish refugee on his Broadway productions, then worked in Hollywood as a dancer for Martha Graham's company before returning to the Federal Theatre Project where Burt himself had learnt the rudiments of his trade.

After his war service, Hecht expanded his literary agency to include actors and directors, in theory at least. When Lancaster met him the reality was somewhat different. 'I know everybody,' Hecht told him, 'but I have few clients. If you sign with me, you'd be important to me. I'd work harder for you because I want to eat and I'd have to keep you working.'

Logical enough, in Lancaster's opinion, and the two men went out to celebrate the deal. Halfway through the meal, the agent paused and looked his new client in the eye. 'You know,' he said, 'I don't like being an agent. I want to produce pictures.'

For Lancaster, it was a moment of truth. 'That was what I wanted to do,' he told Hedda Hopper some years later when Hecht-Lancaster was part of screen history. 'Suddenly we began laughing. Here were a couple of bums without a quarter between us discussing producing our own pictures. Hecht laughed and said, "You never can tell. Maybe in five years we'll make it."'

First, however, they had to sift through the seven offers Hollywood had made to the aspiring actor. Most of them came from major studios and stipulated seven years hard labour in the exclusive service of the moguls but one, from Hal B. Wallis, was more interesting. The Chicago-born Wallis had been head of production at Warner Brothers through its most successful years before leaving in 1944 to set up his own company on the basis of a solid reputation as a shrewd and tough administrator. Interpreting the straws in the wind more astutely than rivals within the Paramount organisation, he offered Lancaster a contract with a difference. It too would run for seven years and require two pictures a year, but there was an outside option clause which allowed the actor to do a third picture each year for whoever he pleased.

The contract was contingent on Burt's passing a screen test and he arrived in Los Angeles in January 1946 to take it. Hecht had negotiated a salary of 100 dollars a week during the preparation period, a flat 10,000 dollar fee if he passed it and a further 1,250 dollars a week when he went to work. In due course, his screen presence proved to Wallis's satisfaction, he joined Kirk Douglas, Lizabeth Scott and Wendell Corey on the producer's books.

Although he didn't know it at the time, the test had been for a leading role in *Desert Fury*, due to roll in August 1946, and this became Lancaster's first Wallis assignment. However the delay infuriated the actor, not least because Norma Anderson was still in Manhattan and he was eager to return to her.

The Gods, however, had other ideas. A New York newspaperman turned scriptwriter, Mark Hellinger, had bought the rights to *The Killers*, a short story by Ernest Hemingway that had first appeared in *Scribner's Magazine* in 1927. It had originally been adapted by John Huston during Army time while he was waiting to be called to war, but Anthony Veiller later took over the screenplay and the credit to avoid embarrassing Huston with his somewhat touchy employers. Now Hellinger was stuck for an actor to play the huge dumb Swede, a boxer who becomes the victim of the assassins of the title. His first choice had been Wayne Morris, a hot property after making *Kid Galahad* for Warners in 1937. He'd just returned to the studio after serving in the Navy, but Warners were asking for a prohibitive 75,000 dollars for the loan. As a first-time producer and his own company a relatively insignificant part of the Universal empire, Hellinger hadn't got that kind of money. He looked instead at Sonny Tufts, but hadn't made up his mind as to his acting ability, when Lancaster gave him a nudge in his direction. Hearing the role was up for grabs, he persuaded Marty Juroc, a member of Hal Wallis's staff who'd once worked for Hellinger, to give his ex-boss a sneak preview of the *Desert Fury* screen test.

The viewing led to a meeting between Hellinger and a seemingly oafish blond giant, alias Lancaster trying to make himself as suitable as possible for the part. That, much to his delight, was entirely suitable. 'I'd always been a Hemingway *aficionado*. I'd read everything he'd ever written. I remember Mark Hellinger asking me what I thought about the script and I said, "Well, the first sixteen pages are Hemingway verbatim, and after that you have a rather interesting whodunnit film, but nothing comparable to Hemingway." He said, "Well, you're not really a dumb Swede after all," and I said I didn't think I was.'

So Lancaster proved the value of his option clause, even before he went to work for Wallis, by signing for *The Killers* and soon he was making his debut in front of the cameras. The director was the experienced Robert Siodmark, whom Burt considered 'particularly well fitted. He is a charming and engaging man and strong dramatic films are his metier.' The German-born Siodmark, who had made his reputation with spine-chillers like *The Phantom Lady* (1944) and *The Spiral Staircase* (1946), was Hellinger's second choice after a young unknown called Don Siegel. Ironically Siegel, who couldn't get free from his Warner's contract on this occasion, directed an inferior re-make of *The Killers*, with Lee Marvin, John Cassavetes (as Swede), Angie Dickinson and Ronald Reagan, in 1964.

The Killers is a classic *film noir*, one of the first to display what would become the fashionable post-war cynicism about man's, and more especially woman's, inhumanity to man. In its irresistible but poisonous heroine (Ava Gardner) and dogged insurance investigator (Edmond O'Brien) who risks his life unnecessarily to uncover a worthless truth, it has two archetypal *film noir* figures. Lancaster's character, on the other hand, is pure Hemingway. He is a simple boxer, a man of honour, silent and slightly stupid, who is rooted in a past in which self-respect and dignity counted for something. Although he's been pulped in the ring, he's never been knocked out, and that is a source of pride.

His fate is sealed from the moment he gives up his faithful girlfriend for the femme fatale who drags him into a numbers racket and then lets him take the rap for her by spending two years in prison. Unable to recognise that the woman he loves is using him, he allows himself to be manipulated after his release and ends up broke and betrayed in Atlantic City, condemned to wander for six long years while he waits for his killers to catch up with him.

In the film, his death by machine-gunning comes quickly, within a few minutes of the opening frames, and his story is subsequently told in flashback. Nor is he the only one to die in a scenario that doesn't leave the bloodshed to the imagination. Siodmark habitually used controlled lighting and striking camera angles to create the dark corners of a sick society, but rarely more successfully than in Swede's dingy room where the doomed giant lies fatalistically waiting for the men who have the contract on him. The claustrophobia of the restricted setting is intensified by the quiet small town darkness outside.

Although the film was officially called Ernest Hemingway's *The Killers*, Hellinger and Siodmark took it on themselves to interpret the elliptical original in more direct and contemporary terms. Where Hemingway's killers are pulp-fiction poseurs, much given to hard-boiled sarcasm, Siodmark's are deadly serious. Where Hemingway focuses on a boy, Nick Adams, who observes the assassination and its aftermath with the baffled innocence of youth, Siodmark concentrates on the insurance investigator, a fearful but indomitable loner who can bring order out of chaos, a solution, as *film noir* requires, out of destruction. With six violent deaths, the occupational hazards of crime are there for all to see, though the film makes no moral judgements.

The end product is a top-class picture that could only do good for anyone involved in it, and that included Burt Lancaster. 'I could be very simple in the part,' he commented. 'There was no need to be highly ostentatious or theatrical. For a new actor, this is much easier than something histrionic. There's no question about the good fortune of being ushered into films in that kind of role.'

As the new boy, he behaved well during shooting, determined to pick up all he could from a director he admired. When Siodmark had to do fifteen or more takes on one small scene, Burt was embarrassed and apologised humbly for his ineptitude. As he'd never witnessed the filming process before, he had no particular ideas on how it should be done, and was content to accept orders as mandatory. In years to come, many a director would wish devoutly that he'd never learned differently.

By August, the shooting was complete and Lancaster could sit back and await the reviews. On both sides of the Atlantic their theme was that he was a sensation, and that a big future was certain to follow. In the *New York Herald-Tribune*, Otis L. Gurnsey Jr recorded that 'he portrays a likeable fall guy in a most promising screen debut', while *Variety* felt that 'he does a strong job'.

When *The Killers* opened in London in November, Dilys Powell described Lancaster as a 'husky, good-looking, straight-browed newcomer' in the *Sunday Times*, while Harris Deans, writing prophetically in the *Sunday Dispatch*, said, 'I have a feeling we're going to see more of Burt Lancaster. I liked his quiet, smooth acting, especially in that first scene in which he just lies on a bed and watches a door waiting for his killers. Doesn't say a word, just watches ... but there is more acting done by the muscles of his face than is often done by another actor using both arms and a voice.' The *Daily Telegraph*'s Campbell Dixon was less whole hearted, but even he gave guarded approval. 'If I am not quite as enthusiastic as the producer about the "sensational discovery", Burt Lancaster, that is not unusual. At least he looks real.'

Burt himself celebrated his triumph with his second marriage which took place on 28 December 1946 in Yuma, Arizona. His bride was the war widow, Norma Anderson, tall, blonde and serenely beautiful on her wedding day. Her husband was asked at the time what feminine trait he disliked most, to which he replied, 'I hate tricks. Most particularly that "you-great-big-wonderful-man-you" routine. Far from flattering, it actually shows no consideration for the person involved. I consider it most unwomanly. If a woman pulls it on me, I dislike her immediately.' Norma was one who didn't, and she won the prize.

The Lancasters lived initially in a house at Malibu Beach, then moved, as custom dictated, into a palatial residence in Bel Air Canyon. Burt's mother had died by this time and his father, newly appointed as his manager, lived with them, as did his brother, Jim, an ex-cop who'd held the family together in the Depression when Burt was at college. Soon there were two children, James and William, in the household and the expenses mounted.

'You know, Mark,' Burt recalled telling Hellinger one day, 'I don't seem to have any money.' 'Well,' Hellinger said, 'you won't. You'll owe the government a great deal of money, you'll be broke for a long while.' And Burt said, 'I don't see how. I lead a fairly moderate life.' And Hellinger replied, 'Well, you have your father out here, don't you? You brought your brother out as your lawyer. You've just bought a car for your brother and one for yourself and you've just bought a house and so forth. Well, if you keep that up, you're going to be broke – in trouble.'

Sound advice certainly, but time made it superflous when Lancaster quickly became one of the wealthiest men in Hollywood. Meanwhile, however, he absorbed it. 'I thought about it quite seriously; that the only responsibility and obligation I have is to try to do my work well and not to worry about those areas in which I am not the wisest man. And the moment I stopped thinking or worrying about

16

finances, I found myself in the black. I began to worry only about m.,
work.'

As *The Killers* had set the careers of both Lancaster and Hellinger on
the right track, this was no great problem, and both men were quick to
capitalise on it. From his own point of view, Burt had no trouble at all
coping with instant stardom. He was arrogant enough to expect it
and old enough to feel that he'd earned it, although his brief Broadway apprenticeship was nothing compared to the years of disappointments and gruellingly hard work for tiny salaries that most of his fellow
actors had to live through before they became 'overnight' sensations in
California.

At this time, Burt's ability to perform was strictly limited, but there
could be no doubting his screen presence, that elusive star quality that
makes or breaks cinema actors. Nor was there any denying his startling
good fortune, as he himself agreed. 'A great case can be made here for
luck, but it was one of those instances of being the right actor in the
right spot at the right time. It might not have happened had I been just
another movie actor who had played bits. That way an actor tends to
come to attention rather slowly. If you're in an important play on
Broadway, you have a better chance because it's the proper showcase.

'If you're in a play and have a good role and you're exciting in it,
and if you have the physical equipment that is important to motion
pictures – how you look, how you move – you are more apt to get a
break that way. And when you do come to Hollywood, you come under
more important circumstances. In my case, it was very much a matter
of being in good physical condition. Movies are, in a large sense, a
matter of movement and physical excitement, and you can get by if you
can move well and have a certain physical presence. And good condition
helps in any kind of acting.'

Hal Wallis, who sat in a spacious office at Paramount because he
knew a good thing when he saw it, hastily ordered a re-write for *Desert
Fury* to accommodate Lancaster's enlarged status. The original part
had been strong, but secondary; the new one would be star stuff.
Meanwhile the producer allowed his tyro to rejoin Mark Hellinger for
Brute Force, on which he had top billing.

Jules Dassin, whose left-wing leanings would soon oblige him to leave
Senator Joseph McCarthy's Hollywood in a hurry, was hired to direct
the brooding prison melodrama from Richard Brooks' screenplay. Lancaster played Joe Collins, one of the five inmates of Cell R-17, whose
stories are told in flashback with a lot of emphasis on their feelings about

17

women. In Collins' case, this means a young wife (Ann Blyth) who has to have an operation for cancer, but refuses to go into hospital unless her husband is at her side. This is sufficient incentive for the small-time crook to lead a jail break in which he and his fellow prisoners are killed. In fact he has walked into a trap set by a sadistic prison officer in the Nazi mould (Hume Cronyn) who knows the escape is on, but lets it go ahead so he can put it down by force.

Brooks, whose combat experience during World War II had stripped away his illusions about the goodness of mankind, wrote a script with a hard core of hatred and futility which is only partly disguised by the close attention given to the prisoners' sweethearts, as required by the Hollywood of the day. Dassin interpreted it in explicitly brutal terms and made points about the prison system that were years ahead of their time.

'Dassin is a very fine director,' Lancaster put on record many years later. 'I was very fortunate to work with him, and with Siodmark before that. Other films I made around this time, like *Desert Fury* and *I Walk Alone*, can only be described as lightweight in their value. But with someone like Dassin I could see that I was working with a man who was knowledgeable and helpful, someone who could excite new ideas in terms of how you wanted to play the part.'

Knowledgeable or not, Dassin had to take a lot of gratuitous advice from his lead actor who started to display his true aggressive colours during the shooting of *Brute Force*. Wherever the credit was due, the material and the finished film pleased the star. 'It was very potent,' he announced, 'and I think for those particular days – the middle of the 1940s – it was a larger-than-life approach to things. The characters were all very strong, and very romantically written – as opposed to the documentary approach to that kind of film.

'Joe Collins was different from the Swede. The Swede was confused and lacked sophistication so when his love affair with the glamorous Ava Gardner went to pieces, he literally didn't care to live any more which is some indication of his limits, if you like. But for Collins in *Brute Force* it was another matter. He wasn't stupid. Of course, he had a very sticky sentimental relationship with Ann Blyth as the crippled girl. But there was one prevailing thing: Collins, in his own uneducated way, was a strong shrewd man with a growing desire to be free. No prison should hold anybody – that's the way he felt. It's a concept that was thought of as romantic in those days, but now, we recognise the fallibility of the penal system, and its inability to do any good. Societies are at last having to face the idea that just putting people in jail doesn't do any good any more, and that maybe society has to come up with a new concept of how to deal with people who break its laws.'

This point of view had considerable appeal to a committed liberal like Burt and he was prepared to tolerate the sexist approach to presentation and publicity in order to get it over. The film's advertising showed one of the actresses, Yvonne De Carlo, in an alluring pose with a caption that read, 'This kind of woman drives men to prison – and then drives them crazy to get out.'

As far as Lancaster was concerned, if that was the way it had to be that was the way it was. 'The emphasis was always with the love story. A film could be about Gable or Tracy, but the conflict that people always wanted to see was with a woman who loved Gable or Tracy. The feeling was that there always had to be some sort of love story; and the truth is that this still prevails today in the so-called popular film. Or even in a deeper sense, we often say that no story's worth telling unless it's a love story. We don't mean now that it has to be boy-girl or man-woman love. It can be something about the love of an idea or a cause, or the hatred of an establishment which means therefore the love of humanity. But in those days they made films for very safe reasons. They believed that what was known to work well at the box office should not be tampered with.'

Brute Force, and its brutally forceful star, hit the public in the long hot days of the summer of 1947. 'Jules Dassin's staging has called for a great many close-ups of Lancaster looking steely-eyed and unshaven; but these do not become monotonous within Lancaster's brooding effective performance,' wrote the *New York Herald-Tribune*. *Time* was less certain: 'Stars Burt Lancaster but is not otherwise to be compared with *The Killers*. That may have been hammy, but it was a Grade A ham, so adroitly served up that the picture went on several of the year's Best Ten lists. *Brute Force* is a prisoner of all the old jail-break clichés.'

Desert Fury, which Wallis had cannily held up until *Brute Force* had added to his actor's stature, finally appeared in the autumn of 1947. The re-writing had left him with top billing, but in a part that obstinately refused to match it. The screenplay, based on Ramona Stewart's novel, lacked any elements of tension and merely served to pad out an undramatic tale with languid conversation. It wasn't helped by Lewis Allen's stately paced direction, nor by the spectacular Technicolor photography that left the performers with brick-red faces, though it had a distinguished musical score by Miklos Rozsa.

Lancaster coasted through as Tom Hanson, a hard-hitting and very manly deputy sheriff who falls in love with a rebellious girl (Lizabeth Scott), the daughter of the rich owner (Mary Astor) of a desert casino. Initially the girl prefers John Hodiak's ruthless gambler, but a car crash plus ninety-five minutes of Lancastrian glamour set her on the path of true love.

Although he was on the right side of the law and survived until the end credits for the first time, Burt was fortunate that this banal little tale wasn't the foundation stone of his film career because his drearily decent part received little attention. 'If I'd done it first, it's impossible to say how long it would have been before I'd have been given anything that captured the public's fancy,' he admitted honestly.

The *New York Herald-Tribune* critic was equally forthright. 'Lancaster is merely a romantic prop,' he concluded, but third time around the charge couldn't harm him.

If further proof of Burt's gilt-edged position were needed, Hal Wallis supplied it by putting him into *Variety Girl*, Paramount's all-star revue, which appeared in October 1947. Once again he was teamed with Lizabeth Scott in a short sketch. It was his first, but by no means his last or his best, appearance as a cowboy and he had to shoot a cigarette out of the actress's mouth. Then came a puff of smoke, and a shot of Burt putting up a 'Girl Wanted' sign. At this point the audience was supposed to laugh heartily, as the camera moved on to other celebrities.

Whether they did or not hardly mattered for this comic mini-interlude was the exception rather than the rule in the inexorable rise of the House of Lancaster.

three
INDEPENDENCE

If 1947 has seemed busy, it was as nothing compared to 1948 when Lancaster set up his production company and starred in its first film, fulfilled his quota for Wallis and took a massive salary cut to appear in the prestigious *All My Sons* for Universal.

In *I Walk Alone,* based on Theodore Reeves' unsuccessful play *Beggars Are Coming to Town,* Hal Wallis thought that he'd found the perfect vehicle not only for Burt, but for the rest of his stable of recently signed stars: Kirk Douglas, Lizabeth Scott and Wendell Corey. For Burt it was the third and final appearance with the dewey-eyed Miss Scott and the first of many with Kirk Douglas, who was to become the closest he would ever have to a friend and ally in the upper echelons of the acting profession.

The two men played gangsters whose rum-running during Prohibition sets them up against the law. Douglas contrives to frame his partner and Lancaster does his fourteen years in prison. However, the tables are turned on his release in 1947 when he hotfoots it to New York, hell-bent on revenge, to find his betrayer well established in a smart night club. He complicates matters by falling for a singer (Scott) who is also Douglas's mistress, then engages in a final showdown with the silver-tongued racketeer.

Sensing the mood of the moment, Wallis produced the film on a low budget and made a killing with it. It had the right underworld elements: a simple emotionally engaging plot, thoroughly despicable characters and a certain street-sharp style. Kirk Douglas, still something of an unknown in his largest role to date, was a hit. Lancaster however was not. 'He plays Frank Madison with the blank-faced aplomb of Tarzan,' said Bosley Crowther in the *New York Times,* and other critics agreed that the actor was wooden and expressionless, once you'd got over the impact of his physique.

Burt was quick to recognise the problem that was to haunt him throughout the early stages of his career. He had a rather immobile face that could stare moodily into camera or at the female lead and a fine set of large white tombstone teeth that could be bared into a ferocious snarl or grin. His first films exploited these assets by casting him as strong silent characters who relied on passive strength to bulldoze their way through until they met either an immovable object which wiped them out or emerged ahead of the game. So far, so good but it could hardly be called range. Nor was it the stuff that big reputations were built on. Recognising this, Lancaster acted decisively by insisting on working for peanuts for producer, Chester Erskine, in his adaptation of Arthur Miller's play *All My Sons*. Directed by Elia Kazan, it had run for nine months on Broadway and won the New York Drama Critics Circle Award the previous year. Burt appreciated the contemporary relevance, as well as the more universal application, of its message about corruption and guilt among businessmen, and was pleased to accept second billing behind Edward G. Robinson.

Joe Keller (Robinson) is a small-time factory owner who knowingly provides faulty cylinder blocks to an aircraft manufacturer rather than lose a government contract on which his company and his family's well-being depend. As a result, twenty-one American pilots, including his own son, go to their deaths. When the company is investigated after the war, Keller sloughs off the blame and it is his partner (Frank Conroy) who goes to prison. Problems arise when his second son, Chris (Lancaster), already embittered by his war experiences, returns home and falls in love with the partner's daughter, who tells him the truth about his father.

He then takes it on himself to make Joe Keller recognise his guilt, a difficult task because the older man sees his actions as totally justified by his need to make money to support his dependents. Only a letter written by the dead son, saying he'd gone on his last mission knowing about his father's responsibility for the defective planes, convinces him and he commits suicide, leaving Chris absolved and free to marry the girl.

Although *All My Sons* wasn't a box-office winner, Lancaster had no complaints. 'Okay, it didn't make money,' he commented. 'It was too talky, too preachy. But we took a chance. We tried. Why, I'd still be the same punk kid I used to be if I was afraid to take a chance. I wanted to play Chris Keller because he had the courage to make his father realise that he was just as responsible for the deaths of many servicemen as if he'd murdered them. And, as I had been in the Army, I had no difficulty in duplicating his feelings. I believe that each person shares a responsibility for the welfare of others.'

The critics greeted the film with varying degrees of enthusiasm and Howard Barnes, writing in the *New York Herald-Tribune*, summed up the general mood, 'While there are scenes of fine indignation in the motion picture, realised to the full by Edward G. Robinson, Burt Lancaster, Mady Christians and Frank Conroy, they do not off-set fabricated situations and blurred characterisations.'

As for Lancaster, some loved him, some didn't. *Time and Tide* considered him to be 'the blot on the film. His apparent inability to express anything other than dumb toughness or dumb devotion robs the all-important father-son relationship of its significance.' Fred Majdalany of the *Daily Mail* felt differently. 'A thoughtful, dramatic "meaty" film, well performed by Edward G. Robinson and Burt Lancaster – the first time I have seen Mr Lancaster act with more than his biceps and his jaw,' he wrote.

Lancaster himself was content enough. He'd diversified into radio, recreating Frank Madison in *I Walk Alone* with Lizabeth Scott and Kirk Douglas for Lux Radio Theatre in May 1948, and Chris Keller, opposite Edward G. Robinson on NBC's Cameo Screen Guild Players' production of *All My Sons* in November the same year. And he was ready to confront Hal Wallis.

The producer had been reluctant to give the necessary permission for Burt to play in *All My Sons*, but had folded in the end under the Lancaster talent for wearing down the opposition by wearing it out. His father, Jim Lancaster, once warned, 'Don't ever take Burt on in an argument. One Sunday when he was a youngster, his brother Jim did. Burt conked him on the noggin with a baseball bat. That taught Jim never to argue with his brother again. Burt has never grown out of his love of arguing.'

Others were slower to learn the lesson. As an adult, Burt stopped solving disputes with his fists, probably because his obvious strength and fitness deterred potential opponents from offering him that kind of challenge. Verbally, however, he was a menace whose infinite patience with the ins and outs of his case, whatsoever it might be, was disrupted on occasion by short sharp displays of ferocious temper from which no one was immune.

Wallis, as the holder of a contract that Burt already considered he no longer needed, was an obvious target for persecution. Having lost the toss on *All My Sons*, he suffered another defeat on *Sorry, Wrong Number*, when he was unwise enough to go on a fishing trip with his star. While waiting for a bite, the two men discussed Wallis's dilemma which was how to cast the husband in his latest film. He wanted Lee Bowman, a specialist in rather weak characters, but he wasn't available. Lancaster, having decided that the film was good of its kind, had other ideas.

'I said, "Why don't you let me play it?" And Wallis replied, "You're much too strong for it." Those were his exact words. And I said, "But that's the whole idea: a strong-looking boy on the threshold of life allows a woman to buy him and then suffers for it, and all of his character has been drained out of him. And at the beginning of the film, they'll believe I'm strong, and the contrast will make for real dramatic excitement." '

Wallis could think of no reply to that so he discussed the idea with Anatole Litvak, who was set to direct. He agreed, and Lancaster was in. The film belongs to Barbara Stanwyck whose playing of a rich cripple who overhears two men planning to kill her over the phone won an Academy Award nomination, but the secondary role of the murderous husband did no harm at all to Burt's rocketing career.

The plot was adapted for the screen by Lucille Fletcher from her own radio play. The original had been a single hander that had been made famous by Agnes Moorehead over the air waves. For the film, the story was fleshed out with a wealth of subsidiary characters but its core remained the same. It revolves around a self-declared invalid whose bank balance enables her to marry a handsome but ambitious and none too moral young man (Burt). When his gambling activities land him heavily in debt, he homes in on his wife's insurance policy in the classic Hollywood way, and hires an assassin to make sure he collects on it. It is this conversation that the victim unwittingly overhears but, unaware of her husband's involvement, she calls on him for help, so triggering a battle with his conscience. Ironically, by the time he has won it, it is too late.

Litvak directed for taut melodramatic effect and Lancaster developed his role from shallow greed to tortured guilt when he recognises that he's sacrificed his wife's life to save his own. When he listens to her dying in agony, he reaches a new level of achievement in his chosen profession. 'Yes, I really sweated bullets on that one,' he said. 'This was the first part with which I couldn't identify Lancaster on the screen. Usually there's some movement, some characteristics which you recognise as your own. But not this one. Ten minutes after I walked into the theatre,

I gave up looking for Lancaster. Seemed like a different person up there. It's a good movie.'

Harold Barnes of the *New York Herald-Tribune* agreed. 'Lancaster is grimly persuasive as the homicidal husband who gets caught in a mesh of telephone calls', as did *Look* magazine: 'Burt Lancaster continues his steady advance from muscleman to accomplished actor.' In Britain, the *Daily Telegraph*'s Campbell Dixon took a moral stand. 'Both the principals are unpleasant and the playing of Barbara Stanwyck as the tiresome wife and of Burt Lancaster as her husband – Mr Lancaster who cultivates a quiff and a sullen stare, is American girlhood's newest "rave" – does nothing to make them less so.'

Back on Broadway, the name of Lancaster was on the lips of Elia Kazan and Tennessee Williams. They had a play to put on and they wanted Burt badly for leading man. Had he taken it, there is no saying which way his career might have gone for the play was *A Streetcar Named Desire* and the part that of Stanley Kowalski. However he turned it down, leaving an unknown called Marlon Brando to immortalise it in his stead. 'I don't say I would have done it as well as Brando,' he commented, 'but I do think I would have been very good for that particular role, but I never got the chance to do it.'

The reason he didn't was that he was already a major movie star. His name on the credits, after just two years on the job, was sufficient to ensure that a picture grossed a minimum of a million dollars and he himself was earning 200,000 dollars a throw. As Edward G. Robinson put it when he worked with Lancaster on *All My Sons*, 'He was showing that animal vitality and suppressed volcano inside that inevitably made him a star.' It also made him want to go it alone. By late 1948, the time had come to take the plunge.

Hecht-Norma Productions, named after Harold, and Lancaster's wife, came into existence well within the five-year deadline its instigators had joked about during their celebratory dinner eighteen months before. Although Errol Flynn and Bing Crosby had made their own films to take advantage of tax concessions after the war, it was the first actor-producer studio in Hollywood. It set a trend that was widely copied, to the extent that it has become normal. Both men had done better than they could reasonably have expected and Lancaster, in particular, felt that he should be taking advantage of his popularity instead of letting Hal Wallis cash in on him.

Accordingly he used all kinds of legal loopholes to make as few of his contracted films as possible, with such success that he completed only six Wallis/Paramount pictures during the seven-year period he signed on for. Part of his obligation was paid off in lucrative loan-cuts, which Wallis frequently arranged for his stable of stars, but Burt wriggled out of three films he 'owed' altogether. Although he continued to work for his original backer in the mid-fifties once the contract had expired, he made him pay through the nose for his services. Nor was he above putting pressure on him by standing upside down on one hand on a ten-inch ledge outside the third-floor window of Wallis's Paramount office as proof, if more were needed, of his taste for brinkmanship, physical and emotional.

In starting his own company, Lancaster had very definite ideas about the kind of films he wanted to make. As he saw it, Hollywood had to change, and fast, if it was to survive in the post-war world. The films of the future should reflect the growing awareness of social issues, rather than provide escapist pulp for the lowest common denominator. 'I felt that Hollywood couldn't go on doing a lot of what was pure pap, as well as a lot of good films that were purely entertaining. People had to be given some of the realities of life. And, of course, in the years following the war, the USA was going through an enormous catharsis at all levels, and the country today finds itself in a very unpleasant position as a result of the evolution of those years. Films in their own way are history-making. Like all good art, they illuminate something.

'This doesn't mean that all films should be very serious things. There's a great deal of room for the pleasant fun film. But people also need to be aware – because what's going on in the world is in some way affecting the way they're living, and how they're going to live in the future. In the final analysis, the direction life takes will fall into their own hands. They will have to make the decisions as to how they want their own societies to move. All art must take that into consideration – and film can be one of the great art forms.'

So be it, and Lancaster would see that his thinking man's philosophies were translated into celluloid in the years to come. Meanwhile, his purpose was to prove that he could showcase himself as successfully as Wallis had done. Accordingly he picked a commercially, rather than artistically, fitting vehicle for his first production. Called *Kiss the Blood Off My Hands*, its content was as exploitative as its title, and it had the further advantage of putting Burt up front from the start in an electrifying opening sequence in which he runs for his life from an unknown pursuer after the sententious announcement, 'War brings ruin to men and cities, and cities are easier to rebuild.'

26

Based on a novel by Gerald Butler and directed by an ex-actor, Norman Foster, it features Lancaster as a young Canadian merchant marine with a concentration camp history and an uncontrollable temper that leads him to stab a drunk in a London pub. The murder is seen by a Cockney black marketeer (Robert Newton) who blackmails the young man into taking part in a hijacking venture. The love interest is a lonely aristocratic nurse (Joan Fontaine). 'You're everything that's bad,' she tells her lover, 'but I've never felt like this about any man.' Her incautious involvement leads her to kill the Canadian's persecutor, before the unhappy couple turn themselves over to the police in a soggy and unsatisfactory finale.

Having borrowed money to make the film, *Kiss the Blood Off My Hands* introduced its star to the worries of production with a bang. Joan Fontaine was pregnant and had to take time off because of ill-health; then she caught a cold which kept her out for twelve days; unremitting rain delayed the exterior sequences and Robert Newton found it hard to adjust to the sudden changes in the schedule. In the end, it seemed little less than a miracle that the picture was brought in only three days over its planned forty-five day allocation.

The result fell short on quality, though it more than recouped its costs on distribution. Today, when cinema films are made on location almost as a matter of course, it would have benefited from the authentic atmosphere of the East End of London. However, on the soundstages and back lot at Universal, comprehensively wreathed in artificial fog to support the widely held belief that the British capital is never in the clear, it was implausible from the start.

Typically, despite the general mediocrity, Lancaster came out about even. The *New York Herald-Tribune*'s Joe Pihodna considered that 'he walked off with the acting honours, even with stiff competition from Joan Fontaine'. Thomas M. Pryor, of the *New York Times*, who had earlier written, 'Even in a profession where spectacular ascents are more or less routine, the rise of Burt Lancaster is regarded as something extraordinary', was less certain this time. In a piece titled, 'Lancaster Fights the World Again', he reflected that, 'the process of humanising Burt Lancaster is obviously not going to be so easy and it is going to take time. Mr Lancaster is handy with his fists and speaks most eloquently when using them. But to develop fully as an actor and to come over to the right side of society, he will have to make a break someday, for there are only so many variations on the theme of being misunderstood, and Mr Lancaster has just about exhausted them.'

By way of diversification, the thirty-six-year-old star decided to resume his circus routines in November 1948. He had a twelve-foot trapeze erected in the back yard of his bungalow at the studio, and he practised diligently on it with Nick Cravat, much to the horror of the watching moguls. Then he and Cravat went on the road once more, appearing in Chicago, Milwaukee and New York City for a salary of ten thousand dollars a week. This return to the horizontal bars gave him ideas that would radically alter his film career in 1950, but first he had two more regular tough guys to portray.

The first was in *Criss Cross*, a doomed picture not least because its producer, Mark Hellinger, who had become Burt's friend on *The Killers*, dropped dead of a heart attack at the age of forty-four while it was still in pre-production. Lancaster himself took up the sad story. 'There are a lot of behind-the-scene things that people just don't know. In the case of *Criss Cross*, Mark Hellinger had an original idea about the holding up of a race track, and he had gone into an enormous amount of study as to how this would be done: things to do with the guards, and the handling of the trucks that come, and the switching back and forth of millions of dollars from the bank. He had an exciting Rififi approach to the whole thing. But at this time Hellinger had died.

'Now apart from my Wallis contract, I had a contract with Hellinger for three pictures. I had made two, *The Killers* and *Brute Force*. Then this half-finished version of *Criss Cross* was part of Hellinger's estate which under his contract with Universal reverted to the studio. So they came up with a re-hashed script. And I was obliged to do it. Siodmark was in the same position to me: he was obligated to do that film. So we backed into a picture that nobody really wanted to do, and the end result was a poor one.'

Hellinger had seen *Criss Cross* as the completion of his Lancaster trilogy of remarkably realistic crime films. Siodmark, however, with his talent for menace and pacing, shifted the emphasis away from Burt's character, a rather stupid guard who allows himself to be subverted into taking part in a large-scale robbery because he loves his ex-wife (Yvonne De Carlo), onto the slick crook (Dan Duryea) who is her current husband. The end product is a portrait of brooding under-world misery where money is the all important catalyst and in which women, provided they are seductive enough, can break men to achieve their nefarious ends.

If the loss of the limelight irritated Lancaster, the reviews proved even more aggravating. In the *New York Times*, Thomas M. Pryor's

28

dislike of the star had intensified, and he twisted the knife again. 'Burt Lancaster eventually gets around to being the same old tough guy of yore,' he wrote. 'It should not be surprising that his performance is competent for he has been working at the same type of role for some time.' James S. Barstow Jr of the *New York Herald-Tribune* hastened to agree: 'Lancaster is almost forced into a near parody of his previous dumb-brute portrayals. He is given the thankless task of holding down a responsible job as an armoured car policeman and at the same time appearing stupid enough to be led by the nose by a floozie to an improbable group of criminals and his death after a pay-roll hold-up.'

Nor did the London papers rate him any more highly. 'As Mr Lancaster is no great shakes either as a raconteur or as a thinker, the result is a pretty dull monologue in words of one syllable,' was Fred Majdalany's verdict in the *Daily Mail*.

Worse was to follow when Wallis finally attracted the attention of his errant leading male long enough for him to appear in *Rope of Sand*, an old-fashioned adventure in which he plays a tough big-game hunter-guide in Africa who knows the whereabouts of a cache of diamonds. They are hidden on the property of the villains, Claude Rains and Paul Henreid, who are teamed, as they were in *Casablanca*, with Peter Lorre. The result is a pale shadow for Lancaster is no Bogart and Corinne Calvet, who is cast as Rains' mistress in her American debut, is no Bergman. Worse still, the dialogue is in the kindergarten class. 'How did you get in?' asks Rains. 'The door was open,' Lancaster replies. Nor did William Dieterle's direction ever rise above routine rock bottom.

A.E. Wilson, writing in the *Star*, said the best that could be said for actor and production, but it wasn't much: 'Throughout the long sequences of *Rope of Sand*, Burt Lancaster wears an air of extreme bewilderment, quite understandable in one who finds himself enmeshed in a plot of considerable complexity. If Lancaster, who was in search of a secret cache of diamonds hidden in the sands of a South African desert had a clear view of what exactly he was up against, he was luckier than me. I hope I have made it clear that he finds himself in many a tough spot. It is indeed a tough film which, despite some slow passages performed amid a gloom that makes it hard to sort out the characters, has much excitement.'

Burt Lancaster no longer cared. He'd wangled a renegotiation out of Wallis that cut down the number of pictures he had to make for him. Then he persuaded Warner Brothers to give him an advantageous contract by which Hecht-Norma Productions would make three films over the next three years for the Burbank studio. The arrangement put him in the Cagney class, for the veteran actor had just signed a similar deal with the studio, but Burt would make much better use of his. Restlessly he flexed his magnificent muscles and bared his flashing teeth. His next metamorphosis was about to begin.

four
BRAVADO

Question: When did an acrobat turned actor turn stuntman?
Answer: When Burt Lancaster appeared as Dardo in *The Flame and The Arrow*.

The year was 1950, and the picture marked the real unveiling of Hecht-Norma Productions and the culmination of Lancaster's determination to start the new decade with something completely different. Later would come the socially conscious works he'd talked about at the fledgling company's inception but meanwhile he was going to have some fun. And what could be more fun than scooping the pool with a picture in the vein of his childhood hero, Douglas Fairbanks?

In the intervening years no actor, with the exception of Errol Flynn, had leaped and vaulted, balanced and swung, somersaulted and walked the high bar with such panache as Lancaster could. His brilliance as a circus performer had been widely hailed in publicity handouts but few of his fans had seen him in action. Many more had supposed his reputation to be part of the usual studio hype and were astonished at the agile revelations of *The Flame and The Arrow*. Starved of swashbuckling adventures since Flynn's retirement, they responded with a tidal wave of enthusiasm that swept the picture straight into the big time.

Lancaster not only drew shrewdly on his own skills and the action ingredients of earlier films, but showed his producer's muscles by adapting Flynn's sets for *The Adventures of Robin Hood* and *The Adventures of Don Juan* to save substantially on costs. Better still, he added an element that was all his own, a tongue-in-cheek bravado which surprised those who had imagined that his intense gangster's facade was the limit of his potential. Dardo is a medieval hero, a daredevil adventurer who leads his brave band in a revolt against the Hessian invaders of Lombardy. Their leader (Frank Allenby) has hired German mercenaries to help

31

his cause, an act that inspires Dardo to abduct his niece (Virginia Mayo) who then falls in love with her captor. After a series of mishaps brought about by his generosity of spirit, Dardo wins the day in a climactic battle that brings the film to a staggering pole-climbing, sword-fighting, chandelier-swinging conclusion.

Kids' stuff for sure, but just what the doctor ordered to break the mould of any gangster's screen career. Nick Cravat, ever faithful, responded to the call to play the amusing if silent side-kick and to share the acrobatic limelight, so launching a mini-movie career of his own. His lack of acting talent ensured that he'd be forever speechless, but wherever Burt swung, Nick wasn't far behind.

The two men warmed up for the film by joining their estwhile employers, the Cole Brothers Circus, on the road for four weeks. This time their price tag was 11,000 dollars a week, quite a rise from the three dollars they'd been paid in the early thirties. The circus even provided Lancaster with a 65,000-dollar private railroad car so that he could travel from town to town in comfort, but after three days, he borrowed a car and drove himself. 'I couldn't stand the luxury,' he commented.

The Flame and The Arrow was Burt's first picture for a delighted Warner Brothers but, in typical studio fashion, Warners were rather too quick to say that he'd done absolutely all his own stunts. One Don Turner was equally quick to insist that he'd been involved in three sequences, although he allowed that the acrobatics were all Lancaster's. The star offset this injudicious exaggeration by going on tour to promote the film and repeating many of his on-camera feats in person. 'I've got a couple of thousand bucks in this picture,' he quipped, in his new light-hearted vein, 'What's in a neck?'

Variety gave the succinct industry seal of approval to the film and its hero: 'Setting for the bow-and-arrow play is medieval Italy, with a Robin Hood plot of how injustice is put down under the daring leadership of an heroic mountaineer. Burt Lancaster does the latter, portraying the arrow (Dardo) of the title with just the right amount of dash. It's a role right up his alley, permitting a display of acrobatic tumbling skills and plenty of muscle flexing.'

On the other side of the Atlantic, Margaret Hinxman approved Burt's transformation in *Time and Tide*: 'A surprising number of good things: among them the discovery that Burt Lancaster's greatest skill lies not in glumly defying the minions of the Hollywood underworld, but in performing perilous acrobatics; a rollicking, riotous banqueting scene; and a gay air of inconsequence which defies criticism.'

Dilys Powell, of the *Sunday Times*, was not so readily won over: 'As the Robin Hood of Lombardy, Burt Lancaster performs acrobatic feats which remind one of the late Douglas Fairbanks; but the genial boyish charm of Fairbanks is not there, and in its place I find little but a savage grin and trapeze work. Not even the Christmas spirit can persuade me to recommend without reserve.'

Wallis's next plan for his elusive property was *Dark City*, which would have teamed him once again with Lizabeth Scott, but Twentieth Century Fox and MGM made loan-out offers he couldn't refuse and Burt was shipped off to lead in *Mister 880* and *Vengeance Valley* instead. A recent Wallis signatory, Charlton Heston hit the headlines for the first time in *Dark City* in Lancaster's place; he would do so again nine years later when Burt turned down *Ben Hur*, and Heston inherited his chariot. All this was appropriate because before he was signed, the actor had been recommended as 'another Burt Lancaster'. 'Yes, but do we need another Burt Lancaster?' was the persecuted producer's wry reply.

Meanwhile the original was denting his hard-man image still further by playing an amiable US Treasury agent who tracks down a modest counterfeiter (Edmund Glenn). He is the *Mister 880* of the title, a real-life ancient who forged between forty and fifty single-dollar bills a month, just enough to live on without, he hoped, becoming a burden on the tax payer. In fact the screenplay was an adaptation of a roman-ticised version of the story by St Clair McKelway which had appeared in the *New Yorker*, rather than the reality which existed in Treasury files. Either way, it was Glenn, an engaging villain, who stole the show from Burt's dilligent attempt at geniality.

It could only be a question of time before Lancaster appeared in a Western, and it is rather surprising that so much of it passed before he did. *Vengeance Valley* was its name and it was toughly directed by Richard Thorpe who gave an authentic feel to cattle round-up scenes that have rightfully taken their place in the history of the genre. Spectacular locations in the Rocky Mountains in Colorado helped in this respect. The theme was the familiar one about incompatible siblings, with Burt as the good guy who constantly takes the rap for his foster brother (Robert Walker). His misdeeds include trying to take over their father's ranch, cheating on his wife (Joanne Dru) and impregnating a local waitress. Predictably the double-crossing can't go on and there is a fatal showdown between the two men which leaves Burt with Miss Dru and his good name.

As Westerns would take up a fair proportion of his time from now on, especially as he grew older, it is appropriate to record that he rides tall in his first saddle. Too tall perhaps for a trusty cowhand, but safely enough which was his main conern in this newly learned pursuit. 'He can ride a horse pretty good now,' the veteran Australian stuntman, Gil Perkins, recorded twenty years later, 'but at first he was fairly weak at this.' In years to come, he would settle into the classic Cooper slouch as his mastery of the animal improved.

If anyone had any doubts as to the speed with which the Lancastrian confidence was growing, his agreeing to play Jim Thorpe, widely held to be the greatest all-round athlete the world had known, should have dispelled them. For a start, Thorpe was a Red Indian, and no amount of dyeing of Burt's golden locks and re-shaping them into a kind of bouffant quiff could make him look remotely like him, yet he didn't hesitate to take the part on.

The screenplay of *Jim Thorpe – All American* was fairly radically romanticised. Thorpe was a poor boy from Oklahoma who was encouraged by his father to leave the reservation in order to educate himself and to compete in the white man's world. The first he didn't manage, but the second he did to such spectacular effect that he won gold medals in the decathlon and pentathlon at the Olympic Games in Stockholm in 1912, and set world records that weren't bettered for years.

Later he was disqualified because he'd played professional baseball which was against the Olympic regulations. He also had three marriages (reduced to one for the film) and lost a son which contributed to his decline into drinking and drifting through Hollywood in the hope of being given token Indian roles. He was hired as technical adviser on the film and presumably condoned its inaccuracies and its unjustifiably optimistic ending which sees him taking a job as a trucker.

Lancaster's interest in the film was twofold: it showed his athleticism to good effect and, more importantly, it considered the issue of racial prejudice. It had long been Thorpe's contention that he hadn't got the job he wanted as a coach after the Olympics because of his colour and that he had later been exploited by the movie business. In both respects, he was certainly correct and Burt, who had always been a genuinely sincere crusader for civil rights despite his own impregnable position in the White Anglo-Saxon Protestant heirarchy, took pains to stress this point of view in his interpretation of the role.

The finished film, directed by the reliable veteran, Michael Curtiz, had fine supporting performances from Charles Bickford as the coach who spotted Thorpe at Carlisle Indian School in Pennsylvania in 1907 and from Phyllis Thaxter as the wife who deserted him. As for Burt, he showed to advantage in all his sinewy rippling glory.

Released in Britain as *Man of Bronze*, it attracted contradictory notices. Paul Dehn of the *Sunday Chronicle* doubted Lancaster's involvement in some of the sequences: 'It is an act of impersonation made much easier by a camera which works adroitly on the principle of showing us Mr Lancaster poised for, say, the high-jump take-off: interposes a shot of someone quite different clearing the bar at six feet, and then shows us Mr Lancaster again landing with a triumphant smile on his face. At the end I felt only half convinced that this was a true story, which in fact it is; and Mr Lancaster clinched my incredulity by acting as though he felt likewise.'

The *Daily Mail*'s Fred Majdalany took the opposite point of view though his praise was hardly unadulterated: 'Burt Lancaster seems particularly well-suited to play a character consisting almost exclusively of brawn and persecution complex, and he is thoroughly convincing in the athletic sequences.'

An escapist programme filler called *Ten Tall Men* followed. Hecht-Norma Productions made it under the auspices of Columbia, and everybody involved raked in the cash from this astutely commercial choice of material. Burt romped around as the leader of a special squad of French Foreign Legionnaires who are assigned to harass the Riffs and prevent them from attacking a Legion garrison. In a simulated Sahara Desert, they kidnap the Arab chief's daughter (Jody Lawrence), so preventing her from marrying to unite the warring tribes against the French colonisers. The scope for sandstorms and chases and antics was immense, and Burt worked hard to see that no opportunity for bravura action went untapped.

As unmemorable larks go, it was fine and served to fill the time and the coffers until Hecht-Norma, Warner Brothers and Robert Siodmark were ready to roll on *The Crimson Pirate*. This was the inevitable follow-up to *The Flame and The Arrow* and it marked another new stage in Lancaster's development in that he played a very active role in preproduction and even took a hand in the directing with writer, Roland Kibbee.

'I was particularly interested because I'd been faced with the usual problem of a young actor who came to Hollywood: if you're good in a certain kind of role, they tend only to cast you in that. I had the devil of a time previously when I did the first film of that nature, *The Flame and The Arrow*. When I went to Warner Brothers to attempt to do that

35

film, they wanted me to do a gangster film because they thought I was in that general ilk since I'd made *Brute Force* and *I Walk Alone* and *Criss Cross*. I was anxious to get into something different.

'There was a great deal of fun to *The Flame and The Arrow*. It was the kind of spoof we carried to greater extremes for *The Crimson Pirate*. I designed all the action sequences for *The Crimson Pirate*, all the comedy stuff. I worked with a comedy writer as well as with Siodmark himself. And as a matter of fact, the whole last part of the film, the fight on the ship which runs eighteen minutes of screentime, with all the gags and jokes, was shot by a writer and myself while Siodmark was in London shooting interiors for another part of the film.'

Ironically, the need to tap Warner's frozen assets and the lower costs in Europe took *The Crimson Pirate*, a buccaneering yarn set in the Caribbean, across the Atlantic to Britain and the Mediterranean while a film that would have benefited from a London location like *Kiss the Blood Off My Hands* had been confined to studio barracks. But wheeler-dealing was the name of Lancaster's game and he was always keen to use his own company to make a fast buck out of advantageous circumstances. The quality stuff, with the risks it entailed, he contrived to make when others put up the capital. He admitted as much when he said, 'I'll make swashbucklers for my own company. But in my outside pictures, I want to do things that will help me as an actor against the time I have to give up all the jumping around.'

Happily for children of all ages everywhere that time had not yet come, and his performance as Vallo in *The Crimson Pirate* was as athletically superb as ever. Once again he enlisted Nick Cravat as his fall guy, overcoming his inability to act by making him both mute and simpleminded. 'All I do is go on the set in the morning, find out what they want me to do, ask what my relationship is with the other people in the scene and go ahead and play it,' was the diminutive acrobat's view of his work.

Vallo is a bare-chested, sixteenth-century buccaneer who takes a break from piracy to hire himself out to the Spanish colonial overlords. His assignment is to put down a small revolution on a West Indian Island, but he switches sides when he falls in love with the revolutionary leader's beautiful daughter (Eva Bartok). Realising that he lacked Errol Flynn's gentlemanly charm, Burt played the film for laughs, going so far as to start the caper by saying that only half of what is seen is to be believed. He spends the remaining hour and three-quarters providing it in an engaging satire of all that his predecessors had held dear.

36

'Previous to this, the early Fairbanks films, and later the Errol Flynn films played the swashbuckling thing dead straight,' he explained. 'There was a certain amount of humour in the films, of course, but they were very serious about almost everything they did, whereas we spoofed everything. I daresay we were the innovators camping up that type of thing, which later became famous in the Bond series.'

The Crimson Pirate was the most expensive sea-opera of its time, and much of the money was spent on creating a science-fiction fantasy world for the grand finale, so that primitive tanks, submarines and balloon bombers could be launched against the opposition. In this innovative use of technology and reliance on gimmicks for comic effect, the film undoubtedly set patterns which Cubby Broccoli and Harry Saltzman developed a decade later for Bond.

Shooting took place at Teddington Studios outside London and on an island in the Bay of Naples in late 1951. The unfortunate Siodmark found that he had a very different Lancaster on his hands from the compliant beginner he'd coached through *The Killers*. This time there was no doubt who was boss, and it wasn't the director, whom Burt addressed to his face as 'you silly old has-been' as he countermanded his instructions as to where the camera should be placed.

As far as Lancaster was concerned, such transitory rudeness was part and parcel of the enormously high energy levels he put into his work. There is no doubt that by this time he was a workaholic, who devoted his life to his trade to the detriment of human relationships. 'This one is lusty and gutsy,' he said of *The Crimson Pirate*. 'We're throwing everything in. It has taken five years of my life already. This sort of work is killing. There's so much action. I take picture-making seriously. I want to keep some integrity about the business.'

By seriously, he meant that he hired people to do things that he subsequently decided he could do better himself. 'It's not a good idea to isolate yourself in the part. I like to find out how the camera works, then I can try for the best effect in what I'm doing. I want to know the director's angle on things as well. I know it's difficult. But I'm like that, restless and strung up inside when I'm working. I am searching for something and I haven't found it yet.'

It was the nearest Lancaster, a man who, once he'd made his name, never apologised, no matter how wrong he was, ever came to saying he was sorry, about a film whose geniality was strictly skin deep. During its making, he even achieved the near impossible by fighting with the stoical Nick Cravat who was training him for the acrobatics the picture required.

When *The Crimson Pirate* came out in 1952, it swept all before it critically and at the box office. *Variety* gave credit all round: 'Lancaster and his deaf-mute pal, Nick Cravat, sock the acrobatics required of hero and partner under Robert Siodmark's rugged but tongue-in-cheek direction.' Alton Cook dubbed the star as 'one of most amiable and strenuous comedians'.

Many would not have agreed, at least as far as the amiability was concerned, but the film made Lancaster into the man with the Midas touch: he was famous, he was rich, he was acclaimed. He had a beautiful wife and a flaxen-haired brood (daughters Susan and Joanne had been born in 1949 and 1951 respectively). His son Billy had caused family worries in 1950 when he'd contracted polio but he'd recovered quickly, although he retained a slight limp.

As he neared forty, Burt was still prime pin-up material with a forty-one-inch chest, fourteen-and-a-half-inch biceps and a quality of animal magnetism that hadn't faded with the decades. His health was perfect and even those who disliked him – and their number was growing – agreed that he had brains as well as brawn, commercial acumen as well as a handsome face. Unfortunately these enormous advantages, both natural and acquired, inflated his ego far beyond the point of no recall. He could afford to be humble – but he wasn't, though he claimed that he was trying to improve.

'I have a very bad temper, but it isn't as bad as it used to be,' he insisted. 'As time goes on it gets better, a part of the business of making adjustments. I've always tried to control it, but when I really get mad, I go berserk. Really blow my top. Actually I've only given way to it three times in my life. And it's usually an accumulation of things built up over a period of time.'

One who wasn't consoled by the alleged rarity of his bad behaviour was the columnist, Sheilah Graham, who'd admired his physique so much when she first met him on the set of *The Killers*. Her enthusiasm only lasted until their second meeting when she joined him for lunch during the shooting of *Brute Force*. They ate at a communal table and Burt fielded her questions adroitly and repeated them mockingly so as to amuse his captive audience. 'Burt the man lost me as an admirer during *Brute Force*, a very good title for this very physical film star,' she wrote some years later in her book, *Scratch An Actor: Confessions of a Hollywood Columnist*. 'He delights in a display of force and you never know when it's coming.'

'Over the years, I learned that Burt seems to enjoy taking his temper out on people who work for him and are usually not in a position to retaliate. He was using me as a test pattern, to see how far he could go, to prove he was an independent man who could make fun of a columnist and to hell with the consequences.'

To her credit, Ms Graham tried to shelve her animosity and report objectively on Lancaster's films, some of which she admired in print. She also tells one story about him which is worth repeating for the insight it provides into the actor's abuse of his immense personal power at this stage in his career.

'Lancaster's terrible temper is well known in Hollywood,' she wrote. 'He can restrain himself for the screen, and this held-back anger is very effective in his films. But in real life when he is annoyed, his erruptions are alarming. At a party Mr Hecht gave to show off his expensively decorated home, Burt was invited but didn't want to attend. He isn't much for parties, but he was convinced he should go. It would look bad if he stayed away. He had a drink or two – he is too careful of his superb physique to get drunk ever – but those who knew him could see he was in a black mood. Those who did not were startled when Burt asked, "Where's the can?" Absolute silence. "How do you like this? He builds this dump with my money and I don't even know where the can is." His host made haste to show him. Fifteen minutes later, Burt was laughing and joking as if nothing had happened.'

There could be no legitimate excuses for such embarrassing private tantrums, but Lancaster has pleaded frustration at himself as the cause of some of his on-set displays. This time the story is his own, as told in his John Player Lecture at London's National Film Theatre in 1973.

'I once had to walk into this room before three or four hundred extras and walk up to a girl, a cigarette girl, and say, "Hello baby, let me have a cigarette. Keep the change." Give her twenty dollars and so on, and I simply couldn't do it. We shot it twenty-eight times. I was so embarrassed at waiting for them to roll the cameras and to go on again, and I was so nervous and excited and upset with myself that I picked up a chair and smashed it against the wall.

'It took me a long time to be able to take command. In the intimate scenes I was perfectly at home because I could forget about the camera and relate to the person. If I had to play a love scene, I was able to literally be in love. But when I had to come out and take the stage and be the grand seigneur, I was very frightened. Even to this day, it takes a great deal of will on my part to stand there and declaim.'

Undoubtedly his problems, on and off the set, were indicative of the

39

tension produced by the excessive demands he made of himself. His intelligence, developed in the dubious back alleys of circus and vaudeville, was street sharp and allowed him to use those who wanted to use him, like Harold Hecht, to mutual advantage. It did not, however, quite reach the cerebral levels he expected of himself. His thinking, like his pronouncements, was tortuous and convoluted, a ponderously analytical hammer to crack a nut. He once spent forty-five minutes explaining how to make an omelette to a captive art director, a characteristic padding out of a simple process that illustrates his tendency to create complexity where none exists.

Yet he aspired openly to the intellectualism that he couldn't achieve. 'An actor has got to have certain things going for him if he's a truly great actor. I could describe the quality as something innate in him, something that in a sense has nothing to do with any qualification or experience he might have: it's just a God-given talent. On the other hand, a very good actor has to be intelligent, has to be sensitive, and has to have some kind of strength. That applies to women too. A good actress has "balls" in addition to heart and mind.

'As for myself, I had a pretty varied background. I was an avid reader. I was a music buff: I live at the opera and at concerts. I wasn't the little boy coming to town from some place in South Dakota who looked as if he'd just walked off the farm. I was born in New York and I'd spent all my life there, and it's a very sophisticated city. I had a reasonable knowledge of the political aspect of things too. So with these qualities, I was able to look at a script and see the values in it.'

One screenplay that fell firmly into this plus category was Cecil B. de Mille's *The Greatest Show On Earth*, which was hardly surprising because it consisted of two-and-a-half hours of uninterrupted Big Top extravaganza. With a competent story-line and spectacular acrobatic thrills, it should have been a natural for Burt, but for once his luck failed him and it proved impossible to negotiate a deal to loan him out for the duration. The limelight went instead to James Stewart and Charlton Heston, while Lancaster fulfilled some of his overdue commitments to Hal Wallis.

His first assignment for Wallis marked his debut on television, never a medium he has had much truck with. It was on the NBC-TV show, the Colgate Comedy Hour, hosted by Wallis's comedy duo, Dean Martin and Jerry Lewis, and Burt made a rare excursion into humour in a sketch with the irrepressible pair.

His next step was to lean on Wallis to let him appear opposite Shirley

Booth in *Come Back, Little Sheba*. Ms Booth had played the lead, Lola Delaney, opposite Sidney Blackmer, in the acclaimed Broadway production of William Inge's play and had signed for the screen version. She was forty-five and had never appeared in a film before, facts that put the producer under a lot of pressure from doubting colleagues, but he stuck to his guns, rightly as it turned out.

Then Lancaster came on the scene, brushing aside the other candidates with his customary steam-rollering brashness: 'I remember when *Come Back, Little Sheba* was contemplated. Hal Wallis said, "You're not right for it." And I had to agree with him really, because the man in the film should have been about sixty. But I prevailed on Wallis. I said, "I understand this character. I'd like to play it. Now, we both know it's Shirley's film – she's got the lead. But if I can do a respectable job in it, I will lend some weight to the box office for you." And on that basis Wallis let me do it. It was a bold departure for me, to say the least.'

And not, on the whole, a wise one though Lancaster never regretted his decision. It would be hard to imagine a greater contrast between the rumbustious spoofing of *The Crimson Pirate* and the melancholy drama of *Come Back, Little Sheba*. Lola Delaney is a slatternly apathetic wife, a faded beauty whose remaining love is a dog called Sheba. Doc (Lancaster) married her only because she was pregnant, then lived to regret it over many years of childlessness following the baby's death. Meanwhile he had given up medical school, become a chiropractor to pay the bills and consoled himself with alcohol.

At the start of the proceedings, he is on the wagon and working again, but the peace is too good to last. Lola, an addict for mindless soap operas with a tiresome line in nagging, mourns her lost youth and her lost dog as she drifts aimlessly through middle age. The arrival of a pretty lodger and her macho boyfriend serve to jerk Doc out of his transitory stability by reminding him of his squandered life. In desperation, after years as a member of Alcoholics Anonymous, he takes to the bottle and tries to kill Lola with a knife in the ensuing drunken rage.

After hospital treatment, he is sent home to resume his travesty of married life. The play ended on a note of hopelessness which Hollywood in 1952 wasn't ready for. Accordingly it was amended so that Lola accepts the loss of Sheba and the couple are reconciled so that they can live happily – or maybe miserably – ever after.

Daniel Mann directed very competently and Miss Booth capped her stage triumph by winning the Oscar for Best Actress when the Academy Award ceremonies came around. As for Burt, he prepared for his role with analysis, rather than research, refusing to see Mr Blackmer's or any other interpretation of Doc Delaney so as to develop his own straight from the script. As with *Sorry, Wrong Number*, Wallis's reservations about giving his star the go-ahead hinged on the fact that he was too strong for the role. And, once again, Lancaster overcame the producer's objections. He stressed that his physical strength would work in his favour in the part because the character was not essentially weak, but rather undermined by his love of a repellent wife.

It is probable that this was not the playwright's original intention, but Lancaster stood firm: 'I guess I wanted to play the part more than any other I ever got close to. Doc Delaney is the most human, if imperfect, kind of guy ever written into a play or script.'

Whether the end justified the means was a matter of sharply divided opinion. 'Lancaster is an actor of instinctive sensitivity, whose playing has always a certain gentleness and sensibility,' wrote Lindsay Anderson in *Sight and Sound*, 'but his range is limited, and this difficult part goes beyond it. In the simple matter of age he is quite wrong, and the heavy lines of make-up and the whitened hair do not convince.'

Time echoed him: 'Lancaster plays the sleep-walking Doc with great earnestness, but his performance frequently makes the character seem wooden rather than frustrated.' *Variety*, though, had other ideas: 'Opposite Miss Booth is Mr Lancaster bringing an unsuspected talent to his role of the middle-aged alcoholic husband, a character that is a far cry from his usual swashbuckling muscle-flexing parts. It is a fine job and his established film name sharpens the picture's drawing potential. Dilys Powell (*Sunday Times*), John McCarten (*New Yorker*) and Bosley Crowther (*New York Times*), by no means traditional supporters of Burt, agreed. 'The excellence of Mr Lancaster as the frustrated inarticulate spouse, weak-willed and sweetly passive, should not be overlooked,' was Crowther's contribution.

As for the protagonists themselves, Miss Booth was somewhat ambiguous in her advice to her co-star. 'Burt,' she told him, 'once in a while you hit a note of truth and you can hear a bell ring. But most of the time, I can see the wheels turning and your brain working.'

But Lancaster, ego-tripping with mounting self-satisfaction, had no such doubts. 'I don't for one moment fool myself,' he insisted. 'It was Shirley's picture and she was marvellous, and so it should have been hers. Because Bill Inge had written about this kind of woman, and how she was smothering and destroying this man without ever realising it, because she was the soul of kindness, so she thought. But for *Come Back*,

Little Sheba, I got extraordinary interesting reviews for the first time. The tendency of a reviewer is to regard you in the image you have had before. In other words, I was the leading man or the swashbuckler, blab-blab-blab. And suddenly they began to think of me as a serious actor. So that was a progression in my career.'

By any standards, what came next was a regression, but he owed Warners a picture and, when they lined up *South Sea Woman*, he agreed to do it, albeit with resignation. 'This is what they picked. I couldn't change their minds, so I did it, and quickly.' It was, at least, familiar territory for he plays a marine sergeant in pre-World War II Honolulu who is court-martialled for desertion. Flashbacks reveal the reason to be the South Seas woman (Virginia Mayo) who has come between the hero and his mate (Chuck Connors).

The two men enjoy a thoroughly Lancastrian series of boating japes as they burn a Chinese junk, sink a Japanese destroyer, seize a German yacht, release French prisoners and prevent an attack on Guadalcanal in a high-speed exercise that was expertly paced for the programme-filling end of the maket by the experienced Arthur Lubin. 'A terrible lot of nonsense,' said Bosley Crowther (*New York Times*) while *Variety* admired the star's 'expert muscle-flexing and romancing'.

During shooting, Burt took an hour or two out to make a guest appearance in another Warner Brothers film, *Three Sailors and a Girl*. It was a rubbishy old-fashioned musical, starring Gordon MacRae and Jane Powell, and Burt didn't need to change out of his marine sergeant's uniform from *South Sea Woman* to deliver his one-line backstage. 'You'll never make it in show business, kid,' he informs Sam Levene as part of the finale. No such charge could be levelled at him for this un-billed 'now you see him, now you don't' cameo counted as another appearance in a Warners picture – and that was the stuff that lucrative contracts were made of!

five
ETERNITY

After cash, cache – and the film that gave it to Burt Lancaster was *From Here To Eternity*, directed by Fred Zinnemann. By winning his first Academy Award nomination and the New York Film Critics' Award for Best Actor of the Year, it made him respectable in a way that a good 'little' film like *Come Back, Little Sheba* and the reflected glory of Shirley Booth never could. *From Here To Eternity* was a 1,900,000-dollar blockbuster that grossed more than six times that sum in distributors' domestic rentals in the United States alone. It was also a class act, winning eight Oscars, including Best Picture, and five more nominations. Unfortunately for Lancaster, one of these went to his co-star, Montgomery Clift, and the two men neutralised each other out in the minds of the judges, leaving William Holden to scoop the pool for *Stalag 17*. Nevertheless Burt's career, post-*Eternity*, would never be so circumscribed again.

Just before the film came out, he talked about his recent past in a way that suggests he knew that changes were due. 'In a lot of my earlier films, we depended on action to cover up story holes. If the plot became a little fuzzy or unbelievable, we quick like wrote in a sequence where I jumped over a twelve-foot fence or konked the villain with an eighteenth-century bean-bag. Then we'd cut to a beautiful low-key shot of me smooching the girl and the weak spot in the script would suddenly be bridged.'

Ironically, in the light of these words, it is Lancaster's smooching with the girl in *From Here To Eternity* that provides the film's most memorable moments. Indeed coach drivers still stop on the coast of Hawaii to point out the spot where Burt and co-star, Deborah Kerr, clad only in bathing suits, made cinema history with one of the sexiest love scenes ever filmed. In 1953, it was a sensation and in Britain, at least, most of it landed up on the cutting-room floor, victim of the prudish censorship of the time.

However its purpose was not to bridge gaps in a script that Fred Zinnemann rates, alongside *High Noon, A Man For all Seasons* and *Julia*, as one of the four best he ever received. It was based on James Jones's 816-page novel about brutalities in a United States Army infantry unit in Hawaii in 1941, before and during the Japanese attack on Pearl Harbor which forms its climax. Jones used his own military experience, some of which he spent in prison, to paint a grim picture of sadistic sergeants urged on by their officers to humiliate, torture and even kill their men. He pulls no punches in his descriptions of sex, and scatters four-letter words indiscriminately through his mammoth text.

When Columbia's Harry Cohn first bought the film rights, he hired Jones to reduce his opus to cinematic proportions, but in the end it was screenwriter, Daniel Taradash, who compressed it into a 161-page shooting script. In the process, he cleaned up the material and made the language of the soldiers 'fit for a girls' school' as Leonard Mosley wrote in the *Daily Express*. He also shifted the balance so as to whitewash the us Army, much to the author's resentment. In the book, the culpable commanding officer was given promotion; in the film, he was forced to resign as a punishment for his crimes. Out too were perversions, explicit torture and venereal disease. Lancaster and Kerr in the near nude was one thing, but Hollywood still had its lines of propriety to draw.

'Columbia Pictures ass-kissed the Army so they could shoot the exteriors of the film at Schofield Barracks in Hawaii without being bothered,' was Jones's view, and he expressed it frequently to his cronies on the picture, Montgomery Clift and Frank Sinatra.

Jones's characters were taken straight from the pool of American fiction. There is the silent boxer, Robert E. Lee Prewitt (Clift), who refuses to fight because he once blinded an opponent in the ring; the gallant sergeant Milton Warden (Lancaster) who sticks by his men and his old-fashioned values; and the sad young officer's wife (Kerr) who compensates for her husband's vileness and infidelities with sexual adventures of her own; the best friend, Angelo Maggio (Sinatra); the tart with a heart and a desire for security (Donna Reed); and the brutally vicious stockade sergeant (Ernest Borgnine).

When it came to casting Warden, Zinnemann's choice was between Lancaster and his fellow tough-guy, Robert Mitchum. 'I'd seen Burt in *The Killers*,' he explained, 'and I could see he made his mark, he was someone, so he was very much the front runner. Mitchum wasn't available at the time, but fortunately Burt was, to my great delight because personally I couldn't have imagined anyone better.'

Columbia were prepared to go with Burt, though Hal Wallis made them pay dearly for the privilege. In a horse trade, by which they made a picture called *Bad For Each Other*, with Wallis stars, Charlton Heston and Lizabeth Scott, Columbia ended up paying 150,000 dollars outright for Lancaster, of which the star was to receive 120,000 dollars, plus 40,000 dollars extra for the second film.

In the event, he was worth the money, though the picture's bargain was undoubtedly Frank Sinatra who'd been accustomed to receiving 50,000 dollars a throw. However, he was currently in danger of becoming a has-been, and begged the part here, agreeing to a fee of just 8,000 dollars. In return, he gave a performance that won the Best Supporting Actor's Oscar and put his career back on course. Zinnemann laid his own job on the line to hire the mercurial Clift in the face of studio opposition and Joan Crawford was originally signed for Karen Holmes. The mind boggles as to how much her presence might have added to the potential for rifts among these temperamental performers, but it wasn't to be because she fought over her costumes so ferociously before shooting began that there was no alternative but for her to leave the film, allowing the responsible and charming Deborah Kerr to be employed in her place.

The plot had several strands but the two most important ones involved Milton Warden, which meant that Lancaster had the largest part and top billing. Warden is a professional soldier, pragmatic and effective, the opposite side of the coin to the sensitive and rash Prewitt whom he consistently tries to protect from himself. And he is a lover whose affair with his captain's wife runs the gamut of flaring sexual passion through her tender affection to its doomed conclusion. For Karen Holmes, though ready to leave her husband, will only marry an officer, and Warden, though prime officer material, hates the breed. On the evidence of the ones he has to work with, he is entirely right to do so, but it doesn't help his romance.

The part of Warden demanded a certain honest toughness that Lancaster had often given before, plus a sensitivity and sexiness that were not so familiar in his work. 'Warden was a very forthright character and actually had less dimension than some of the other people,' Zinnemann commented. 'He was not as neurotic or as complex as Prewitt or Karen so I didn't call on Burt to analyse and project in the same way as

Monty and Deborah had to. His ambition was to be a good soldier and, in a sense, he was the catalyst, the commentator on the whole situation. He was a very straight man, very gung ho, and he knew all the tactics for keeping alive and getting along. He was a survivor, but he was very compassionate towards Prewitt, a victim who was determined to stick to his guns even if it killed him, as it eventually was bound to do.

'Burt had a very impressive way of putting across that sympathy in the reverse as it were. By being tough, he was able to project a great deal of actual tenderness and a feeling of comradeship. To me it was a very moving performance.'

The other demand Zinnemann made on Lancaster was to flesh out the love scenes convincingly. 'Those things always depend on chemistry between two people,' he explained. 'Deborah was cast very much against type because at the beginning of the film it's made clear that she'd slept with a lot of people. With a sexual star, that wouldn't be news. With Deborah, she didn't look or move like that at all. In fact up to that point, she'd mostly played the Virgin Queen of England. She was very remote and very, very dignified so people became curious. Burt was in his prime, in splendid physical shape and very athletic so it really worked out well.'

Zinnemann was under constant pressure to get the job done fast. The unit spent four weeks in Hawaii and seven in the studios at Burbank, a period that would be unthinkably short in modern times for a film of this weight and status. When they flew in a chartered plane to Hawaii, arriving at five a.m., Cohn had them shooting by mid-morning, despite Zinnemann's request for a sightseeing rest-day before work began in earnest.

As a result of the pressure, Zinnemann had no time, and certainly no inclination, to involve himself in the disputes among the stars, although he admits that the men could have been calmer. 'I can't say that Burt was easy, but then neither was Monty and neither was anybody, except Deborah and Donna Reed. The men were always a bit highly strung, shall we say. It's understandable because it is nerve-wracking to be there exposing yourself emotionally, as it were, before a bunch of strangers. It takes a colossal amount of concentration. I imagine it must be harder for men than women. Normally I've found that women just get on with it and men psychologically have to overcome their difficulties. Of course, there are exceptions, people like Marilyn Monroe and Judy Garland who start out feeling they're no good as actresses, but those

47

who've grown up in the business like Deborah are professionals. They're easy to get on with.'

No love was lost between the exceptionally thin-skinned Montgomery Clift and the tempestuous Lancaster, two men who were in any case as different as chalk from cheese. Clift had years of stage experience and years of study in the Actor's Studio under Lee Strasberg behind him, and he bitterly resented Burt's name at the top of the credits.

'He'd ring me up in New York,' his friend, Pat Collinge, recalled, 'and analyse Prewitt exhaustively. He'd be making superb actor's sense, then out of the blue he'd start ranting against Burt Lancaster. "He gets top billing, he doesn't deserve to," he'd yell. "He's a terrible actor. He thinks he's a dynamo; he's nothing but a big bag of wind, the most unctuous man I've ever met!" And then he'd drop the subject and go back to talking about Prewitt.'

Lancaster admired Clift's thoroughness. 'He approached the script like a scientist,' he said, 'I've never seen anyone so meticulous.' But he had no time for the long drunken nights of hell-raising that Monty shared with Frank Sinatra and James Jones. During the Burbank days, the three men would eat out in a little Italian restaurant in West Hollywood, then sit on the pavement under their special lamp-post discussing their grievances, their lives and lovers, before returning noisily to the Roosevelt Hotel. Twice they were threatened with expulsion, and twice Columbia had to intervene on their behalf.

By holding himself aloof from such roisterings, Burt seemed sanctimonious and boring, and so found himself isolated from the main axis on the film. However such internal stresses did no harm to the end result which was widely praised. 'Rates as one of the all-time greats in the ranks of motion pictures, having armed forces background,' stated *Variety* unequivocally, adding, 'Burt Lancaster, whose presence adds measurably to the marquee weight of the strong cast names, wallops the character of Top Sergeant Milton Warden, the professional soldier who wet-nurses a weak, pompous commanding officer and the GIS under him. It is a performance to which he gives a depth of character as well as the muscles which have gained marquee importance for his name.'

A.H. Weiler in the *New York Times* had a different but equally favourable point of view: 'In Burt Lancaster, the producer has got a top kick to the manner born, a man whose capabilities are obvious and whose code is hard and strange, but never questionable. His view of officers leaves him only with hatred of the caste, although he could easily achieve rank, which would solve his romantic problem. But he is honest enough to eschew it and lose the only love he has known.'

In Britain, Leonard Mosley, who didn't like the film, applauded the performances: 'Miss Kerr and Burt Lancaster succeed in conveying with some skill the ecstacy and despair of an illicit affair they know can't work out.'

Where critics led, audiences queued to follow and the Capitol Cinema in New York was kept open round the clock to accommodate them. In 1954, when the box-office returns were reflected in the balance sheets, Columbia's income rose by 20,000,000 dollars to 80,000,000 and its profits quadrupled to 3,500,000 dollars. Burt Lancaster was on top of the world.

His next, thoroughly unimaginative step was to wrap up his deal with Warners by making *His Majesty O'Keefe*, a routine romp set in the South Seas in the 1870s. Filmed on location in Fiji from a brisk script by Borden Chase and James Hill, Burt's partner-to-be, it has the actor in the title role of a Yankee sailor whose mutinous crew throw him overboard. Happily this occurs when he is near the island of Viti Levu so he swims ashore, looks around and, quick as a flash, comes to the conclusion that he should stick around to make his fortune out of copra – if only he can persuade the natives to pick coconuts.

Initially he can't overcome their habitual idleness and by the time he's single-handedly defeated German merchantmen – this was the fifties when, in the aftermath of World War II, even historical stage villains were apt to be Teutonic – and some of the last of the slave traders, he no longer wants to. Instead he accepts the islanders' gracious invitation to be their king and takes up with a beautiful Polynesian girl (Joan Rice) with whom he can be presumed to live in regal idleness ever after.

His Majesty O'Keefe was the final Hecht-Norma Production. Thereafter the company was re-christened Hecht-Lancaster, and a new deal was struck with United Artists to distribute its films through offices at the Sam Goldwyn studio, headquarters of all the UA enterprises. The first picture under these arrangements was *Apache*, one of Burt's more absurd exercises in social concern. It also marks his first collaboration with Robert Aldrich, a director whose work was remarkable, then as now, for its explicit visual brutality. Not for him such Hitchcockian subtleties as fear that can be felt rather than seen; the Aldrich way is that if it's worth killing, it's worth killing as violently as the censor will permit. As *Apache* stars Burt Lancaster, WASP-ish as ever, as Massai, a lone Indian who attempts to improve the lot of his beleagured people by taking on a large section of the United States Army circa 1880, there is a lot of scope for Aldrich's bloodbath mania.

The film attempts to be pro-Indian and thoroughly entertaining simultaneously, and contrives to fall squarely between two stools in the process. It panders to its star's sincere feeling for the under-privileged minorities, while giving him as much scope as possible for performing the acrobatic stunts that come so naturally to him. Historically, in Westerns Indians had been two-dimensional villains with feathered head-dresses and no saddles. Now they had a blond blue-eyed champion ready and willing to make one of their number into a hero. Of course, this was 1954, somewhat before the rise of the ethnic actor, and Hollywood had nothing to offer as an Indian warlord except a blacked-up white.

Even so, Lancaster must have been among the least well-suited physically to the part of Massai. Nor did his 'squaw' (Jean Peters) score much more highly, as the *Monthly Film Bulletin*, noted: 'We remain conscious that these two actors are doing a very decent best in an impossible task. The strangeness is missing: Indians are not just white Americans with a different coloured skin and a simplified vocabulary.'

Quite so, and to play them as such would now be considered as racist and patronising as making them into cardboard cutouts of savagery. Well-intentioned though it certainly was, the production was too soapy to do more than nod in the decent direction. '*Apache* is a film that would seem to have a guilty conscience,' wrote *The Times*. 'It does not hesitate to imply that the treatment meted out to the Apache after the surrender of Geronimo was unimaginative, to say the least of it, and the comparisons drawn between Massai, with his honest blue eyes, his faithful squaw, and the white enemy are in favour of the former. But *Apache* is not a sociological document so much as a coloured excuse for some spectacular feats by Mr Burt Lancaster before he declines into sentimental domesticity.'

The finale so scathingly referred to was, in fact, an alternative ending to that in Paul I. Wellman's book, *Broncho Apache*, on which James Webb's screenplay was based. The original Indian rebel, having escaped from a deportation train which was taking him to exile in Florida, confronted his enemies once more and died bravely when the odds against him became overwhelming. That was the conclusion Hecht-Lancaster and almost everyone else wanted and expected. The exception was the studio which demanded that Burt shouldn't die. What's more, they demanded it so vociferously that they overcame the objections of the normally implacable Lancaster and tacked on a ridiculous climax in which the enormously outnumbered Massai hears the cries of his new-born child and gives himself up to the American troops so that his boy shall have a father.

Later Burt regretted this uncharacteristic bow towards the front office: 'In the original ending of *Apache*, I was killed by Charles Bronson. We shot an alternative ending because the distributors said, "Burt, you can't die in a film." That's the kind of thing the Hollywood scene is about sometimes. And it wasn't just them. The exhibitors came with bended knees saying. "Please don't die, your fans won't want to see you die." I must say that though I hated the idea, I went along with them and the picture was very successful, so I will never know how the other ending would have done. As I have done many times in my life, I sold my soul to the Devil.'

Presumably his fans had no such qualms about his lack of immortality in his next film, *Vera Cruz*, in which he is killed by Gary Cooper in the final shootout. Perhaps it had something to do with the second billing he accepted in order to appear in a buddy-buddy wide-screen spectacular with the evergreen veteran of a thousand simulated Western battles. Once again the setting was historical – the Mexican Revolution in 1866 – and the action hyper-acrobatic. Robert Aldrich who'd found Burt 'not an easy man to get along with, but quite responsive' on *Apache*, agreed to direct again, from a Roland Kibbee/James Webb script. The task, he would discover, wouldn't be so simple second time around.

Cooper and Lancaster play two soldiers-of-fortune who become mercenaries and fight for whichever side pays the most, in a story that relies entirely on double-dealing and stabbing in the back for its pacing. The pair meet a countess (Denise Darcel) at a ball, accompany her to Vera Cruz and fall in love with her dastardly plan to steal the Emperor Maximilian's gold en route. Lancaster remains villainously faithful to the precious metal throughout, but Cooper comes to believe that it should belong to the Revolutionaries so that they can use it for the good of the Mexican people. Such credulousness is the stuff that heroes are made of, in this kind of picture at least, and it is enough to ensure that he wins out over his ex-partner.

At the box office, however, it was Hecht-Lancaster and Burt Lancaster who walked off with the financial and critical honours. The film cost 1,700,000 dollars to make and amassed 11,000,000 dollars in return, a fifth of that, its connections calculated, being directly due to Gary

Cooper's presence. It was billed as the 'Battle of the Giants' with Lancaster's ever-grinning villain confronting Cooper's dispossessed Southern gentleman for the heavyweight championship of Hollywood. But there was more to their screen relationship than that. Indeed, had it been developed in a better script, the cautious friendship that emerges from the instinctive distrust between the opportunist and the idealist could have been extremely interesting. As it is, it is diffused by Aldrich's smash-and-grab direction which lays heavy emphasis on gratuitous violence to women and mass extermination of everyone else.

This, of course, was what produced queues around the block, though the critics howled in protest. 'Guns are more important in this shambles than Mr Cooper or Mr Lancaster. In short, there is nothing to redeem this film – not even the spirit of the season. Some Christmas show indeed,' said the *New York Times*, while the *Daily Telegraph*'s cynical Campbell Dixon observed, 'In a life-time's film-going, I have never seen a film quite so bloodthirsty and brutal. The gringos think it fun to lassoo Mexican girls; Mr Lancaster twice slaps a larcenous countess hard across the face; whenever a new twist is needed, they shoot somebody from the saddle or mow down a squad. This sadistic school-boy fantasy is well made, except for the frieze of Mexican soldiers who keep popping up on walls, and Mr Cooper, Mr Lancaster and some of Hollywood's toughest-looking characters wade effectively through the blood.'

The violence against women in Lancaster's films was real – or anyway realistic – enough to set them apart from those made by earlier acrobats, especially Douglas Fairbanks. In his day, maidens had been shy and docile and he rescued them with lustless pre-Freudian honour. His encounters with what the characters he played saw as the fairer sex were unremittingly romantic, never complicated by temptation. By the mid-fifties, things had moved on a bit and Lancaster's exceptional physical vigour made it inevitable that he would mix red-blooded desire with a dash of brutality here and there, especially when Aldrich was around.

Although his women were almost invariably Hollywood pretties, decorative but essentially characterless as tradition still demanded, fashion dictated that the male should tame the shrew, and this Burt proceeded to prove he could do. One unlooked for and surely unwelcome result in the wake of the film's release, was a story in the scurrilous *Confidential* Magazine in May 1955 by one Charles A. Wright, alleging that Lancaster was an habitual abuser of women, among them Francesca de Scaffa (Mrs Bruce Cabot) who had come to a studio in Santa Monica to test for a role in *Vera Cruz*. Another suggested victim was Zina Rachevasky, the playgirl daughter of the head of a banking concern. Lancaster, Mr Wright claimed, had picked up the habit during a rough youth and had 'been handing out lumps ever since. Not a few of these have been collected by some of the world's best-known beauties.' However none of them stepped forward to complain, probably because they had no cause to.

Robert Aldrich, on the other hand, took on Lancaster at just the time when he thought he could direct as well, or better, than any man alive. 'I had always felt that I had a kind of director's attitude towards my work,' the actor stated with conviction. 'I was constantly worrying about the writing of the scripts I acted in, always wanting to change the staging of the scenes, always feeling it could be done in a different way. I never lost that tendency. For some reason, many directors found it difficult to work with me.

'But that's the way any actor works who's worth his salt. Very few actors just stand and allow themselves to be directed. They're the ones who have to do it, so they have to have some concept as to what they want to do – some approach to it that will make their work that much more effective, and bring off the idea they're trying to express.'

Translated into the context of *Vera Cruz*, that meant, according to Rene Jordan, Gary Cooper's biographer, that Aldrich allowed Lancaster to steal the picture: '*Vera Cruz*, for what little it is worth, belongs to Burt Lancaster, who seduces Denise Darcel and performs many an acrobatic feat with a glittering, malevolent grin, as if his very teeth were high on adrenalin. It is a divertingly hammy performance that Aldrich vainly tried to control; co-producer Lancaster was on his way to directing himself as *The Kentuckian* and was trying his new britches on for size all over the location.'

In retrospect, it is strange that Burt picked an old-fashioned Western, a genre he never particularly admired though he played in plenty of them, for his directorial debut, yet that is exactly what *The Kentuckian* is. Based on a novel called *The Gabriel Horn*, by Felix Holt, and translated for the screen by A.P. Guthrie Jr, it tells of a pioneering widower, Big Eli (Lancaster) who leaves Kentucky with his young son (Donald MacDonald) for the wide open spaces of Texas where men can still be men. The time is 1820 and family feuds are rife, even in a state that is beginning to become over-settled in the hero's eyes, so it comes as no surprise when the opposition appears before he has reached its frontiers.

Eli is sidetracked romantically by a schoolteacher (Diana Lynn), then spends his passage money on freeing an indentured servant girl (Dianne Foster) from her contract, so initiating a new conflict with the town bully (Walter Matthau). Only after he's got rid of several murderous brothers and disposed of the bully can he be free to leave for the land of his dreams with the girl he loves.

The film is beautifully shot in wide sky locations in Kentucky and Indiana by Ernest Laszlo, who'd also worked on *Apache* and *Vera Cruz*; it has a resounding musical score by Bernard Herrmann; and the cast, which also include John Carradine, is well selected. The only problem is the director who produced a leaden-paced, monolithic pup, enlived only by three action sequences, the first of which occurs eighty long minutes into the film. This is the key scene in which Matthau wields a bull whip against the bare-fisted Burt, and it is only matched by a free-for-all on a river boat and a climactic shootout. Lancaster, it seemed, has some talent for putting together movement, as indeed he's proved earlier in the grand finale of *The Crimson Pirate*, but little idea of how to fill the gaps.

While he was working on *The Kentuckian*, Lancaster imposed all the ferocious disciplines he usually burdened his employees with on himself. He tinkered constantly with the script which never quite satisfied him. He rose at five a.m. in order to get to the locations and make sure everything was meticulously set up. He appeared in almost every scene, then got home late at night. The rushes would be waiting, and he'd pore over them with the editor until after midnight deciding on the game plan for the next day.

It is easy to believe him when he said, 'I actually found it the hardest job of my life. I had no time for anything. It's no life really. Nobody works harder than the director if he's at all serious. His work is never finished, simply never finished. You make all the decisions, you deal with temperamental actors, then the next day you start the same grind all over again. But it's the best job in pictures because when you're a director, you are God. And, you know, that's the best job in town.'

Few of the critics believed in his directional deity. 'A bit too self-conscious, as though the director and the actor couldn't quite agree,' wrote *Variety*, while Bosley Crowther of the *New York Times* drew a parallel between an actor who wanted to be a director and a Kentuckian who wanted to be a Texan, but neither is successful. 'There is no excuse,' Crowther added, 'for letting the whole thing run wild in mood and tempo with no sense of dramatic focus or control.'

Lancaster was gracious enough to admit defeat. 'Long ago I learned it's no trick to being a director,' he told the press. 'The tough job is being a good director. I will probably never again act in a picture I also direct. Much as I've enjoyed working as an actor in the past, it's possible I may quit that phase of show business and concentrate on being a director. That's been my real ambition ever since starring in motion pictures.'

Neither of these predictions were realised, though it was nineteen years until he directed himself again. As for taking the helm full-time, he'd discovered on *The Kentuckian* that it was a very tough job indeed. Not that that would have deterred a workaholic like himself but later reflection persuaded him that his talents lay in front rather than behind the cameras.

It is also possible that, accustomed as he was to instant success, Lancaster took the decision to become a director too hastily and for the wrong reasons. Expecting overnight acclaim and discovering instead that he was as vulnerable as anyone else, he never gave himself a real chance to develop as a director, yet, the highly intelligent C.A. Lejeune was one who saw considerable promise in *The Kentuckian* when it came out in London in the same week as a revival of John Ford's *The Wagonmaster*.

'I should make it clear at once that I am not discussing the relative merits of the two films,' she wrote in the *Observer*. 'As a manipulator of material, Mr Lancaster stands to Mr Ford in much the relation of a kindergarten pupil to a professor. The one knows next to nothing of the controlled flow of visual imagery of which the other has been a master for more than thirty years. He is still comparatively artless, but he is learning. Burt Lancaster is an ex-circus artist, chiefly renowned on the screen for his agility, his magnificent teeth and his courage in "performing his own deeds of daring". But I think he must also be a man with an untaught love for the fine and imaginative thing.'

Later in her column, she sums it up as, 'a rough buckskin type of film, with a glint of poetry here and there, and plenty of clean air blowing through. Perhaps I am not being over altogether fanciful in believing that *The Kentuckian*, artless and rawboned though it is, has some distant kinship with the great John Ford studies of pioneering days; wagons rolling west, railroads hammering east, stagecoaches lurching perilously from post to post, and always the sense of fresh communications, of new highways opening.'

Perhaps Burt didn't read the *Observer*, but in any event he failed to respond to this encouragement. However he compensated by fighting hard for the most creative piece of producing ever achieved by Hecht-Lancaster. For several years, the company had been trying to make films without Lancaster as star. One such was *The First Time*, a feeble farce, with Barbara Hale and Robert Cummings as the struggling parents of a prima donna child. The film had been released in 1951 by Harry Cohn of Columbia as part of the package for the first Lancaster Western, *Ten Tall Men*, but the crowds had stayed away in droves.

A similar fate was predicted by United Artists for *Marty*, a small film with a modest budget of 330,000 dollars. The Paddy Chayefsky screen-play had been already made for television, with Rod Steiger playing the title role. The programme had lasted just one hour, and both its shortness and its exposure were held in the corridors of power.

But Burt was not to be deterred. 'We had the devil of a time trying to get the money together to do *Marty*, even though it was an extremely small-budget picture, because people in Hollywood said, "Who wants to see a story about two ugly people?" It was a heart-breaking story and a beautiful film, but that is what you constantly run up against.'

Lancaster had already worked with Ernest Borgnine on *From Here To Eternity* in which the Italian American actor had played the sadistic Sergeant Fatso Judson, so he knew what he was getting when he signed him up on a five-year contract.

Nevertheless, the choice of a man who was well on his way to becoming a classic screen villain for *Marty*, a lonely thirty-four-year-old bachelor, was inspired, as was the selection of the veteran Delbert Mann as director. He brought the picture in in a brisk eighteen days and made such a good job of it that it won the Golden Palm at Cannes and four Oscars, including Best Picture, Best Actor (Ernest Borgnine) and Best Screenplay (Paddy Chayefsky).

Marty is a lower-middle-class butcher whose friends and relations assiduously provide dates so that he can fit into their conventional pattern of husbandry and paternity. Yet when the worthy man chooses a girl as plain and decent as himself, they find they need him as drinking companion, spare man, or dutiful son, and so try to smash up his romance. Although fundamentally a soap opera, the film was well ahead of its time in that it aspired to show life as it was lived by very ordinary people in a lower-middle-class neighbourhood of the Bronx. Such realism may have been fashionable in fifties' Britain where John Osborne and John Braine, to name but two, were setting trends, but it certainly wasn't the stuff that Hollywood considered that films should be made of. Why should any respectable dream factory be expected to peddle the masses to themselves? If they wanted to see dim primeval streets with families crammed into lousy housing and lonely misfits drooling over sex magazines and comic books in bars, they had only to look around them. So why would they pay to go and see it at the cinema?

Marty showed up the flaws in this logic by making 5,500,000 dollars at the box office. Not that that satisfied United Artists in the very least. When *Vera Cruz* had made nine million plus, why should they be content with a mere five million from *Marty*? Prestige didn't feed film stars or fuel limousines. That took folding money – and the more of it the better.

Ernest Borgnine was another who was quick to state his dissatisfaction with Lancaster when he sued the company, claiming that he'd only received ten thousand dollars of the fifty thousand due to him under his contract. When the case was eventually settled out of court, Borgnine delivered his own verdict: 'a very tough hombre'. And he said it with conviction.

It may have been post-*Kentuckian* blues or the fact that Brando's triumph in the part Burt had missed out on in Tennessee Williams' *A Streetcar Named Desire* was always there to rankle, but he went comparatively quietly to fulfil his next commitment to Hal Wallis. It was Williams' interesting but rather uncommercial play, *The Rose Tattoo*, which had been produced on Broadway with Maureen Stapleton as Serafina. However Williams had written the work with Anna Magnani, whom he'd known in Italy, in mind and, when he sold the film rights to Paramount, he stipulated both that she should play the lead and he should write the screenplay.

This gives the project a touch of international class and an intellectual gloss that Lancaster couldn't resist when Wallis asked him to play the genial if oafish truck driver, Alvado Mangiacavallo. Both Wallis and Lancaster knew from the outset that the actor would be out of his league but the producer wanted a name to bolster the picture's marquee image and the player was prepared to stick his neck out for the reflected glory it would bring him.

In the event, the director, Daniel Mann, whom Lancaster had worked for on *Come Back, Little Sheba*, another film in which the honours went to an untypically unglamorous woman (Shirley Booth), kept the show on the right road, and the results did Burt no harm at all.

The plot was pure Williams. Serafina (Magnani) is an earthy Sicilian peasant woman living in a steamy town on the Gulf of Mexico. She has remained faithful to the memory of her dead spouse for many years, even to the extent of keeping his ashes in a vase on the mantelpiece. Suppressing her natural sensuality, she lets her appearance get sleazier and sleazier until her teenage daughter calls her 'disgusting' to her face. She also learns that her revered spouse kept a mistress, knowledge that paves the way for the arrival of Mangiacavallo, his muscles rippling under his bared torso. Not only does he remind her of her husband, but he has a rose tattooed on his chest just as the dear, if faithless, departed had. These fortuitous circumstances combined with the amiable New Orleans truckdriver's capacity to amuse and entertain in buffoonish fashion gradually strip away her bitterness and she begins to live again.

One of Williams' more optimistic plays, this is Serafina's show. Maureen Stapleton, who'd played the part on Broadway because Magnani's English was inadequate, had done a professional job, but there was no doubting the splendour of the Italian actress's performance in the film and it was duly rewarded with an Oscar for Best Actress. Many years later Lancaster gave credit where it was due to both his award-winning leading ladies: 'In my opinion,' he declared, 'Shirley Booth is the finest actress I have ever worked with. And I would put Magnani next. Really superb artists, these two women. You're awed working with them, they're so good. Nevertheless, glamour is still a prerequisite (in Hollywood), although like everything else it's not what it used to be.'

For his own part, he could take some comfort from reviews that insisted that he'd tried and, in some cases, suggested he'd succeeded. Arthur Knight (in *Saturday Review*) said, 'He attacks the part with zest and intelligence ... But one is always aware that he is acting, that he is playing a part that fits him physically, but is beyond his emotional depths. His strong-toothed grin, his cropped, slicked-back hair, his bent-kneed walk are, like his precarious Italian accent, mannerisms and devices carefully acquired for the occasion and barely more than skin deep. The earnestness of his effort only serves to highlight Magnani's own complete submergence in her role.' By contrast the *New York Times* considered he'd 'superbly' matched Anna Magnani, while John McCarter of the *New Yorker* felt that he 'wasn't bad as the dim-witted suitor'. That however was damning with faint praise after his eulogistic comments on the leading actress. 'Miss Magnani is one minute moving you to tears and the next reducing you to helpless laughter, but no matter what your emotional state, she holds on to you like a limpet with her incredible talent.'

In Britain, the coolly rational Dilys Powell, after stressing Magnani's magnificence, found quality in her overshadowed leading man. 'He seems to me to have not the clown's mug which the widow sees, but the face of a good-looking wolf,' she told *Sunday Times* readers. 'All the same, Mr Lancaster, a much better actor than a few years ago one had any reason to suppose, contributes much of the boobyish sympathy and gentleness which the role needs. Indeed the whole film is finely acted.'

As consolation prizes go, it wasn't bad at all.

six
ENIGMA

By 1955, Burt Lancaster was at the height of his power. He had a string of acting successes behind him and *Marty* had given credibility to his activities as a producer of distinction. His 'Mr Teeth and Muscles' image had been tempered to the extent that he could command parts in serious films like *The Rose Tattoo* and *Come Back, Little Sheba*. With assets worth at least three million dollars, he could only be described as immensely rich by the standards of the time. He had completed his family when his fifth child and third daughter, Sighle-Ann (pronounced Sheila) was born in 1954 and the family was luxuriously installed in the kind of Bel Air home that befitted the status of its breadwinner. Burt could write his own pay cheques, underwrite his own projects and do whatever else he liked, yet he was not, by all accounts, a happy man.

Meeting him in those days was an experience that made brave men quail. His physical size was intimidating enough, but it was his ability to freeze people with a single disdainful glance that destroyed them. He didn't suffer fools gladly, and those whom he put in that category were never left in any doubt about it. He could be terribly stern one minute and terribly funny the next, cracking jokes with dry humour and smiling his terrifying smile, but few people were totally at ease with him.

Among those who were not was his wife Norma, who developed a slight twitch in one eye as the years went by. Life with such a monumental presence could not have been easy, especially for one of a slightly nervous disposition. However she learned that smiling benignly through Burt's more outrageous bursts of temperament was the best means of survival.

Sheila Graham tells of one such incident when the Lancasters were having a screening in their private projection room for a couple who worked for them. Burt and the wife had an argument about pre-marital sex, before the film began. He was for it, she against it. Then the lights

60

went out and the quartet settled down to watch. Towards the end of the film, Burt, having had an hour or so to mull over the discussion, could control himself no longer. He stood up and raged at the woman: 'Get out of here and don't ever come back.' To make sure they understood, he escorted them to their car and kicked the door savagely as they climbed in. All this with not a drop of alcohol to drink. Norma remained calm and remarkably unembarrassed by the proceedings, which indeed turned out to be the familiar storm in a tea cup. Before long the couple were visiting as regularly as ever.

Lancaster reserved his most vitriolic displays for journalists and photographers, two professions he instinctively loathed. He was undoubtedly one of the few genuinely knowledgeable actors when it came to the technicalities of film-making, with an excellent grasp of the finer points of editing, lighting, advertising, even make-up. He was also professionally vain, in the best possible way, in that he'd never be late and he'd always know his lines. As a producer he was shrewd and, as he himself has noted, quite capable of sacrificing art to commerce where finances dictated it should be so.

But publicity was another matter. He recognised the need for it, without accepting its nuts and bolts. 'Don't bother me with any of these creepy press people', was the line he habitually gave his press agent. The sight of a photographer waiting for him at an airport could set off a twenty-minute tirade while a question he didn't like could result in the unfortunate newspaper man being banned for life. Having slung one journalist out of his hotel suite in New York for just such a crime, he recognised him when he turned up with a photographer to do a location piece on a later film.

'You guys are assholes,' he told them. 'You ask people to do things and you do nothing in return. You waste our time and there is no guarantee that the story will appear. I can go into a market and buy a can of beans and I pay for it. That's good business. But you guys ...'

'You're spending all this money [on ads] in our magazine,' the writer replied. 'Wouldn't it be a good investment to give us thirty minutes of your time and you'd have several pages of publicity free?'

To which Burt, irrational and pig-headed as ever where this *bête noire* was concerned, retorted, 'Absolutely not. I don't care what you do. You can take pictures of me picking my nose or scratching my ass, but I won't give you any of my time.'

When it came to personal vanity, Burt was a strange mixture of physical perfection and peripheral bad taste. His long-time make-up

61

man, Bob Schiffer, who later became head of make-up at Disney, claimed that he never saw his employer look in the mirror. On a train going to Kansas City after *The Kentuckian*, Burt was talking about his next film, *The Rose Tattoo*. 'I hadn't read the part or anything,' Schiffer commented, 'but I said to him, "You can't play it with all that hair." He had all this long golden hair for the Western, and I ended up cutting it all off to about a quarter of an inch. With nail scissors. I think if you smeared dung all over his face and told him he looked great, he'd believe you!'

His body, though, was a source of continuing pride. Finely tuned by early-morning running sessions round the UCLA track and continuous practice on the trapeze with Nick Cravat, it was as impressively muscled as ever. He exerted iron discipline over his diet to keep it that way. Lunch in his offices consisted of hard-boiled eggs, cottage cheese and crackers. His secretary prepared the same meal every day. In the evening he'd drink two scotches and eat a plain steak with green salad. He chewed the meat with his perfect bite, a dental technique pioneered by a Californian in the early fifties. It involved remodelling a man's mouth so that the upper and lower teeth didn't grind against each other, a process that allegedly eliminated the need for future fillings. The treatment cost about 10,000 dollars and Hecht had it too so as not to cause his star any embarrassment. Although Burt was primarily interested in the avant garde preventative aspect of it, there is no doubt that his flashing almost hypnotic trademark grin was even more prominent afterwards. His one indulgence, smoking untipped Camels, showed a most uncharacteristic disregard for his health, but presumably the frustrated gourmet in him felt that this was the lesser of several potentially damaging evils.

In his daily life, the body beautiful was concealed under some of the most unappealing clothes that even Los Angeles could provide. One favoured outfit was an electric-blue suit, worn with a white shirt, a canary-yellow tie and heavy brown shoes. When he dressed to go to the opera, he'd look like a hood, in a black shirt and white satin tie. Norma matched him in the matter of garish dressiness. A white cashmere jacket lined with lace, with a white mink collar and diamanté model sleeves was just her style.

The offices of Hecht-Hill-Lancaster at 202 North Cannon Drive reflected the actor's liking for visual opulence. The scriptwriter, James Hill, was Rita Hayworth's fifth husband at the time and was brought in as a kind of buffer state between Hecht and Lancaster in 1955. 'Hecht and I complement each other. Harold is the best executive I ever saw and an exceptional critic. He's not creative but infallible when it comes to knowing what's good. Jim Hill, our story man is wonderful. And let me tell you, good material is the life and breath of this business. No actor can make a bad story good.'

Hill's office was all spartan practicality, in sharp contrast to Burt's which faced it across the corridor. The star sat behind a huge kidney-shaped desk covered entirely in white leather. Behind him there was a pool with an electric waterfall and an artificial tree, with orchids stuck into its branches. In the morning the secretary would turn on the waterfall and a man would come in to change the flowers. The white walls were hung with Impressionist paintings and there was a television set in a cabinet covered with semi-precious stones with a lion's head to lift the screen into the viewing position.

As he didn't involve himself with interior decoration, it is unlikely that Burt specifically ordered this high-priced vulgarity, but by this time he certainly felt at home in such surroundings. The circular entrance hall was equally startling, with a white carpet and a cage full of tropical birds reaching from floor to ceiling. The corridor was hung with original Rouaults, bought as investments, while the executive washroom counted an electric shoe polisher among its accoutrements. It was used exclusively by Hecht, Hill and Lancaster, as benefitted the despotic rulers of a strictly hierarchical organisation.

Hecht and Lancaster could always count ambition among their similarities, but by this time they had little else in common. Burt was a tall golden gentile, Harold a short dark Jew, and the jealousies that were built into their relationship were beginning to come out of the woodwork. Burt referred to his partner as 'The Mole' or 'Lord Mole' and to his slender-legged wife as 'Ladybird Legs'. No doubt the nicknames were lightly given but they were gall to Hecht who would have liked to equal his vibrant star verbally, given that it was impossible for him to do so physically.

On one occasion, he offered the journalist, Hollis Alpert, a huge sum to compose one liners for him to say in the style of Sam Goldwyn, whenever the occasion arose. When Alpert asked a mutual friend why the proposition had been made, the man replied, 'He wants you to make him into a tall gentile.' Although such divisions didn't make for the happiest of working relationships, the two men would need each other for five more years during which time they would produce some of their best films. Meanwhile they rubbed along by using Jim Hill, a rather more easygoing character than either of them, as an intermediary.

Both Lancaster and the organisation were noted for their generosity, especially at Christmas when there were splendid presents and an extravaganza of a party for the employees. Back in the Bel Air mansion, the festivities were equally lavish, with a huge lighted reindeer mounted on the roof of the house and celebrations that went on for days in a thoroughly Irish tradition. However Burt didn't confine his open-handedness to Christmas week. One of his nicer traits was that he never forgot anyone who had been kind to him or done him a favour. He always found a place for Nick Cravat on his staff and also for his stand-in, Tom Conroy.

Likewise his father, now in a wheelchair, and his elder brother Jim, were protected from harsh economic reality by being given jobs under the Hecht-Hill-Lancaster umbrella. The fact that Jim with his strong Brooklyn accent and ordinary appearance was so totally unlike his brother that it was impossible to imagine they came from the same background, cut no ice with Burt. Jim had supported the family during the Depression so he was owed a living for the rest of his life. And he got it. Another plus for Lancaster, who hated references to his generosity, was that he arranged his handouts with as much secrecy as possible.

Such behaviour stemmed from the innate sense of justice that influenced his choice of films and, even more importantly, his political line. When Hollywood was sharply divided by the witch hunts of Senator Joseph McCarthy and his House of Un-American Activities, Burt wasn't afraid to stand up and be counted. With Humphrey Bogart, Lauren Bacall, Judy Garland, William Wyler, John Garfield and about 500 other like-minded Hollywood luminaries, he joined the Committee for the First Amendment, an organisation that was soon listed as a 'communist front'. In fact it was fairly toothless in its defence of the Hollywood Ten, a group whose left-wing political beliefs had endangered their careers, but it did make a plea for sanity in what were very vicious times.

As a lifelong Democrat, Burt has consistently supported civil rights and racial equality. He was also willing to open his home for fund-raising events, in a way he'd never had dreamed of using it for parties, a form of social communication he particularly abhorred.

Under normal circumstances, his home life was family orientated, though he had a circle of friends taken from most of the professions with the notable exception of acting. Doctors, businessmen and lawyers were among his regular partners for golf and bridge, the two games he liked best. Both offered plenty of scope for obsessive analysis over long periods which kept his interest in them alive. They were also impossible to perfect which made them into on-going challenges of the kind he particularly enjoyed.

During the middle and late fifties, he played golf almost every day, returning on occasion with a broad grin to announce proudly that he'd got round in seventy-six. He also practised the game on his office carpet, shouting 'fore' whenever the door opened. As for bridge, he set up the Savoy Club with some friends, but got into a fight with a lady player who threw her cards in his face after he'd quibbled about her bidding. After that, he preferred to have two tables at home so that he could switch to the second if he fell out with the people at the first. Although he was a good player, many of his guests refused to return to be outrageously insulted again. One who did was the faithful Nick Cravat who still partners him today, having survived some thirty years of recriminations over the green baize.

The rest of his limited spare time was taken up with reading which he still does voraciously, and with regular visits to concerts. He'd acquired a comprehensive knowledge of the arts that included ballet and painting as well as music. As a father, he was surprisingly benign. Both he and Norma believed that children should be brought up without any limitations on free expressions so the five young Lancasters ran amok as they wished. James was something of an oddball, given to singing the entire score of *My Fair Lady* to anyone who would listen and to coming up to stangers and tickling them under the arms. Billy had a slight limp from the polio he'd had as a baby and a more easygoing disposition than his brother.

As a husband, Burt was less than faithful, according to Shelley Winters, though no breath of scandal was ever attached to the name of Lancaster by the vitriol-tipped pens of Hollywood's gossip columnists. Although other names have been bandied around as possible partners, it is Miss Winters who comes clean in her racy autobiography, *Shelley*. By her accounts, New York lifts were places of destiny for Burt. Not only did his break into Broadway in *A Sound of Hunting* stem from a between floors encounter, but his first significant meeting with Miss Winters, born Shelley Schrift, occurred in just the same circumstances.

There they were, strangers in the night at the Gotham Hotel in 1947, shortly after Burt's marriage. He had two centre stalls tickets for the second performance of *South Pacific* in his pocket and no one to accom-

65

pany him to the show, and she had a single for the back row. They'd nodded to each other across a crowded studio commissary back in Hollywood so what could be more natural than to make an instant date before they reached the lobby?

For the blonde honeypot from Brooklyn, a true professional who was never so foolish as to go downstairs without her borrowed mink, it was lust at first sight, an emotion she'd previously felt for Lawrence Tierney, John Ireland and Errol Flynn and would soon feel for Marlon Brando, William Holden and her second-husband-to-be, Vittorio Gassmann. Of Burt, she wrote, 'He was charming and funny and, oh God, so handsome. And he was, I think, one of the most gracefully athletic men I've ever seen. Just to watch him walk was almost a physical pleasure.'

It wasn't the only delight she was to have in his company. During *Some Enchanted Evening*, the couple held hands and shed sentimental tears and, when the curtain finally came down, the gallant Lancaster carried her to his limo. At Le Pavillon, once she'd seen off Norman Mailer who'd dropped into their booth to try to sell the film rights of *The Naked and the Dead* to Lancaster, they swapped ancestor anecdotes until closing time, then 'skipped and sang and ran along the middle of an empty Fifth Avenue like kids'. Later there was a ritual laying of a blue and white bedspread on a thick white rug and, to the strains of Gigli singing 'O Paradiso' on the gramophone, the affair was on.

It lasted for about two years whenever their respective film commitments permitted until Miss Winters, learning from the *Hollywood Reporter* that Norma was expecting her third child, found enough consolation with Marlon Brando to give her the courage to break it off.

In the meantime, she'd been ostracised by her Orthodox Jewish parents for consorting with a married man, and forced to move out of their house into a penthouse apartment at the Villa Italia found for her by Lancaster. It was furnished with a leopard skin couch, and a uniformed maid was hired to look after the buxom beauty when her lover was unavoidably absent. She recalls him as an attentive swain, ever ready to dispose sables around her shoulders and send limos to her door. When he'd claimed that his marriage was in difficulty she had high hopes that he would leave Norma permanently, though she admits that, in her heart of hearts, she knew that he'd stay with his children while they were so young. Events were to prove her right. The Lancasters overcame their problems to such good effect that their marriage survived until 1969 when their youngest daughter was fifteen.

Shelley Winters gives an early clue to the enigma of Burt Lancaster when she writes of their first evening together, at *South Pacific*. 'When Bloody Mary sang the words, "Most people live on an lonely island," both Burt and I were weeping. I knew why I was weeping, but he seemed so strong. I couldn't imagine what could make him relate to that song so deeply. He was rich, famous and at the beginning of what promised to be a great career. He was married and had children and a beautiful home. How could that song evoke such sadness in him?'

Superficially he had everything, but ten years later, the search for the real Burt was still more obscured by the trappings of success and wealth. Those who knew him at the time felt that being a producer/actor was too limiting for him. He has been described as an enormously intelligent man who could have been President of the United States, or at the very least a businessman in a position of great power, a tycoon of the stature of Felix Happer whom he played in Bill Forsyth's *Local Hero* in 1982. However when he was asked to stand on the Democratic ticket for the governorship of California in the 1970s as the antidote to Ronald Reagan, he refused, possibly because the offer came too late.

It certainly seems as if his time of greatest doubt coincided with his period of professional invincibility in the middle and late fifties. In 1954, *Cinemonde* described him as a 'Colossus wounded by life, a beautiful brute', as if his dissatisfaction was clear for all to see. Certainly he was at the point of no return in the sense that a man in his forties must either continue on his set course or make fairly rapid and drastic decisions to change it. Yet Lancaster was obsessive about meeting challenges. If, deep down, he'd felt that he wasn't fulfilling himself, he would surely have taken action.

He was an enigma in other ways too. For a sensitive and generous man with an appreciation of beauty in many artistic forms, he was remarkably rude, even loutish at times. He hadn't been polished by either his parents or his education and his wealth hadn't turned him into one of nature's gentlemen. Clifford Odets, who part-wrote the script of one of Lancaster's most successful late fifties films, *The Sweet Smell of Success*, is on record as saying that he couldn't think of Burt as one man. He listed his traits as: (1) the cocksure; (2) the wild (inexhaustible physical energy plus unreflected enthusiasm); (3) the paternal (and slightly patronising); (4) the cruel (the Hyde side of Jekyll); (5) the would-be gentleman; (6) the con man. If they seemed incompatible to Odets, they must have seemed even more so to Lancaster himself, as he tried to deal with his own complexities. To his credit, he progressively mastered his terrible temper to the extent that he could use it when he wanted to rather than when he couldn't stop himself. Yet the cruelty and the conmanship tended to increase, rather than decrease, over the next decade.

Sheila Graham summed up the fifties' Burt very well when she wrote: 'He has a monolithic personality. He is a giant single. He is made of steel but he listens to far-off cries for help, and gives it. Nothing is too much trouble and he will knock himself out for a cause. He is a great salesman, he can talk you in and out of anything, an idea, a property, how to play a scene, money for a good cause. He has a tremendous ego and he is very opinionated, but perhaps he is entitled to it.'

It is hard to say fairer than that.

seven
SWINGING HIGH

So beginneth the five-year heyday of Burt Lancaster, producer/star. The discovery and recognition that he had feet of clay as a director, an occupation which he'd hitherto seen as the natural outlet for his talents, inspired him to new creativity as a producer. Relentlessly active as ever, he backed a whole string of projects that were notable for being very good of their kind. Better still, they showed a commendable variety of purpose as Lancaster tested himself on Shaw and Rattigan as enthusiastically as on the high wire. It was in this period, that he controlled his destiny most surely. Perhaps as a natural corollary, it was also a time of bitter dispute as the man of steel attempted to impose his wishes on people like Lawrence Olivier and Clifford Odets. Hiring class and making it work for you is always a tricky business, and there is no doubt that Burt was less tactful than most.

An habitual analyser, he has explained his film-maker's philosophy in the following terms. 'I enjoy doing a film as an actor, particularly if the part is exciting or the subject matter appeals to me, but the real satisfaction is in production, in seeing it through from inception to completion. I think that in the main, film has to be entertaining. This is an industry and its nature is to sell entertainment. People go to the theatre for the most part to relax, to escape the tensions of life and the pressures in the world. Most picture-makers try to make pictures which have the broadest possible appeal, for the obvious reason they are profitable and you have to stay alive. I like to get a point across but I don't see myself as a crusader. I think that every honest producer tries to say something. Everything, whether we like the term or not, has a message – even if the message is nothing more than "sit back, we're just going to have some fun".'

Trapeze, James Hill's first project for Hecht-Hill-Lancaster, fits very neatly into this last category, being a high-wire extravaganza filmed in and around the celebrated Cirque D'hiver in Paris. Clearly this was a project after Lancaster's own heart, a definitive circus film which he intended to set the seal on his many years as an acrobat. At the age of forty-three, his tensile strength was unimpaired, but he was realistic enough to know that the elasticity wouldn't last much longer, and indeed he never put together so agile an act again. The script alone, written by James R. Webb from Max Catto's novel, *The Killing Frost*, cost a hundred thousand dollars and *Trapeze* turned out to be the most expensive of all Hecht-Lancaster films. No money was spared to make the tribute worthy of the star and Sir Carol Reed was lured with a share of the profits into the director's canvas chair. A bright young actor, Tony Curtis, whom Lancaster had worked with and liked on *Criss Cross*, was cast as his protégé and the shapely Italian beauty, Gina Lollobrigida, then at the height of her very considerable sex appeal, was signed up for the love interest – and paid one hundred thousand dollars, an astronomical sum at the time, for the privilege.

The Cirque d'Hiver had been built a hundred and three years before at the instigation of Louis Dejean, the most acclaimed circus manager of his day. Originally called the Cirque Napoleon, it was opened in the presence of the Emperor Napoleon III in December 1852. Under Dejean, who remained in command for twenty years, it was established as one of Europe's greatest circuses. One of the highlights came in 1859 when a Frenchman called Leotard, who'd invented the flying trapeze, demonstrated it to wildly cheering Parisian crowds.

There could be no more historic place for Lancaster to make *Trapeze*, and he must have felt an affinity with the shades of dead aerialists as he climbed the ladder, his muscles showing as impressively as ever through a diamanté-studded leotard and white tights, to face the cameras. Curtis and Lollobrigida had been trained to do as many of the acrobatics as possible themselves and doubling was cut to a minimum. Lancaster, of course, did most of his own stunts and those that were too dangerous even for him were performed by Eddie Ward of Ringling Brothers Circus. The two men had worked together in 1935 in the Gorman Brothers Circus and Lancaster had enough respect for Ward's skill to appoint him technical adviser on *Trapeze* as well.

The story is pure corn, with Lancaster as an ageing and embittered high-wire artist who is persuaded by Curtis's brash would-be circus star to teach him his repertoire of tricks. The two men agree to do a new act when a go-getting beauty (Lollobrigida), also an aerialist, comes between them. She falls first for the younger man, then sees the error of her ways and chooses Burt's maturer charms instead. This of course causes ructions in the male ego department, but the matter is resolved by Lancaster getting the girl and the tranquillity he needs for his declining years, while Curtis has the consolation prize of being one of only a handful of artistes capable of doing a triple aerial somersault.

The audiences may not have been queueing around the block for the narrative, but there could be no doubting the attractions of the aerial thrills. The film was made in blaze of publicity, uncharacteristically so far as Burt was concerned, and all of it emphasised how genuinely perilous the stunts had been for the stars. Burt may not have liked the bright lights but there is no doubt that he enjoyed the end result which was that the picture made a packet for Hecht-Hill-Lancaster, earning seven and a half million dollars in domestic rentals alone. For a producer/star with acrobatic leanings, it was a dream come true.

Lancaster gave exuberant proof of his post-*Trapeze* well-being when he did a back flip during a mock fight in the aisle of a passenger plane en route for Boston. Unfortunately he landed in the lap of Artur Snabel, the famous, and at that moment, very worried pianist. Fearful for his hands, he expressed his lack of amusement in the strongest possible terms. On arrival, Burt vaulted over a ten-foot wire perimeter fence to avoid the reception committee.

Ten years after *The Killers*, Lancaster was still in the grip of Hal Wallis; and *The Rainmaker*, his second picture for 1956, was his penultimate role for Wallis before he severed the connection for good. Although Paramount had originally cast William Holden in the title role, it was a part tailor-made for Burt. Starbuck is essentially a con man, a wandering jack-of-all-trades who arrives in his horse and buggy in a drought-wracked South western township, and promises to open the heavens for a modest fee of a hundred dollars. He is a colourful, persuasive character, with all the brash confidence of a super salesman, and he backs up his act so effectively with drums and machines that it seems inevitable that rain will fall – as indeed it does.

There is a second more important strand to the plot which matches Lancaster with one of the legendary figures of Hollywood, Katharine Hepburn. Because she'd been out of the business for four years, she had to give pride of place at the top of the credits to Burt, but that in no way inhibited her portrayal of Lizzie Curry, the frustrated, leathery spinster, who looks after her farmer father and her two brothers. She is parched metaphorically as the land is literally, and again it is Starbuck who

71

convinces her that she is beautiful and worthy of any man's love, in a touching middle-aged romance.

'Once in a life you've got to take a chance on a con man,' says Starbuck to Lizzie at a key point in the film. Many felt that the sentence was equally appropriate in reality and that Hepburn was putting herself on the line by agreeing to co-star with Lancaster. His reputation as a scene stealer had preceded him, but no doubt she felt, rightly, that she had more than enough talent to cope with his flamboyant screen presence.

The making of the film was attended by rumours that the two stars weren't getting on, as seems likely given their forceful characters. Hepburn despised Burt's Hollywood approach to acting, and especially his preference for learning his lines every morning for the next day. Given his habit of insisting on last-minute script changes on all his pictures, it was a sensible precaution but Hepburn, with much more stage experience behind her, considered it essentially sloppy and unprofessional. As for Lancaster, he allegedly found the most celebrated leading lady he'd appeared with too affected for his taste. Their personal animosity is reflected in an end result that lacks the chemical spark of romance. Lancaster is the charlatan rainmaker to his finger tips, but Hepburn, with her educated New England voice and her civilised manner, is not a natural country cousin. Nevertheless it was she who walked away with most of the plaudits – and the Oscar nomination for Best Actress, though she lost out at the award ceremony to Ingrid Bergman in *Anastasia*.

Typically of Hal Wallis, money-maker par excellance, the film was shot in studio, so missing out on some potentially splendid dust-bowl locations. Nevertheless, several critics considered it better than N. Richard Nash's Broadway play, on which he'd based his screenplay and one, Paul Holt of the *Daily Herald*, ascribed the improvement to the stars. '*The Rainmaker*,' he wrote, 'is much better than the play, mainly because of the magical combination of Lancaster, as the con man with dreams as tall as skyscrapers, and Hepburn, who plays a gangling frustrated spinster. He has never done anything as good as this. She is at the height of her talent. Together they push the film to greatness and hold it there.'

Fulsome praise indeed, and it was echoed, though more analytically, by Dilys Powell in the *Sunday Times*: 'The glib visitor is played by Burt Lancaster. His gestures and poses are a shade athletic, and once or twice I had the fancy that he was still impersonating the Crimson Pirate. He is saddled too, with awkward stretches of dialogue, fake-imaginative phrases which, however well they may accord with the character on stage, on the screen make one restive. But when it is needed, he brings a hint of uncertainty to the part and the result is a very likeable pathos.' Flawed it may have been, but *The Rainmaker* was a box-office success. Better still from Burt Lancaster's point of view, it established him as the stuff that celluloid con artists are made of, so paving the way for *Elmer Gantry* which would prove to be his pinnacle four years later.

Meanwhile he went to work for Wallis for the final time on *Gunfight at The O.K. Corral*. Appropriately the picture teamed him up once again with Kirk Douglas who'd played second fiddle to him but outclassed him as an actor in *I Walk Alone* in 1948. The pair were christened 'Burt and Kirk, the Terrible Tempered Twins' by Sheilah Graham, who summed them up with these two taut sentences: 'Burt was autocratic from the start. Kirk waited three years and seven films before he dared to be himself.'

Given that Hal Wallis had fathered the careers of both men, it is ironic that he now found himself on the receiving end of their capacity to drive a hard bargain. By this time, Douglas, like Lancaster, had his own production company, and Wallis eventually had to agree to pay them a hundred times as much as he had nine years before. Even taking inflation into account, it must have hurt like hell. However he was astute enough to know that they were the actors he needed so he bit on the bullet and capitulated to their joint will with as good grace as he could muster. Later the picture's takings would give him the last laugh in his eleven-year association with Lancaster.

Wallis hired Leon Uris, who has since produced a whole string of blockbuster novels that rely on fleshing out the bare bones of history with highly imaginative fiction for their success, to write the screenplay. Working from an idea culled from an article by George Scullin, Uris uses the talents that were to make him famous to build a suspenseful scenario out of the brief real-life battle between Wyatt Earp, his brothers, Morgan and Virgil, and Doc Holliday on the side of the angels and the outlawed Clanton gang. This encounter took place at Tombstone, Arizona on 26 October 1881, and it is re-staged every year in the same town for the benefit of tourists.

As historical fact gives way to celluloid fiction in the Uris version, the characters are sanitized for the audience's convenience. The original Earp was not such a fine upstandingly honest Marshall as Uris - and indeed Lancaster - would have us believe, while Holliday was an altogether meaner consumptive doctor than Douglas portrays. The

73

Clanton Brothers were re-written in appropriately villainous vein and a lady gambler (Rhonda Fleming) and a Madame (Jo van Fleet) were added to give the picture 'dimension', otherwise known as curves.

True or false, there is no doubt that Lancaster and Douglas thrived on their gun-toting stereotypes, nor that the film turned out to be a fine wide-sky horse opera. Charles Lang Jr's beautiful colour photography and Dimitri Tiomkin's rousing score can take their share of the credit, as can director John Sturges, who contrives to mould some fairly unrelated Earp-Holliday anecdotes into a structured picture that builds steadily towards its tense climax. It may not be a classic Western, but it's a fine piece of entertainment.

Lancaster makes Earp into a quiet well-dressed hero who speaks improbably good English and prefers to knock an adversary out with his gun rather than shoot him full of bullets. Initially full of zeal for the law, he has to adjust his priorities in the final analysis to ride out to O.K. Corral to avenge his murdered younger brother. The part is well within Burt's range and provides him with opportunities for measured soul searching and walking tall.

Few would have envied John Sturges his task with Lancaster and Douglas, particularly because this was during their period of greatest rivalry. 'The strangest Alliance This Side of Heaven or Hell' read the film's publicity poster, referring to Earp and Holliday, but those in the know in Hollywood thought it could apply equally convincingly to the men who played them. Kirk Douglas had started in the business at much the same time as Burt, but hadn't made quite the same instant impact so that he always felt that he was a few steps behind. The gap allegedly gave him a Lancaster complex, so that he wanted to prove that anything Burt could do, he could do better. It must be said that, on occasion, Burt enjoyed exploiting his psychological edge.

One such opportunity came up when autograph hunters were hounding Burt as the two men walked towards the cars when shooting for the day had ended. 'Why don't you ask Mr. Douglas for his?' the actor enquired. 'Great performer. Of course, you don't recognise him without his built-up shoes.' Although Kirk was only a couple of inches shorter than Burt, his ego was so bruised that he was weeping by the time he was driven away.

In later life, Douglas said that he'd always considered himself a character actor. Lancaster, on the other hand, was indubitably a star. However *Gunfight at The O.K. Corral* gave Douglas a chance to come out ahead because he had the more colourful part and he was riding high after being nominated for an Oscar for Best Actor for his portrayal of Vincent Van Gogh in Vincente Minnelli's *Lust for Life*. He was also smarting under the gauntlet thrown down by John Wayne who said to him, after seeing that film, 'Jeez, Kirk, why in hell did you play this pantywaist? Guys like us, we should play the heroes.'

In the final film, the two men were roughly equal, which means that Sturges did a good job. Presumably his memories weren't too horrific, because he also directed the less successful sequel, *Hour of the Gun*, ten years later with two more actors who were reputedly not the easiest: James Garner as Wyatt Earp and Jason Robards as Doc Holliday.

The reviews of *Gunfight at The O.K. Corral* concentrated on the film, rather than the performances. 'No single event in the movie will surprise anybody. But everything is done with an extra degree of quality,' observed William K. Zinsser in the *New York Herald-Tribune* while Hollis Alpert of *Saturday Review* thought it was 'far more relaxed than most movies of this type'.

When Lancaster returned to Los Angeles from Old Tuscon, the cactus belt Western facsimile city in Arizona where the O.K. Corral had been reconstructed, he was possessed by a new resolve to make quality productions on his own account. Whether or not this determination stemmed from his prolonged location rivalry with Kirk Douglas over the relative merits of their respective companies, it had the effect of making him break his own mould. Previously he'd looked for class when he was being paid by someone else, usually Hal Wallis, and made sure fire box-office winners like *The Crimson Pirate* for himself. The exception to his rule had been *Marty* which he hadn't appeared in. He'd followed his Best Film Oscar winner up in 1957 with *The Bachelor Party*, which again combined the scriptwriting talents of Paddy Chayevsky with the directional ones of Delbert Mann to good, if less award winning effect.

Now he would make five films in a row for Hecht-Hill-Lancaster, and break the company apart in the process. Harold Hecht was a man who could sniff out money-spinners blindfolded and understandably, as he was always behind the scenes, he had no interest in financial failures. Lancaster, on the other hand, was motivated at this stage in his career by a desire to carve himself a niche in history. His athletic powers were inevitably on the wane and, for a man whose tastes were not extravagant in the Hollywood sense, he had more money than he could possibly need. 'I am terribly wealthy. I am worth three and a half million dollars, I am very happily married. I have five children. I've everything

I want. What more could I possibly need?' he enquired of the *Evening Standard*'s Thomas Wiseman.

The answer was immortality. Burt was also well aware that flops could keep him nearly as rich as triumphs. As a producer he could have his company hire him at a minimal salary so avoiding personal income tax. Instead he'd pay a much lower corporate tax on his company's profits. Heads or tails, he was bound to come out the winner.

With this in mind, Burt commissioned Ernest Lehman to convert his novelette, *Sweet Smell of Success*, for the screen. On one occasion, according to the indefatigable Sheilah Graham, the two men had lunch together and the conversation went something like this:

Lancaster: I've got a good mind to beat you up.

Lehman (astonished): Why?

Lancaster: I think you could have written some of the scenes better.

Lehman: Go ahead. Beat me up. I'd like to get my hands on some of your money.

Lancaster didn't take up the invitation to litigation. Instead he hired Clifford Odets to lend a helping hand, then passed the completed screenplay on to Alexander MacKendrick to direct. A British director, whose greatest claim to fame was making the best-ever Ealing comedy, *Whisky Galore*, can hardly have been an obvious choice but MacKendrick gave the film both the tension and the seediness it needed to make it nearly great.

The picture reunited Burt with Tony Curtis with whom he'd got on so well on *Trapeze* two years earlier. They'd resolved at the time to appear together in *The Ballad of Cat Ballou*, as adapted from the novel by Roy Chanslor. In fact that project was a further seven years in the melting pot before Lee Marvin won his Oscar for the putative Lancaster role, with Michael Callan as his side-kick. However, *Sweet Smell of Success* proved an adequate substitute.

To prove just how serious he was about his change of tactics, Burt put on spectacles for J.J. Hunsecker, the first morally corrupt villain of his career. J.J. is a vicious Broadway syndicated columnist with sixty million readers who uses his ill-gotten power with total ruthlessness to make or break as he pleases. He is neither a cardboard cutout villain, nor a gangster, both of which Lancaster was familiar with, but a genuinely evil character whose obsessive adoration for the sister (Susan Harrison) effectively ruins her life.

Hunsecker hires an equally devious and go-getting publicist called Sidney Falco (Curtis) to carry out dirty work that includes breaking up a romance between his sister and a jazz guitarist (Marty Milner) by smearing him as both a Communist and a drug addict. After the jazz player is fired due to false gossip to this effect planted by Falco in a rival column, J.J. decides that he must be destroyed totally by being framed for possession of marijuana.

The film is a savage exposé of the reprehensible moral code of the hack journalist who becomes megalomaniac under the influence of his own sadistic invention. These villains wear lounge suits and exude respectability, yet their moral turpitude is as total as the vitriol drips from their typewriters. 'He's a man with forty faces – all of them false,' says J.J. of his hatchetman at one point, and at another, 'I'd hate to take a bite out of you. You're a cookie full of arsenic.' Falco too has no illusions about his pact with the devil: 'With him for a friend, you don't need an enemy', is his summing up.

J.J. Hunsecker is one of Lancaster's favourite parts, and friends have suggested that he identified fairly closely with the power-hungry monster. When it came to review time, it was noted that Burt's interpretation of Odets' authentically sour dialogue had the ring of truth, and it is possible that Sandy MacKendrick went along with that point of view for he had this to say of hs first experience in control – albeit remote control – of a Hollywood star: 'Burt has never faltered in his career. One of the things he has, that the stars had, is that he can walk into a room and there is a change in the heartbeat. If you had some instrument, you could measure it. It's like having a wild animal there suddenly. It has to do with aggression and potential violence. I think some politicians have it, but no English actor.

'I was very conscious that there was an ego different to others. The stars had this, a neurosis which goes right to the edge. You somehow use this to get performances from these deep-sea monsters. There was this enormous difference between him and Tony Curtis. Tony has a fantastic vanity, but no ego. He could act Burt off the screen, but he will never be a star. He hasn't this granite quality of the ego.'

Variety noticed 'a remarkable change of pace for Lancaster, who appears bespectacled and quiet but smouldering with malice and menace', while the *New York Times* felt that the film was 'Meanness ... rendered fascinating.'

Neither Harold Hecht nor the audiences who were conspicuous by their absence agreed. Hecht said openly that he hated the picture and wished it had never been made. He even shook his head when Burt, delighted with the film's reception at the premiere, threw his arms expansively around Clifford Odets. Time has proved both men were right according to their creeds. *Sweet Smell of Success* has never made money, but it was and is a very good film, and Lancaster found a new outlet for the inner turmoil and burning energy that haunted him. Instead of being physical or heroic, he became convincingly and grandiosely vicious. At the very least, it was an extension of his range.

eight
INTENSIFICATION

Burt set the first part of 1958 aside for repairing his fences. Pairing up the greats was a familiar Hollywood device for bringing in the crowds, and he'd worked it profitably enough himself with Gary Cooper in *Vera Cruz*. The man who received the clarion call this time was Clark Gable. He also received top billing, something Lancaster was never too proud to forgo in the interests of business. It didn't matter that Gable, at fifty-seven, was on the wane in the popularity stakes, nor that he was too old for the part he was to play. He was the man who'd immortalised himself in *Gone With The Wind*. He was in.

The submarine drama they collaborated on, *Run Silent, Run Deep*, was hailed as one of the best-ever slices of life as it is lived on the ocean floor. Gable plays a World War II submarine captain who loses one vessel to the Japanese in the Bongo Straits in 1942. When he takes command of another sub in Pearl Harbor his sole preoccupation is the chasing and sinking of the enemy destroyer that had fired its torpedoes against him. His vengeance trail is opposed and obstructed at every stage by his crew and his second-in-command (Lancaster) who had wanted and expected the top job for himself. Gradually Gable wins respect for his mission and, by disobeying orders from above, contrives to exact his just revenge. He then avoids the inevitable reprimand by dying a hero's death and leaving room at the controls for Burt.

This fairly routine patriotic plot was moulded by director Robert Wise into a graphic account of the way a submarine works and how the fear felt by the men is intensified by cramped and claustrophobic conditions. 'A better film about guys in the "silent service" has not been made,' stated Bosley Crowther in the *New York Times*.

In 1973, when he was interviewed by Rui Nogueira for *Film on Focus*, Wise recalled that shooting the picture hadn't exactly been a piece of cake: 'We had a lot of problems with the script we started – getting something we could all agree on. Then, as we were shooting, there was a lot of behind-the-scenes fighting and pulling going on between the three partners in the company.

'Gable started to sense half, two-thirds of the way through the film what was going on with the script and, since it was Lancaster's company, he started to be concerned about what was going to happen to him. So he started to raise a little fuss about wanting to know what the end of the script was going to be.'

In the event, he need not have worried because many of the reviewers compared the Gable-Lancaster tandem with the Gable-Spencer Tracy ones of earlier years. At the box office, *Run Silent, Run Deep* had to compete with Blake Edwards' riotous submarine comedy, *Operation Petticoat*, with another he-man duo, the evergreen Cary Grant and Tony Curtis, following up his excellent notices in *Sweet Smell of Success*. Typically it was a no contest, with the laughter-raiser scooping the pool over its more thought-provoking rival.

Nevertheless Hecht-Hill-Lancaster did well enough out of it to allow Burt to impose another of his exercises in artistic intensity on his nervous partners. Since *Come Back, Little Sheba*, he'd been careful to select parts that would stress his fortes: vitality and especially the ability to express strong emotions hard held just beneath the surface, rather than roles that would show up his limitations. Now he bought the rights to Terence Rattigan's two-act play, *Separate Tables*, with the stated aim of hiring Spencer Tracy to play the American writer, John Malcolm, to Sir Laurence Olivier's Major Pollack.

On stage the work had been done as two playlets, with Margaret Leighton and Eric Portman playing the two leads in both, first in London and subsequently on Broadway. For the screen version, it was thought that the rather esoteric material would be enhanced at the box office by having four star roles, rather than two and Terence Rattigan, who'd made it a condition of selling the film rights that he should do the screenplay, agreed to work along those lines.

On the distaff side, Lancaster selected Vivien Leigh, then married to Olivier, and Deborah Kerr, whom he'd worked so well with in *From Here To Eternity*. Olivier was to direct, and contracts were signed to that effect in Los Angeles in February 1957.

Tracy had always had an ambition to work with Olivier, but when he heard the glad tidings, the film actor, better versed in the ways of Hollywood than the star of the English stage, was instantly on the alert.

'Won't Burt Lancaster want the part?' he enquired. 'No,' said Olivier, 'he's agreed that you do it.'

They had a celebratory party, and the Oliviers flew back to London. As soon as they arrived, Lancaster was on the line. He'd changed his mind and decided to take the part after all.

'Either Tracy does it or you can't have us,' Olivier replied. Which was exactly what happened. Olivier saw Burt's 'try out' for the project, then withdrew as an actor and a director, because he wasn't confident of getting what he thought the play needed out of the American star, and Vivien Leigh pulled out as well.

Lancaster had always relied on being able to lean on his directors, as he recognised obliquely when he said, 'It depends on the conviction. It's no great trick to know that a scene is right, but you must be malleable to the extent that you are aware that no one knows for certain what is the best way to get the best results. But there shouldn't be any confusion about what you want to say with a scene. That should be clear in everybody's mind, what the end result, what you're after, should be.'

With Olivier, he came to the end of that particular line. Rehearsals began and both men were equally clear in their own minds as to what they wanted to achieve. The problem was that their visions were poles apart, and the malleability was conspicuous by its absence. Discussions soon turned into acrimonious arguments as the irresistible force met the immovable object. Neither man budged artistically but Olivier moved out, taking his wife with him.

As his retreat cost him something in the region of 300,000 dollars, it was a formidable demonstration of his steely integrity. However it didn't stop *Separate Tables* which went ahead in 1958 with David Niven and Rita Hayworth replacing the Oliviers.

Niven, in particular, was delighted at his good fortune. 'Terence Rattigan is an actor's playwright,' he wrote in his autobiography, *The Moon's a Balloon*. 'To perform the characters he has invented is a joy because they are so well constructed that so long as you can remember lines and don't bump into the furniture, you can't go wrong. *Separate Tables* is one of Rattigan's best plays and The Major is one of his best-written characters so I was, naturally, overjoyed when I was offered the part in the film version.' To which he added, 'It was a dream company to work with,' a comment that would have strained the credulity of many of his peers.

The film, like the play, is set in the Beauregard Hotel in Bournemouth, 'a frowsty, tragi-comic Betjemanish place with permanent "residents", stained-glass lozenge windows, and the aspidistras and gentility and ghastliness no more exaggerated than you find them in such places'. It becomes a microcosm of some of the more pathetic aspects of society. Major Pollack (Niven) bores the assembled company with tales of wartime heroism while Burt's alcoholic author romances the hotel's mature owner (Wendy Hillier) and Kerr's timorous Sybil Railton-Bell is trodden under foot by her snobbish mother (Gladys Cooper). No sooner is this pattern of desperation set, than it is burst apart by a newspaper story which reveals the Major as a fraud, and the arrival of Lancaster's estranged wife (Hayworth) seeking a reconciliation with her erstwhile mate.

Filmed in melancholic black and white, *Separate Tables* turned out to be a class act, under the direction of the up-and-coming Delbert Mann who'd honed his skills in the lion's den of live television. Sadly Lancaster did little with his well-written role, apart from running his fingers through his hair and looking weary as he struggled to decide betwen the two women who were vying for his affection.

'The camera tells us with brutal frankness that in Burt Lancaster we have a not-so-able actor acting,' commented Arthur Knight in *Saturday Review*, but Campbell Dixon (*Daily Telegraph*) disagreed: 'He powerfully suggests the tensions and violence locked up in a man fundamentally tolerant and good.'

The lack of depth in his portrayal was reflected when the Oscar ceremonies came round. The film was nominated for Best Picture, but lost to *Gigi*, and David Niven, giving the performance of his life, won his only Academy Award for Best Actor. Wendy Hillier was adjudged Best Supporting Actress while Miss Kerr received her fourth Best Actress nomination, although she had to give best on this occasion to Susan Hayward for *I Want to Live*.

Isabel Quigley, writing in *The Spectator*, found both Burt and Rita Hayworth unconvincing, 'because they don't give the air of being lonely has-beens. They are too obviously in their prime, on top of things, altogether far too competent and tough for failure and self-pity.'

If Lancaster's absence from the roll of honour vindicated Olivier's judgement, the producer received a handsome consolation prize from the receipts of *Separate Tables* in cinemas nationwide. Nor did he have to wait long for a return match with the great British actor. While *Separate Tables* was shooting, Sir Laurence had retired hurt to London where he made yet more theatrical history by taking the lead in the first production of *The Entertainer*, the twenty-seven-year-old John Osborne's follow-up to *Look Back in Anger*. The part was Archie Rice, a pathetic, lecherous song-and-dance comedian; the director Tony Richardson, working with a big name for the first time, and the theatre the Royal Court.

Olivier, who earned a most unprincely £50 a week, immortalised Archie Rice and gave what many considered to be his best performance outside the classics, but even that was not enough to persuade financiers to lend him the 1,500,000 dollars he needed to produce, direct and star in *Macbeth*, with his wife as his Lady. Instead, the need for money thrust him back into the arms of Burt Lancaster for *The Devil's Disciple*.

By no stretch of the imagination could the auguries be considered good. Olivier was smarting under the rejection of *Macbeth*. 'I don't think I'd ever given up on anything before,' he commented. And it didn't help that Lancaster, ex-army private and circus acrobat, had no trouble raising the money to make *The Devil's Disciple* in England, whereas he, the greatest Shakespearean actor of a generation couldn't command less than half the amount for his own cherished project. The fact that Burt's choice was also by a British classical dramatist merely rubbed salt into open wounds.

Lancaster had got his backing by doing a deal with Kirk Douglas's Byrna Production Company. Under its terms, Kirk took the part of the scoffer, Richard Dundgeon that had originally been earmarked for Montgomery Clift, while Burt did the best he could with the stolid pastor, Anthony Anderson, who decides to give up religious pacificsm to fight the good fight for American Independence. The third lead, the Commander of the British forces, General 'Gentlemanly Johnny' Burgogne, went to Olivier who decided that it was worth patching up his quarrel with Lancaster for a salary of 200,000 dollars. Cynics have suggested that his acceptance may have been partially motivated by the hope that Burt might be persuaded to use his hustler's talents on behalf of *Macbeth*, if he was offered the sop of playing Macduff. If so, he was doomed to further disappointment.

Shaw himself had looked upon *The Devil's Disciple* as one of his least successful plays and the two-million-dollar film version could only be a commercial gamble, especially as it was shot in black and white. In an attempt to make it more palatable to the masses, something Shaw himself would have approved of, The Terrible Twins hired scriptwriters John Dighton and Roland Kibbee to revise the play. The liberty replaced Shavian wit with diatribe and action spiced with sex thought to be better suited to the producer-stars.

Pre-production completed, Lancaster arrived with his wife and five children and installed them in a rented house in Shenley for the duration. The behaviour of the incorrigible quintet was as uncontrolled as ever – even carte blanche in Harrods toy department didn't satisfy them – but the lack of tranquillity at home was as nothing compared to the ructions on the set. After only two weeks, director Sandy MacKendrick, who'd worked successfully with Burt on *Sweet Smell of Success*, was fired and replaced by Guy Hamilton, also from Britain, but thought to be more susceptible to Lancastrian suggestion.

'Look, we didn't agree with how the picture was being done,' an angry Harold Hecht, his crew-cut hair bristling, informed the press. 'I don't know which one of us is right – Hecht-Hill-Lancaster or Mac-Kendrick. Before we started filming, we were in agreement, but things don't always work out I guess. That's all there is to it.'

Lancaster, however, was prepared to elaborate when he described MacKendrick as 'A very clever director, and a very nice guy. But he took one helluva lot of time. He would get hold of a scene that was five-and-a-half pages long and attempt to do it in one take by moving the dolly around and through his characters – an incredibly difficult task. We would arrive on the set ready to go at nine in the morning and we'd be hanging around till three in the afternoon rehearsing the moves we had to make. Then we'd shoot, and sometimes he'd say, "No, I don't like that much. Let's do it a different way." At the end of the first week we had two days of film. It was impossible to continue like that.'

Didn't he know that time was money, his tempestuous employers asked themselves, and unloaded him as quickly as possible so that the filming could be completed in forty-eight days. Meanwhile Olivier was having a miserable time in his few scenes as the urbane General. Burt invariably called him 'Mr Olivier', with scrupulous politesse if little regard for titles, but there was no love lost between the two men and no way of concealing the Englishman's irritation at working on a less worthy project than *Macbeth*. Harry Andrews, who'd been scheduled to play Macduff, then given the consolation prize of Major Swindon in *The Devil's Disciple*, considered that Sir Laurence was 'treated disgracefully' and that he lacked confidence for the only time he could remember.

If so, Olivier concealed it by acting his American peers off the screen and so taking his revenge for any insults, real or imagined. 'The Greatest Actor of Our Day,' read the *Evening Standard*'s front page headline. 'It is a film to see,' Donald Edgar's text read, 'just because Laurence Olivier gives the performance of his life. And because in his superb self-confidence, he dared to take the third lead. Knowing that he would steal the film from Burt Lancaster and Kirk Douglas, the two male leads. And he does. Those two able actors look like stupid oafs who have wandered back from a Western into the American War of Independence.'

The writer may have been prejudiced, even chauvinistic, but the American reviewers weren't much more enthusiastic. 'Lancaster glooms away Shaw's most romantic scenes as if he were lost on a Bronte moor,' commented *Time* magazine.

'As Anderson, Mr Burt Lancaster finds himself for long periods in charge of the screen for little discernible purpose and with nothing in particular to do,' stated *The Times*. 'Towards the finish he is the central figure in a farcical free fight which ends with his exploding the British ammunition. From the point of view of the play as Shaw wrote it, Anderson is a dead loss – whenever the film, as it all too often does, seems to think it knows better than the author, its mistake becomes glaringly apparent.'

Although *The Devil's Disciple*, like its predecessor, *Separate Tables*, earned better notices for his employees than for himself, Burt Lancaster refused to be discouraged in his pursuit of intelligence. No one could doubt his courage in pitting himself against the genius of Olivier, nor his honesty when he assessed himself as a competent artisan. 'In terms of popular appeal, what counts is appearance and personality,' he told Thomas Wiseman. 'Skill as an actor, that's something extra. I like to think of myself as a craftsman rather than as an artist. It is not my ambition to be a great actor like Mr Olivier, nor would I be capable of becoming one.

'I am not moved by the desire to make more money or win more fame; I've got enough of both and there comes a point when you can't get any more of either. I'm just interested in doing things that interest me. When I first started in the movies I was unsure of myself. I would flare up easily. When success comes as quickly as it came to me, there are bound to be problems. You ask yourself, how do I come to be here and do I have any right to be here. ... It took me a certain amount of time to adjust. Now I'm adjusted, I keep calm.'

He analysed his situation in even greater detail in *The Devil's Disciple* days when he had lunch at the Grosvenor House Hotel with television personality, Robert Robinson, who was then writing for the *Sunday Graphic*. His premise was that his 'selfhood' was the strongest draw. 'People go to the movies to see the star. Whatever you are playing, they come looking for *you*. The real you. The star's unique personality must never be submerged. And how to be yourself? The most difficult thing of all. The script gets in the way, so does your own lack of self-confidence. But even when I played a cripple – in *Trapeze* – people came along. They came to see Burt Lancaster in those circumstances, to see how he would behave as a cripple.'

When Robinson went to meet the forty-six-year-old Burt Lancaster he saw 'a tall, square statue of a man who would not look out of place set up in a Scandinavian national park as a symbol of industry. In repose he has a stony aspect, in conversation he gives the impression that there is a coiled spring situated somewhere in the region of the thorax which, at the slightest impact, may impel him to uproot a set of swinging bars at a single bound. And also – strangely – I felt he would display great intellectual energy, that his speech would be fluent. He did. It was.'

As Burt ate his cold roast beef he expanded on his creative producer's theme tune. 'If you make good films, you are a good businessman. Being a businessman, a producer is like giving birth to a baby. I enjoy the business side of the films I make in association with Mr Hecht more than the acting. You feel it's more yours – as an actor, you're at the whim of the producer. Someone else is laying down the rules. I prefer to be in the driver's seat. Films ought to make money. Shaw said that about plays. If they make money, it's proof they've communicated. And anyway, if you don't make money, you're out of a job.'

Back in Los Angeles, facing the dismal receipts of *The Devil's Disciple* which had been as far above the heads of the bulk of cinemagoers as he'd anticipated, Mr Hecht was less certain of his enjoyment of his mercurial partner's whims. His doubts could only be exacerbated by the company's final film for 1959. Lancaster didn't act in it, but it's subject matter, racial prejudice, was one he was perennially willing to tackle. Called *Take a Giant Step*, it starred a popular singer of the future, Johnny Nash, as a young black boy who has to adjust to racist attitudes and adolescent sexual urges as he moves towards manhood in a northern American town. The *New York Times* considered it to be 'a cross between a social justice brochure and a Negro Andy Hardy Film' but the *Saturday Review*'s Arthur Knight was more enthusiastic. 'No film to date – not even *The Defiant Ones* – has attempted to describe so explicitly what it means to be a Negro in a white man's world.'

The public wasn't ready for the forthright statements *Take a Giant Step* had to make but the film has stood the test of time well and is now seen as going some way towards living up to its title. Unfortunately its subject matter and some fine acting by non-stars didn't inspire theatres to book it nationwide so it was seen only by the minority who like quality cinema. From Burt's point of view, that was preaching to the converted; from Hecht's it was a dead loss.

The film was the final nail in the coffin of Hecht-Hill-Lancaster. But Lancaster couldn't extricate himself instantly from his commitments and so lined up for *The Unforgiven*, directed by John Huston and produced by James Hill. Faced with rising costs in the United States and competition from the television sets that were now installed in nearly every American home, producers had begun to realise that while skies were as wide south of the border down Mexico way, prices were substantially lower. Consequently the old mining town of Durango had become the Western capital of the Spanish-speaking world, a position it held until the late sixties when Spain, which was cheaper still, took over for the 'spaghetti' era.

Burt ensured that his contribution was worth his while, by taking a three-hundred-thousand-dollar pay cheque. Audrey Hepburn, improbably hired to play his foster-sister after her triumph in *The Nun's Story*, received a similar amount, as did John Huston. Miss Hepburn, an inexpert horsewoman, then upped the ante considerably by falling off her Arab steed on set and breaking her back, causing a long and costly delay while she was hospitalised in Los Angeles. Her injury was complicated by her first pregnancy after five years of marriage to Mel Ferrer. The producers, who hadn't known she was expecting the baby she later lost as a result of the fall until after she'd signed the contract, had reason to be aggrieved. That was only the first mishap in a very accident-prone production, in which three technicians were killed in a plane crash and Audie Murphy, who played Lancaster's hot-headed brother nearly drowned in a boating disaster.

On the credit side, Lancaster, who both admired and was overawed by John Huston, behaved exceptionally well during the shooting and lived up to the intimations of future calmness he'd given in London after *The Devil's Disciple*. He played Ben Zachary, the stiff-necked head of a pioneer family, to Hepburn's Rachel. She is a foundling, who may or may not be of Indian blood. When the Kiowa chiefs arrive to claim her, Ben demands her against the advice of the head of the other family of settlers who recognises that keeping the girl will put all their lives in jeopardy.

Ben remains obdurate, so earning the hostility of his peers, and once the Indians have been defeated in the ensuing battle, he is left a social pariah. However, the knowledge that he is in no way related by blood

87

to Rachel leaves him free to marry her and live unhappily ever after, along with the hatred and prejudice of neighbours of all colours.

Ben Zachary was a gift to Burt after the subtleties of John Malcolm and Anthony Anderson. He is a classical figure in American films, a man with a simple code and honest values who stands by his family come what may. No threats and no danger can shift him from his course once he's convinced what it should be. On the outside, he is tough, impassive and leathery, qualities the middle-aged Lancaster had in abundance, but inside, he has feelings too, and they run all the deeper for being so well concealed.

By 1960, Burt was totally at home in the Western genre. Although he never rode a horse for pleasure, he'd settled down into a convincing slouch in the saddle that was a far cry from his erect posture when he'd begun his career in oaters with *Vengeance Valley* nine years before. Now he portrayed Zachary with just the right blend of uncompromising strength and vulnerability caused by being out on a limb. Unfortunately Audrey Hepburn was totally miscast as the simple Kiowa girl. Act her heart out though she undoubtedly did, her elfin looks and her cultured voice militated against her playing an ignorant pioneer with the necessary conviction. Nor is being English any substitute for being Indian.

Not that the cynical Stanley Kauffman saw it in quite the same light. 'That Huston could not get a good performance out of Lancaster cannot be held against him,' he wrote, 'but he has achieved what no other director has done: he has got a bad performance out of lovely Audrey Hepburn.'

John Huston gave a sombre poetic quality to his impressive two-hour portrait of life on the Texan plains in the 1850s. Where *Take a Giant Step* had been a contemporary attack on racial prejudice, *The Unforgiven* used historical metaphor, but the message of man's inhumanity to differently coloured man was equally clear. It was also equally unpalatable at the box office. A grim purposeful Western with a downbeat ending, superbly photographed though it was, was not what people wanted to see, and the majority made sure they didn't have to. For the fifth time in a row, a Hecht-Hill-Lancaster production starring Burt failed to live up to its financial expectations. It was the end of the line.

In one sense, the company was a victim of changing times. The late fifties was the cinema's nadir because it hadn't learnt to adapt to the rivalry of television. Indeed it would be a further fifteen years before the industry hit on the pyrotechnical formula of *Star Wars* and *Superman* that inspires queues around the block in an age in which anything without special effects can be seen as well for free on the small silver screen.

Nor was it an easy era in which to balance Lancaster's very commendable wish to produce stimulating if potentially hazardous projects with Hecht's determination to use big names in opulent settings. Good 'small' films like *Marty* and *Separate Tables* drew huge crowds when they came off, but Hecht was always aware that the bankers in the business were the star vehicles that appealed to the lowest common denominator.

Burt recognised just how detrimental the investment in time and money they demanded could be to his ideals when he explained the decision to wind up the company. 'We had built an organisation that was too big for the things we wanted to do. We had taken on some of the overhead-aches of a major studio, and could no longer afford to operate in the way we wanted to. You can't spend two or three years preparing for a film that will have limited appeal when your overhead is the size of ours.'

In the twelve years of the company's existence in its various manifestations, it had served its purpose so far as Burt Lancaster was concerned. It had enabled him to set the pace in breaking the total power of the studios and it was no part of his plan to set up a similarly monolithic organisation of his own. In addition, he could be proud of several of the films it had made, if not always of his own part in them. *The Flame and the Arrow*, *The Crimson Pirate* and *Trapeze* were muscular classics for the mass market and he'd used their massive profits not to repeat them, which would have been easy, but to make *Sweet Smell of Success*, *Separate Tables* and *The Devil's Disciple*. This trio, plus *Marty* and *Take a Giant Step*, are proof of Lancaster's intention to produce a worthwhile body of work outside the Hollywood glamour mould, while *Run Silent, Run Deep* and *The Unforgiven* are respectable programmers, at the very least.

In the final analysis, Lancaster and Hecht had used each other in much the same way, in order to launch twin careers that had taken both to the commercial heights of their profession. Now their paths, after several years of escalating internecine strife and jealousies, had diverged to a point where parting was the best solution. Hecht and Lancaster would work together on projects that were already in the pipeline, as the links between them gradually dropped away.

For Lancaster, it was time to scale the heights as an actor, and once again his phenomenal luck held out. In his very next film he would give the performance of his career.

nine
CON MAN

Elmer Gantry and Burt Lancaster went back a long time, to 1947 to be precise when Richard Brooks, having written the screenplay of *Brute Force*, was around to meet its star. When he saw what Lancaster was doing with his fourth film part, his first question was, 'Have you ever read *Elmer Gantry*?' 'No,' said Burt unequivocally, to which Brooks replied, 'I'll get you a copy. And maybe one of these days, we'll make a movie of it.' 'Fine ... fine,' Burt spoke with the vague politeness of the unconverted, but the point had been made.

Brooks's own determination to make a film based on Sinclair Lewis's blistering attack on the shyster preachers who made a killing out of hellfire religion in America's Southern Bible belt dated back still further. Early in the forties, he'd written an anti-war novel while serving in the US Marine Corps. It was well received by reviewers, but not by his employers who felt it should be punished by court martial. While Brooks was waiting for his trial, some strangers sent depositions saying they'd come to his defence, and one of them was Sinclair Lewis, author of *Elmer Gantry*. Faced with this show of force, the authorities settled for taking Brooks' typewriter away and putting him in Coventry.

That might have been the end of it had Brooks not met Lewis in a bar and told him what a fine movie he thought his 1927 novel would make. 'If you ever get around to making it, do yourself a favour,' said the author. 'For God's sake, make it a movie. Don't be afraid of the book.' It was good advice and Brooks, having acquired an option on the title, was all prepared to take it.

Hollywood, however, had always had reservations about attacking religion. Biblical spear-carrying epics like *The Ten Commandments* were fine but even the fringe zealotry in Lewis's sights was strictly taboo and studio after studio gave it the thumbs down. On occasion over the next ten years Brooks and Lancaster would meet by chance, at a boxing match, for example. 'What about *Elmer Gantry* one of these days?' The writer kept his pot on the boil. 'Great idea!' his quarry would reply, in the tones of one who knew that seeing was believing.

Then Brooks cut loose from his regular employers, MGM, and got on a freighter for Europe. For twenty-six straight days he attacked his material. On landing in Belgium, he took to the canals, then rented a car and toured the Continent. At the end of it he had a screenplay. It was 1956 when Burt read it and said prophetically, 'I'll do it!'

Five years later United Artists agreed to the project, but had no free studio at the time, so space was rented at Columbia. Brooks and Lancaster moved into a modest forty-five-dollar-a-week suite and set to work. 'The independent producer-star has one factor in his favour which studios can't afford,' said Lancaster, 'and that's time. For *Elmer Gantry*, Richard Brooks did four complete drafts of the Sinclair Lewis novel, discarded them all and finally settled for a fifth version! He worked on the script week after week. In all we worked for seven months until he had a script in which he believed. Of course, we had no earnings during this working period; but we did have time, one of the most precious of all film-making elements. As a producer-star I can afford this luxury. A studio with its tremendous overheads cannot.'

As one of his main reasons for disbanding Hecht-Hill-Lancaster had been the escalating costs of running it, it was appropriate that Lancaster should fall so easily into a project whose *modus operandi* conformed so closely to those he considered ideal. Sinclair Lewis's exhaustive book had covered thirty years in the life of Elmer Gantry, but Brooks, no doubt remembering the author's advice, condensed it into a few short months for dramatic effect by concentrating on a single episode in the Bible-bashing evangelist's life.

When it was done and the cameras were ready to roll, the head of Columbia came to the Brooks/Lancaster suite with a letter from the head of Paramount asking him to deny the production the space it had hired. 'We have a contract,' said Brooks, in righteous indignation. 'And what have Paramount got to do with this?' The studio head said, 'Well, he's a Baptist and he thinks it would be a terrible thing. When he offered me money to recoup my investment and forget the whole thing, I said, "No, we've rented the space and we're going to make the picture." And we did. And Burt just ... blossomed.'

Although the period is the early twenties, Burt's Elmer Gantry is the kind of guy anyone who goes to bars today will recognise instantly, so it is fitting that we first see him in a saloon. He is surrounded by hard-drinking patrons and gives an early demonstration of his incomparable con man's skills when he effortlessly soft talks his companions into donating some Christmas money to two Salvation Army girls who are threatened with ridicule as they go about their temperance mission. This brief scene is a microcosm of the man in all his plausible and, at times, kindly duplicity.

Gantry wears sharp check suits and a bow tie, and has stubble on his chin. He tells jokes with sexual innuendoes in their punch lines in too loud a voice and claims to be a crack vacuum cleaner salesman to anyone who'll listen. His turquoise eyes and even his crisply crinkled hair exude dishonesty. 'People in fourteen states call me by my first name, Elmer,' he intones with fake jollity and bared teeth. 'Ah yes, indeedee.' It is his stock phrase.

His private life, in a series of cheap hotel rooms with only flat pints for company, is a depressing contrast to this public bonhomie, but everything changes for the better when he chances on a revivalist meeting in a small community. It is held by Sister Sharon Falconer (Jean Simmons) and the womanising Elmer, scenting an opportunity to exercise his talents, instantly joins her congregation. As an ex-divinity student who has been expelled from college for seducing a deacon's daughter, he feels he's well qualified for his new metier. How right he is!

Religious fanaticism, as practised by Sister Sharon without the assistance of drink, cigarettes, gambling or sex may not be exactly to his taste, but of the efficacy of his tub thumping oratory, there can be no doubt. As a teetotal golden-tongued preacher speaking out forthrightly against the sins of the flesh, he makes 450 converts from a congregation of 1,200. Where Sister Sharon demands a hard, pure spirituality of her audience, Gantry puts religion in terms everyone can understand. 'Prayin's the cheapest first rate medicine I know,' he declaims, betraying his alley cat's values as he rakes in the contributions and lifts Sister Sharon, born Katie Jones, into the big time.

Their relationship, which starts out as mutual need, develops into something approaching love, at least on his part, though his unaccustomed monogamy is interrupted in a brief interlude with his ex-girl-friend (Shirley Jones). Gantry is a natural male chauvinist pig – 'every woman competes with every other woman for every man' is his philosophy – but, in this one instance, he is capable of genuine feeling to which Sister Sharon, at heart a colder, more manipulative person than he is, responds as they move into the dinner jacket and evening gala class. Of course it can't last and Elmer Gantry, a hero in the final analysis, is saved by fire from lifelong temperance, though he loves his love in the process.

Lancaster's Gantry is certainly not Lewis's, but a cleaned-up version masquerading under the same name. In the book, Gantry was an ordained minister, but he is defrocked for the film. More seriously, Burt thought the original too one-dimensional, too unsavoury and too emotionally limited to be a success in the cinema. Accordingly, he was humanised so that audiences could identify with him.

'Gantry was essentially a ham,' his portrayer explained. 'He liked having his voice stir up excitement. He was a super salesman, the hail-fellow-well-met type. He wanted the boys to like him. In a sense, we were trying to say that this man was looking for something, and in the process of looking for it, he wanted somebody to be with him and reassure him.'

After his triumph as the charlatan in *The Rainmaker* no one should have been surprised at Burt's consummate mastery of his part. Brooks chose him because, 'He is one of the most professional actors there is. He really knows what goes into making a movie. He's got a good sense of his own character, isn't afraid to let it all come out ...'

Quite so, but it was Burt himself who hit the nail on the head: 'Some parts you fall into like an old glove. Elmer wasn't acting. That was me.'

Though much of the action was shot in a mock-up of a revivalist tent on a stretch of Columbia studios, which has now been turned into tennis courts, it has a remarkable feeling of the grass-roots South where ripping people off in the name of God was, and is, big business. Love, hate and sin combine with crude vulgarity into the essence of the frontier spirit and, in the process, Elmer Gantry's God, 'an all-American football player with a long white beard', becomes accessible to all.

Brooks added to the verisimilitude by scouring Long Beach for old people who habitually went to Baptist meetings and bussing them to the set to fill the tent, instead of using regular – and often familiar – Hollywood extras. 'They really knew the songs,' said Jean Simmons, who later became Mrs Richard Brooks, 'and they really believed they were in one of their own churches.'

Such attention to detail paid off when *Elmer Gantry* was unveiled to wide acclaim, albeit accompanied by the anticipated howls of Baptist protest. By 1960, when revivalism was no longer much of an issue, Sinclair Lewis's once explosive novel wouldn't have shocked too many Americans, nor yet inspired them to go to their local cinemas, but Brooks' stream-lined screenplay and Lancaster's spellbinding hustler had turned it into a winner. As a sop to Protestant churches, United Artists recommended that the film should be certified as suitable for adults and accompanied under-sixteens, although its content wouldn't normally have restricted it so much.

Next came the plaudits. American critics led the way with: 'Lancaster pulls out virtually all the stops to create a memorable characterisation' (*Variety*); 'Without the performance of Burt Lancaster, the film's overall effect would be vitiated. He is an Elmer Gantry who would have delighted the cold enquiring eye and crusading soul of Sinclair Lewis' (A.H. Weiler in the *New York Times*); and 'Lancaster's portrayal may not be the subtlest performance of his career, but it is certainly among the strongest' (Beckley in the *New York Herald-Tribune*).

It was left to Gordon Gow in Britain's *Film and Filming* to explain Burt's triumph more eloquently. 'There are those winning occasions when a Lancaster performance, in quite a serious film, will recall just a slight and very discreet flavour of the old circus flourish, a little something he has doubtless retained from the time when he gave a grand air to the finish of an acrobatic feat or when he verbalised elaborately in the capacity of MC. This element was needed and handsomely provided, for the guy with the evangelistic kick in *Elmer Gantry*.'

Lancaster received his second Academy Award nomination for Best Actor for *Elmer Gantry* and his celebrated smile has never been wider when he collected the elusive statuette from Greer Garson in the spring of 1961. He is on record as saying, 'When Hollywood gives out its Oscars, you generally feel political manoeuvring's been going on.' Even so, beating Jack Lemmon (*The Apartment*), Trevor Howard (*Sons and Lovers*), and especially Sir Laurence Olivier (*The Entertainer*) and Spencer Tracy (*Inherit the Wind*) to the trophy, must have made his success particularly sweet. He also received his second Best Actor Award from the New York Film Critics for the film. Richard Brooks was given a well-deserved Oscar for the screenplay of *Elmer Gantry* and Shirley Jones was dubbed Best Supporting Actress.

With the world as his oyster, it was perverse of Lancaster not to pick a better follow-up than *The Young Savages*. There are several reasons why he might have selected this moody melodrama from the vast range of potentially more rewarding things he was offered. One was that it was adapted from a book by Evan Hunter called *A Matter of Conviction*, and Hunter's previous novel, *The Blackboard Jungle*, had been turned into a top-class 'message' film in 1955 by Richard Brooks, no less. Even if Brooks didn't encourage Burt to take *The Young Savages*, there is the likelihood that its content, based on real events, was an inspiration to his justice-monger's soul.

Secondly, it was set in a tenement district of East Harlem where Italian and Puerto Rican gangs ran amok, a location that would take Lancaster right back to his own childhood. Thirdly, there was the curious irony of Shelley Winters, cast as a woman he used to love.

As Burt was a selfless and habitual sucker for social themes, he probably thought he could do some good through the character of Hank Bell, a politically ambitious assistant district attorney who is ordered by his superior, a candidate for governor at the next elections, to investigate the murder of a blind boy by three Italian brothers. He is also told to get a conviction, which he sets out to do against the wishes of his well-born wife (Dina Merrill), who feels that the boys shouldn't be sent to the electric chair for a crime they've been forced into by their under-privileged circumstances. Gradually with the help of the boys' mother (Ms Winters), Bell comes to share her opinion and refuses to allow thoughts of personal advancement or pressure from his boss to come between him and justice at the trial.

The film is the first of five collaborations between Lancaster and John Frankenheimer, a young director who'd made a brilliant name for himself on television, then switched to the larger screen in 1957 for *The Young Strangers*, also about troubled youth. *The Young Savages*, perhaps re-titled in this way against Frankenheimer's wishes to suggest continuity, was only his second feature but he used it to establish the parameters of future achievement. He was obsessive about detail and insisted on locations rather than studio sets whenever possible. In this instance, he was allowed part of his schedule in Manhattan, the rest in Hollywood, largely because New York was a vastly expensive place to shoot in as he explained ten years later: 'Those were the days before Mayor Lindsay, and that's when you had to pay off every other cop on the beat, and also you had to have a full New York crew covering the Hollywood crew so you were paying two crews. It was also a matter of scheduling. It was just impossible to do it all on location.'

When people mentioned John Frankenheimer to Lancaster in those days, a beatific grin would spread over the actor's face. 'He's a wonderful director,' he was apt to say, 'absolutely wonderful, and he always does exactly what I say.' Which goes a long way to explaining what, in Burt's case, was a record-breaking association. Nevertheless, *The Young Savages* was not an auspicious start. The forty-eight-year-old Lancaster, perennially youthful though he looked, was kicking on a bit for a rising assistant district attorney, and Shelley Winters, frequently immune to direction but compliant enough here, stole such acting honours as were going, which can only have irked the man she claims as her erstwhile lover.

The script, which Frankenheimer had described as 'pretty bad' before he and his friend J.P. Miller re-wrote it, still had serious limitations afterwards, but the black and white photography highlighted a convincing portrait of urban poverty and despair.

'The direction is fast and forceful and, if Mr Lancaster wears that habitual expression which makes him first cousin to a bloodhound confused as to the trail, that is not through any lack of pace in the action or, indeed, to any weakness in Mr Lancaster's own performance. There are a number of shots that drive home truths,' wrote *The Times*, though it wasn't sure whether *The Young Savages* was a 'fearless social document' or a 'gratuitous exercise in violence'. *Time* didn't care, but thought the film was 'at its best when at its ugliest'. Nor did audiences who felt, rightly, that they'd seen it all sooner and better in *The Blackboard Jungle* – and looked elsewhere for their entertainment.

The Young Savages marks the beginning of Lancaster's repressed period when the extroverted ebullience that had marked his swashbuckling and con man days gave way to a dour intensity which was frequently described as wooden. It is as if he'd decided that growing up meant throwing fun out of the window. In due course, he would return to a lighter mood, but meanwhile he was not so much the man of steel, which is tensile, as carved out of solid rock.

Judgement at Nuremberg, a 189-minute marathon, based on Abby Mann's television play, is marked by one of his grimmest performances, appropriately in the light of the subject matter. The director, Stanley Kramer, originally had Sir Laurence Olivier earmarked for the part of Ernest Janning but the British actor was in the process of marrying Joan Plowright at the time so Kramer had to let him go. In the light of the hammy and over-accented celluloid Nazis Olivier produced in the seventies in films like *Marathon Man*, it was perhaps just as well.

In a star-studded cast, Burt received second billing behind Spencer Tracy, but ahead of Maximilian Schell, Richard Widmark, Marlene Dietrich, Judy Garland and Montgomery Clift. The judgement in question doesn't take place at the main body of war trials in 1946 when Goering, Goebbels and Hess were arraigned, but two years later when four Nazi jurists are accused of perverting justice. The most senior of them is Janning, a man whose international reputation as an intellectual

96

supporter of the law was destroyed when he accepted the post of Minister of Justice in 1935. Subsequently he sent political offenders to the concentration camps and administered the sterilisation laws.

The fact that the accused weren't directly responsible for the atrocities, yet by their actions condoned them, adds an interesting dimension to the long trial. They represent the silent majority of Germans who later claimed they hadn't known what was going on in the name of the Third Reich. 'Concentration camps? What concentration camps?' was a popular line of defence among ordinary people, and it is taken up here by Janning's three fellow prisoners as they whine about their innocence.

Janning, however, is a man of more dignity and more perception. For many days he remains silent, aloof and enigmatic. Witnesses come and go, among them Judy Garland who fills the screen (in more ways than one because she was substantially overweight) for ten minutes as a distraught *hausfrau* who has been accused by the Nazis of consorting with a Jew old enough to be her father. Another is Montgomery Clift, who turned down the part of prosecuting counsel that went to Richard Widmark because the 130,000 dollars offered by Kramer was far below his normal fee. Quixotically he rejected the 100,000 dollars on offer for playing the sad Jew who has been sterilised because of unproven weakness of mind. 'Since it's only a single scene and can be filmed in one day, I strongly disapproved of taking an astronomical salary. But in the business I felt it was more practical to do it for nothing, rather than reduce my price or refuse a role I wanted to play,' he explained, and accepted large expenses only.

Lancaster's Janning watches them come and go and listens with equal impassivity to the homespun philosophies of the venerable American judge (Tracy) appointed to the trial, the sharp logic of his own defence counsel (Schell) and the chilling indictments of the prosecutor (Widmark). Only when he is on the stand himself does he come to life with a speech that runs for eight minutes and eleven seconds and effectively destroys his own defence.

'Why did we participate?' he asks. 'Because we loved our country.' He sets the scenes for the familiar tug between expediency and conscience, but later, and also for the love of a country that he feels can't be purged until it understands why it condoned National Socialism, he is more honest. 'It is not easy to tell the truth,' he declares, 'but if there is to be any salvation for Germany we who knew her guilt, must admit it whatever the pain and humiliation. My counsel would have you believe

97

we were not aware of the concentration camps. Where were we? If we didn't know the details, it was because we didn't want to know.'

The speech is the crux of the trial. Janning not only condemns himself, but his three fellow jurists, before he sits down to cries of 'Traitor' from his compatriots, and it can only be a matter of time before all four are sentenced to ninety-nine-year terms, though with the tacit understanding that it won't be very long before they're released.

It is easy to get bogged down in a long trial, particularly one that bogs down of its own accord from time to time, and it is to Kramer's credit that, despite his decision to double the original length of Mann's *Playhouse 90*, he sustains the tension so well for so long. Although part of the film was shot in Germany where Spencer Tracy was received like a king, the Nuremberg courtroom was reconstructed in exact detail in Hollywood's Revue studios. It was ingeniously mounted on rollers so that the camera could move in at any angle and Lancaster did all his scenes there.

During shooting, Burt briefly renewed his old rivalry with Monty Clift, and set up a new and much more bitter enmity with the elegant and cosmopolitan Maximilian Schell with whom he fought continuously. Come the Academy Awards, it was Schell who had the last laugh when he picked up Best Actor. Nevertheless, Lancaster worked hard on Janning, a part for which his flamboyant looks made him physically unsuited, as *Variety* noted: 'Lancaster's role presents the actor with a taxing assignment in which he must overcome the discrepancy of his own virile identity with that of the character. This he manages to do with an earnest performance, but he never quite attains a cold superior intensity.'

His problems were complicated by the need to react rather than act through much of the film. Spencer Tracy was a master of that particular art, as he proves in his seven-minute scene with Clift, but Burt was always more relaxed on camera when he had something positive to do or say. Then came the monologue, with the problems of sustaining interest while putting over essential information in this fundamentally indigestible form. Many critics felt that Paul Lukas, who'd played Janning in the television version and had a proper air of European scholarliness and culture, would have been a better choice but credit must go to Lancaster for his attempt.

One who gave it was Alan Dent in the *Sunday Telegraph* when he wrote, 'Burt Lancaster, wearing an expression of undeviating grimness as the most remorseful of the doomed men, has a confessional outburst near the end which is easily the most striking thing this actor had ever done.'

The subject of collective German guilt between 1933 and 1945 has been re-worked constantly over the years, but *Judgement at Nuremberg* was somewhat ahead of its time in its brutally honest presentation of delicate issues, and Burt certainly expanded his range by tackling a man of considerable intelligence who'd swum with the tide and effectively destroyed both his life and his self-respect.

The juggernaut was launched at a glittering premiere in West Berlin, newly divided by the infamous Wall. With a sense of timing that smacked of rampant commercialism, it took place the day before Eichmann was due to be sentenced in Israel. Three hundred newsmen were flown in from 26 countries, with the New York contingent alone numbering 120 columnists and political writers. When Kramer eventually picked up tabs, they totalled 150,000 dollars, making it one of the most expensive press junkets of its time.

Considerable pressure was put on the stars to attend and Spencer Tracy, Judy Garland, Maximilian Schell and Richard Widmark allowed their arms to be twisted, as did Monty Clift who was in Germany anyway making *Freud* for John Huston. Notable by their absence were Marlene Dietrich, who'd played an elegant widow who puts up Tracy's judge in her house during the trial, and Burt Lancaster. Both were expected when the charter plane landed in Berlin but Dietrich pleaded an inescapable concert engagement and Lancaster claimed pressing involvement in previews for his next film.

As the premiere date had been set for months, no one believed these excuses and there was considerable resentment from the citizens of Berlin, particularly against Miss Dietrich who they looked on as one of their own. Certainly the thought of a three-hundred-strong press corps with a licence to ask pressing questions have appalled Burt, and no one who knew him was surprised at his last-minute defection.

He had however done his bit for Kramer publicity-wise the year before, on 16 March at the Golden Globe Foreign Press awards. They were introduced by one Ronald Reagan, B movie actor, and there was another award for Burt Lancaster for *Elmer Gantry*. 'Ladies and gentlemen,' he announced in his thank you speech, 'if you want to see some real honest-to-goodness acting, you should come to our set of *Judgement at Nuremberg* and watch Spencer Tracy and Miss Judy Garland do some real emoting for you.'

The premiere hit further quicksands when Spencer Tracy was taken ill just before the film was shown to a distinguished audience, headed by Willy Brandt, then mayor of the city. The actor had to leave the Congress Hall, leading to accusations of cowardice from many of the hundreds of largely hostile local journalists at Kramer's press conference after the screening. Although Brandt set the tone by declaring the film to be an event of great political importance which was welcome, 'even if we had to feel shame at many of its aspects', his compatriots were stunned into silence when the final credits came up. The applause came almost exclusively from the foreigners, who included members of the diplomatic corps as well as the press.

Kramer was vigorously attacked by German scribes who felt that the past should be decently buried, or at the very least, disinterred by their own compatriots, rather than by the erstwhile enemy. Kramer however stood firm: the past was not best forgotten, the truth was important and the Germans should certainly make their own films about the Nazi era. In this last he was prophetic, but it would take another fifteen years before Germans who'd been young enough to know nothing during the war would be old enough and brave enough to tackle a subject that remains hyper-sensitive to this day.

Of the stars, Tracy stood up to be counted as believing every line of dialogue he had to speak, while Judy Garland stated that she was impressed by the sincerity with which the delicate subject was treated and Maximilian Schell, Swiss born but German raised, added a more forceful plea for making the film. Meanwhile Burt Lancaster sat in his ivory tower 6,000 miles away. Despite its unwieldiness, *Judgement at Nuremberg* would be seen by many of his fellow Americans (it took 5,500,000 dollars in domestic rentals which was only 200,000 less than *Elmer Gantry*) and that, in his opinion, was communication enough. On Ernest Janning, he refused to be drawn. The ex-Minister of Justice had had screentime enough to state his point of view. Now his celluloid alter ego had other fish to fry.

ten
BIRDMAN

In the essence, that fish was already in the pan because Burt had been working on his next project, *Birdman of Alcatraz*, before he started on *Judgement at Nuremberg*. However the picture had to be shelved for some months while it underwent radical surgery which left its star free for Kramer's epic. *Birdman* was a quintessential Lancastrian project from the first: fraught, committed, cumbersome and ultimately successful. Coming so shortly after *Elmer Gantry*, it confirmed him as one of a tiny handful of actors whose work combined quality for the perceptive viewer with a cash bonanza for the backers. It was a heady combination, though sadly *Birdman* proved to be a peak from which the only way was down.

Robert Stroud, alias the Birdman of Alcatraz, was a double killer, whose original imprisonment for shooting a bartender in a fight over the girl he was living with in Alaska started in 1909, when he was nineteen years old. The charge was manslaughter and the sentence the maximum for the offence: twelve years in jail. In 1916, when the authorities denied him the right to see his beloved mother when she came to visit him, he compounded the crime in front of 1,100 inmates at Leavenworth Federal Prison in Kansas. In a face-to-face confrontation in the dining hall he went berserk and stabbed a guard to death. Three trials and four years later he faced the death penalty, but eight days before he was to be hanged, President Woodrow Wilson intervened at the request of his mother. The act of mercy was minimalised by the Attorney-General who, in common with the prison officials, wanted to see Stroud dead. As it was now out of his power to kill him, he resolved to do the worst he could for him by ruling that the rest of his natural life should be spent in solitary confinement in a cell twelve feet by six.

The intention was to lock Stroud up and throw away the key, but they reckoned without the spirit of the man. One day, during his brief exercise period in the prison yard, he spotted an abandoned fledgeling sparrow and carried it gently to his cell. Raising it and teaching it tricks stimulated a hitherto unsuspected flair for ornithology and he took more birds into his care. A kindly warden, Bill Ransom, allowed him books, and eventually expanded his privileges to include an aviary of canaries. From these small beginnings, he wrote a classic textbook on the subject, Stroud's *Digest of Diseases in Birds*, and also studied English, Latin, astronomy and law in an attempt to while away the eternity at his disposal.

Though he was a model prisoner in the physical sense, his mental attitude of bitterness, impenitence and contempt didn't endear him to the authorities and in 1942, he was moved to Alcatraz, the island fortress in the middle of San Francisco's harbour. Stripped of his birds and his laboratory, he endured another seventeen years of solitary before officials gave in to public pressure and moved him to the US Prison Hospital in Springfield, Missouri in 1959. There he was allowed to work as a librarian and bookbinder but visits and letters were still severely restricted, and birthday cards sent by well-wishers in response to the pathos of his story were returned unopened. In 1963, after more than fifty years behind bars, he died in his sleep of 'natural causes and the infirmities of old age', leaving a defiant epitaph: 'They can't take from me the lesson I have given the world – that no man is licked until he stops fighting.'

Clearly this was the stuff that stories could be woven from. However Mr Bennett, the Director of the Federal Bureau of Prisons, was consistently determined to keep Stroud as much under wraps as possible, no doubt fearing a public outcry if the full facts of the prisoner's excessively long sentence were to be revealed. When Thomas E. Gaddis wrote Stroud's biography in 1955, Bennett went so far as to protest to his editors and publishers and three years later he succeeded in discouraging a major production company from making the book into a film.

However Bennett had reckoned without Burt Lancaster, who saw in *The Birdman of Alcatraz*, everything he'd ever dreamed of in a film role. For a start, Robert Stroud had been wronged in his own and many other eyes by the prison authorities which made him into a suitably liberal cause. True he'd killed twice under provocation before he was thirty, and escaped the death penalty only by presidential intervention that may, at times, have seemed something less than a blessing to a highly intelligent man. However, by 1959, when Hecht-Hill-Lancaster first got hold of the film rights, there was a very good case for releasing the sixty-nine-year-old prisoner on humanitarian grounds. At the very least, the authorities couldn't claim they were holding Stroud out of fear that he might kill again, which meant that Lancaster had a valid and respectable campaign on his hands.

Another bonus was the research into the Stroud case that he'd need to do to present the stiff-necked independent from the age of twenty-two to sixty-nine. He went to it with a will: 'All the events in the film are absolutely true. I tried to see Stroud but I couldn't. I tried to see members of his family. I found his brother but he refused to see me. I thought I'd found his wife in Alaska but I was wrong. Still I did a lot of research. I read everything that was written about his case, millions of words. And I've spent a lot of time with his lawyer.

'When I'm a papier mâché character, I feel lost. I feel that if I am not contributing anything to myself, who is the most important thing to contribute to, then I cannot make any kind of contribution. *The Birdman of Alcatraz* is an example. I have a very strong, almost maniacal concern with the whole problem of penology. I read every letter that Stroud ever wrote and though I never met this man who'd spent over forty years in solitary confinement, I felt I knew him intimately. I would actually begin to weep during some of the scenes. I've never been so personally involved in a part before or since. The film wasn't a great success, but people consistently talk to me about it. It proves something, but I don't know what. If I could prepare myself as thoroughly for every part as I did for that I'd be happy. But then in films you get as involved as you can. Sometimes you have to stop yourself walking through parts when you are what people like to call a star. But one should never, never take the easy way out.'

The original script for *Birdman* was written by Guy Trosper, who co-produced with Stuart Miller, with Harold Hecht as executive supremo. Lancaster described it as one of the best two he'd ever read (the other was *Ulzana's Raid*) and hired an Englishman, Charles Crichton who, like Sandy MacKendrick, had made his name in Ealing comedies, to direct. As Bennett had no intention of letting subversive camera crews into his prisons, Norma Productions, which was revitalised for this one last time, spent $150,000 on back lot reconstructions of Alcatraz and Leavenworth.

Crichton lasted for three gruelling tempestuous weeks before he was fired, to be replaced by John Frankenheimer, who came to the project on the understanding that he, not Burt Lancaster, would have the final word of command. The fact that he'd had a previous interest in the

Birdman story when he'd committed himself to making it for live television meant that he was particularly well suited to take over at short notice. At the time, the Bureau of Prisons had told the television company in question, CBS, that they'd never again get co-operation on anything they wanted to do if they went ahead, an embargo that Frankenheimer would later realise was a blessing in disguise.

'I don't know what possessed me to think I could have ever realised it on live television with the birds, because birds are very, very difficult,' he said ruefully. 'It took days and weeks and months to get these birds to react. There is no such thing as a trained bird. We had to wait until the bird was hungry enough to do a particular thing. Thank God the film was in black and white because for the one sparrow in the story I think we had to use twenty-seven different ones, each looking like one bird, but had it been in colour we would have had to paint all the birds.'

Frankenheimer may have had his patient way with the birds, but he lost out on the prison which he wanted to be for real, in line with his principle of always shooting on location. 'I did not have the power then to be able to insist on my decisions being respected,' he admitted. Burt, it seemed, was steam-rollering along as usual.

When shooting was completed and the first rough cut was unveiled, it ran for close on four-and-a-half hours. The viewing produced a pregnant pause, followed by a desperate plea to Frankenheimer by the producers to cut the mega-epic to more manageable proportions. For the director, who claims he was thwarted all along the line when he suggested the script was too long, it was a moment of triumph. 'You can't cut it,' he told them. 'It's a film called *Birdman of Alcatraz* and it's an hour and twenty minutes before he sees a bird. What kind of nonsense is that? The only thing you can do is re-write it.' Lancaster, canny as ever, was the first to agree, and his team fell in behind him to such good effect that version two was ready for centre lens when he returned from *Judgement at Nuremberg*. This time the first of the sparrows come up twenty minutes into the action and although it was still on the long side at 147 minutes, everybody breathed again.

When Frankenheimer talks about the star who made him famous, he is ambivalence itself. *Birdman* was undoubtedly their best collaboration artistically but the in-fighting was gruelling. 'I wasn't completely happy in the environment of film during *Birdman*,' said the newly-ex-television director gloomily. 'I thought there was much too much interference from various people. I didn't feel the control that I had had in television, which after all is total. I felt the producer was trying to interfere, the writer was trying to interfere a great deal and Burt was interfering. I didn't really feel free. I had to make myself free. I would just have to take time to relax and do it my way, because I wasn't interested in what the producer had to say, or what anybody else had to say. And that was my breakthrough in film because I did it the way I wanted to.'

But only up to a point, as he confirmed when he recalled that it was Lancaster who approved the director because he owned the script. 'He was really not ideal casting but he was very very good, and I don't know who could have played it better,' he recalled with the combination of perception and sychophancy his employer was coming to value so highly. 'Whenever I think of this film, I think of Burt, how he really applied himself to that role. He loved doing it and, in my opinion, he did a beautiful job. Strangely enough, it was a much more difficult part for him to play than the one in *Elmer Gantry*.'

Burt's transformation into the Birdman required a shaven pate which he wore like a badge of office throughout the schedule. He went bareheaded to such industry functions as he deigned to attend and allowed candid stills to be taken from any angle the photographer wished without regard for personal vanity, something most of his peers would have had forbidden in their contracts.

Such was his commitment that when his brother Jim, the ex-policeman, died of a heart attack on set one afternoon, he ordered the body to be removed and went on working for the rest of the day. That is not to say that he didn't feel grief for his brother. Jim was working as assistant director, one of his perennial sinecures, at the time and Burt had never failed to provide for him since he'd followed him to Hollywood in the late forties. However he was well used to concealing his feelings from all but the intimate members of his circle and the habit stuck. He did his mourning in private, and only when work permitted.

Lancaster's Stroud is a painstaking, patient character who brings the same kind of detailed study to his research as Burt brought to his career. Harold Hecht may not have been so far wrong when he claimed that 'Burt became obsessed by Stroud. People are compelled to become what they are by the special circumstances of their lives. Look at Stroud and look at Burt. Burt became a good actor because he's locked in too.'

Lancaster is supported by Edmund O'Brien who introduces the film as Stroud's biographer, Thomas Gaddis, Telly Savalas as the rough prisoner in a neighbouring cell who relieves his loneliness by looking after one of Stroud's birds, Karl Malden as the prison governor, Neville Brand as the sympathetic warden, Thelma Ritter as Stroud's over-possessive mother and Betty Field as the bird-loving widow who sets up a company outside the prison to market the medicines he develops in his laboratory.

Frankenheimer creates a universal metaphor out of his caged man with his caged birds by extending his loneliness and confinement to encompass the isolation of every human being. The prison may be too pristine for credibility, but its principal inmate, the sullen violent killer, who is first seen in 1920 when instant death is replaced by lingering distintegration, is entirely credible. What's more, he remains so over the years of slowing down to an emotional pace at which he can remain sane and become a useful member of a society that wants to exclude him for ever.

How like the real Birdman he is, is another matter. Stroud's alleged homosexuality in prison is certainly not touched on, in line with what was permissible in the cinema at the time. However, the length of his solitary confinement makes it unlikely that he would have had many opportunities to practise any such proclivity, unless it was with a prison warden. Nor can the film entirely diffuse the mystery that surrounds the Stroud case, let alone explain why twenty-four applications for parole were turned down without reasons being given, despite decades of non-violent behaviour.

In the light of this, it was inevitable that there would be accusations of whitewashing. When the film came out, the omnipresent Mr Bennett, Director of the Federal Bureau of Prisons, was persuaded to give his reasons for opposing it on a radio programme. 'I thought the glamor-ising of a murderer like Stroud would not be in the public interest and would be detrimental to our national well-being, harmful to our impres-sionable youth and a handicap to law enforcement,' he said, predictably enough.

Lancaster replied with a public statement of his own: 'Mr Bennett is not the censor of what the American people shall see, nor is he paid for this purpose. The public interest must not be confused with the hurt feelings of a group, nor does any such group represent the public. It is this "sacred cow" psychology which represents a real threat to the right of the public to freedom of expression. The President's Committee on National Goals has drawn attention to the need for controversy, not for unanimity of expressions.'

Later he enlarged on his reasons for making *Birdman* and his convic-

The settlement house where the young Burt
Lancaster learnt his acrobatic stunts.

An early publicity pose with Ava Gardner.

With Ava Gardner in *The Killers*, 1946.

Judy Lawrence and Burt Lancaster having a break during the filming of *Ten Tall Men*.

With Shirley Booth in *Come Back Little Sheba.*

A superb publicity shot taken during filming of *The Crimson Pirate* in 1952.

A birthday party on the set of *The Crimson Pirate* at Teddington Studios. The director, Robert Siodmark, wears a Tyrolean hat.

In *From Here to Eternity* with Deborah Kerr.

A dramatic change in the usual Lancaster style for *Apache*, made in 1954.

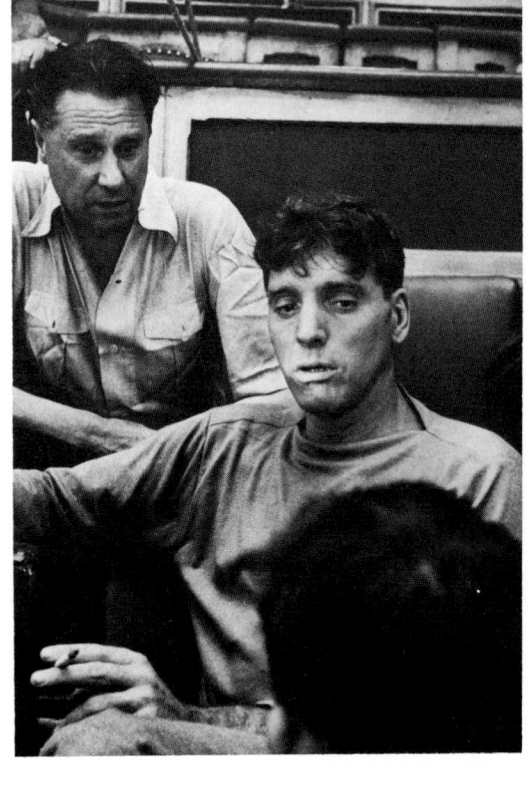

Taking direction from Carol Reed during *Trapeze*.

Wearing glasses for the role of Hunsecker in *Sweet Smell of Success*.

Rehearsing a routine with Kirk Douglas for the 1958 Royal Command Performance.

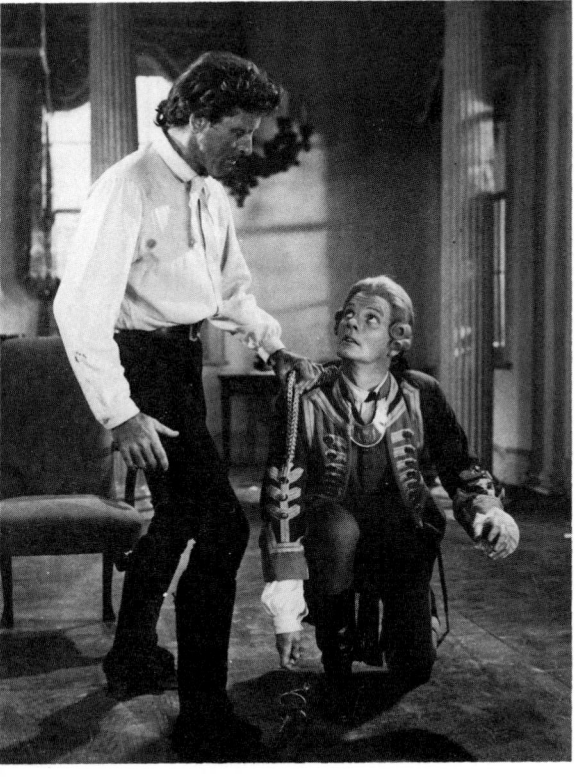

Arriving at Southampton docks to make *The Devil's Disciple*, with (LEFT TO RIGHT) James, William, Susan, Joanna and Sighle.

Burt Lancaster, as the pastor turned swordsman, in *The Devil's Disciple* with Alan Cuthbertson.

Burt Lancaster with Jean Simmonds in *Elmer Gantry*.

After hurting his back playing with the children, Burt Lancaster leans on his wife Norma's arm at the gala premiere of *The Viking* at Leicester Square.

As the *Birdman of Alcatraz*, the convict who became a world authority on ornithology, Burt Lancaster poses for a publicity shot.

Burt Lancaster and Judy Garland in *A Child is Waiting*, 1963.

Released from Hollywood commitments, Burt's first starring role was in Visconti's international classic, *The Leopard*.

As Moses in 1975.

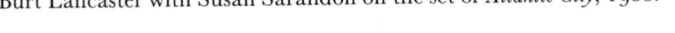

Burt Lancaster with Susan Sarandon on the set of *Atlantic City*, 1980.

A return to Britain for *Local Hero*, 1982.

tion that the public should be kept informed about the inequities of the penal code as it stood at that time. 'I believed principally that it was a very good story. The fact that it dealt with the inadequacies of our penal system was important and worthy of being exploited, but the most compelling thing to me was the emotional story of this man and what he had gone through. We hoped to make people aware of the inadequacies of the treatment of prisoners in general and the room for improvement in the handling of criminals.

'The authorities will quarrel that Stroud was not exactly the kind of man we portrayed him to be. In a certain sense that might be true. But in a very real sense it isn't true. It is not a question whether Stroud was a good man or a bad man. Society simply hasn't found out yet how criminals ought to be treated. They are still part of the old school of punishment. I don't mean to imply that the answers are easy. It's very difficult to know what is the best system. But society tends to want to shut them away and put out of sight those who have offended society. Those who are left with the task of being the keepers are not sure how to treat them. They work under deplorable conditions themselves. There have been great steps taken in recent years, now that we understand the psychology of man more than we did. But it is still at best a faulty operation, and so in that respect *Birdman of Alcatraz* is unquestionably true and no reasonable man could deny it.'

But it was not, he insisted, a condemnation of the prison system on grounds of physical maltreatment. 'This man has been behind bars for the last forty years and should, in my opinion, be freed. They say there is a new charge against him on grounds of homosexuality. Don't make me laugh. The first murder he did was for love of a woman. As for American prisons, they're clean and the inmates are properly fed and looked after. I think that such institutions are terrifying machines for destroying the human spirit. That's what I object to. But society evolves very slowly. I don't despair.'

Although the film was not a world-beater at the box office, many of those in the know agreed that it was one of, if not *the* most poignant pictures of the deadening despair induced by unnatural confinement the cinema had produced. 'The finest prison pic ever made,' stated *Variety* unequivocally, while other publications hastened to give credit where it was due. 'It couldn't have been an easy role, yet much of the supressed power in the man and the film is due to Lancaster's performance,' wrote Robert Beckley in the *New York Herald-Tribune*, while *Time* advised its readers that, 'Burt Lancaster plays with a firm restraint that never conceals a deep-felt conviction that Stroud should not be in stir at all.' Even the *New Republic*'s fussy Stanley Kauffmann, who'd had it in for the actor in the past, was insistent that 'the pleasantest report about the film is that Burt Lancaster gives one of his few good performances.'

The Academy thought so too and Burt was duly nominated for Best Actor for the third time, despite having won the Oscar only two years previously. On Award night he lost out to Gregory Peck for *To Kill A Mockingbird*, but he received the considerable consolation prize of Best Actor at the Venice Film Festival.

He won no prizes though for his appearance on Mike Wallace's PM video talk show on 24 April 1962, a thoroughly ill-mannered occasion on which he proved that he burned on as short a fuse as ever. With characteristic forethought, the actor had laid down parameters before he turned up at the studio. No personal subjects, no reflections on his character, no discussion of those well-publicised disturbances on *Judgement at Nuremberg*. In Lancaster's defence, it was Wallace who broke the rules by questioning him on his supposed inability to get along with his fellow performers.

'There's no reason to talk about it. My temper belongs to me,' Burt gave fair warning of what was to follow. Wallace replied that he was only being honest, at which Lancaster blew up. 'I am suggesting you are not. I think this line of questioning is unreasonable.' Guests, Wallace unwisely persisted, were there to answer questions, any questions that he, the host might choose to put.

He was asking for trouble and he got it. 'I say you won't have the advantage long if we keep going on like this,' Burt fumed. Shortly afterwards he got up and walked out on the startled host. Fortunately the show was taped.

Birdman of Alcatraz was the last time that Harold Hecht and Burt Lancaster would work together as the commitments made by Hecht-Hill-Lancaster finally ground to a halt. 'When a marriage is over, it's over, and there's no use staying together for the sake of the children,' said Lancaster of the split. As he was doing just that in his private life at the time, it was a notably inconsistent statement. However it wouldn't be long before the bonds that attached him to Norma were similarly loosened and discarded.

Nevertheless he reserved much of his affection for his children, now aged eight to sixteen. His hatred of publicity was particularly vehement when applied to them and they were jealously guarded from the Hollywood glare. Fortunately none of them showed any wish to be child actors, an activity their normally over-indulgent father frowned on. Nor were they allowed to talk much about films at home. 'I don't want to involve my family in the business. It's difficult enough when children are the offspring of any well-known person because they come in for a great deal of unnatural attention and it can make their lives strange. They become the butt of jokes at school. So I've always tried to set up conditions where they live like other children.'

This concern for his own brood spilled over onto children in general, and it was in a spirit of high-mindedness that he signed up for his next picture, *A Child is Waiting* at the request of Stanley Kramer, now wearing his producer's hat. Kramer had a liking for 'message' pictures, and the more controversial or offbeat the better. *Judgement at Nuremberg* came into the former category; *A Child is Waiting* into the latter. On paper the auguries were promising, with Judy Garland set to share the star spot with Lancaster and John Cassavetes committed to directing it. The script, again by *Nuremberg*'s Abbey Mann, was a heart-warming original about retarded children and the location selected was the Pacific State Hospital in Pomona, California.

Burt plays the superintending psychiatrist of the hospital, a rather authoritarian figure who initially appears in an unsympathetic light to a muddled do-gooder (Garland) when she comes to teach there. Where she oozes sentimental love and, even more subversively, singles out one child (Bruce Ritchey) who has been abandoned by his parents (Gena Rowlands and Steven Hill), for special attention, the earnest doctor helps the children to help themselves. Only when the new staff member has absorbed this golden rule, can these semi-documentary proceedings be brought to a hopeful conclusion.

No one could deny the effectively weepy nature of this material, nor the shock that audiences felt when they were faced with the mentally defective and in many cases grossly deformed children of the Pacific State Hospital who, with the sole exception of Bruce Ritchey, played themselves. However, audiences resented being manipulated by Mann's glib and occasionally hysterical script and, more especially, by Ernest Gold's repetitive gloom tunes.

The presence of the waif-like Garland, though heart-tugging on screen, made the shooting of the film into a nightmare. With the exception of her cameo in *Judgement of Nuremberg*, she hadn't taken a film part for seven years, but her liking for the screenplay made this one irresistible. Already in poor health, she consistently brutalised her body by taking uppers and downers to get her through the working day. Her addiction wasn't helped by the presence of the handicapped children who brought back painful memories of her own stay at the Peter Bent Brigham Hospital in 1949. There she'd broken through a wall of silence to communicate with an autistic six-year-old girl. 'Don't leave, Judy, don't leave,' the child had screamed when her visit was at an end, and the constant repetition of similar scenes exacerbated the star's depression.

Kramer must have known that it was risky casting two such mercurial performers as Garland and Lancaster together, but in fact Lancaster wasn't responsible for the hiccups on this one. Indeed, he got on well enough with Judy and attended her funeral in 1969.

As for *A Child is Waiting*, it was non-commercial to the core. Reviewers pondered over it and some, like Arthur Knight of *Saturday Review* came up trumps: 'Miss Garland and Lancaster radiate a warmth so genuine that one is certain that the children are responding directly to them, not merely following some vaguely comprehended script.' England had to wait for three years before the film was released to muted notices in the silly season. The *Sunday Telegraph*'s Margaret Hinxman noted Lancaster's 'authoritative restraint' and considered that Kramer's message 'rises above the melodrama, staking its claim to our attention truly and clearly'. Maybe, but no one wanted to hear it in the middle of their summer holidays, and the picture sank without a trace.

Burt's next film, *The List of Adrian Messenger*, didn't suffer a similar fate, mostly because it was a merry murder jape involving a wealth of stars in a variety of improbable disguises. The man behind several of the masks and the charade itself was Kirk Douglas, and he invited his pals, Frank Sinatra, Bob Mitchum and Tony Curtis as well as Lancaster, to dress up for the kill. The thriller format borrowed the premise that a man with twelve inheritors between him and a fortune would be well advised to dispose of them, from *Kind Hearts and Coronets*, but there all similarity ended. John Huston directed what is essentially a badly acted idiocy, mostly because he needed the fee to restore his Irish castle at St Clerans. He shows most conviction in a notable hunt which follows fox and hounds in considerable detail until the former is devoured by the latter, scenes that reflect Huston's own hard-riding passion for the chase.

Otherwise audiences must wait for the ritual de-masking which takes place when all hope – and the final credits – have gone. Burt, stripped of the trappings of a brazen lady suffragette, beams, suggesting that he at least had fun.

These two exercises in financial self-denial dropped him significantly down the list in the annual Motion Picture Herald-Fame poll which assessed the money-making status of the stars. In 1961, *Judgement at Nuremberg* put him in eleventh place; in 1962, *Birdman of Alcatraz* elevated him to tenth; but 1963 saw him falling behind at eighteenth. Clearly he was overdue for a change of pace and, rising to the challenge as vigorously as ever, he made sure it was the most dramatic one he could make.

eleven
UP AND AWAY

Burt Lancaster was always open to offers he couldn't refuse from abroad. The only problem was that to date no one had made any. Many Americans of his generation considered that the cinema industry began and ended in greater Los Angeles, but Burt claimed a history of intrepid foreign viewing. 'Long before I got into films, when I was a kid, I was aware that fine films were coming from abroad,' he commented. 'Some of the early French and English films had a great deal to say. They were not necessarily popular in the USA. You'd see them in New York in small theatres ... It's ironic that a film like *La Grande Illusion* should only play at a small theatre, but it did. The feeling of exhibitors was that people wouldn't be interested. Even later on, I can remember the first time I saw *Great Expectations* I thought, Gee, that's a marvellous film. But it wasn't a successful film in the USA. Yet on every level it was superb. Now when people see it on TV, they think, "My, what a marvellous film". But at the time when it was new, the theatres were reluctant to show English films because they thought that Americans wouldn't know what the actors were saying. The reactions were terribly basic. But all that's changed now. The world of film is international.'

Maybe, but when *The Leopard*, by Guiseppe di Lampedusa, became the literary sensation of 1958, it is unlikely that anyone would have bet folding money on Burt Lancaster playing Don Fabrizio, Prince of Salina, in the film. The book is about torpor and fatalism in mid-nineteenth-century Sicily where the backward island was drawn into Garibaldi's fight for the unification of Italy. There, as in most civilised parts of the world, circa 1860, the power and money of the aristocracy were being eroded by parvenu businessmen who were establishing a new order over the disintegrating body of an outdated class. Di Lampedusa was a member of that class so he knew what he was writing about each day as he sat, pencil in hand, in his favourite ice-cream parlour in Palermo, briefly free of the burden of his own crumbling palace in La Marina.

Italy's legendary director, the sophisticated Luchino Visconti, was also an aristocrat but, as a committed communist, he found the theme of social change, and especially the lemming-like self-destruction of a privileged class, much to his liking. Accordingly he and four co-writers prepared a film script which emphasised that aspect of the book. He then looked round for his Leopard, in the reluctant realisation that his vision of crumbling palaces and elaborate set pieces wouldn't be cheap.

Hollywood was the obvious solution if the five-million-dollar picture was to get off the ground. So the producer, Goffredo Lombardo, travelled to Los Angeles where he contrived to interest Twentieth Century Fox in the project. He also met Burt Lancaster who, alert to his own interests as ever, eagerly pitched for *The Leopard*. 'I told him what a wonderful book it was and how much I'd like to do the film,' he recalled. No doubt surprised that he'd read it, Lombardo returned to his master to promote Burt's cause. Visconti, who seriously doubted that any American could play the part, threw up his hands in despair. 'No, that's ridiculous,' he exclaimed. 'He's a cowboy, a gangster ...'

Fox however were adamant. They did not want Marlon Brando. Visconti should choose between Anthony Quinn, Spencer Tracy and Burt Lancaster. The director went to see *Judgement at Nuremberg* and made his decision. Later that evening, he dialled Burt's number. The offer he made was five hundred thousand dollars.

Later still he came clean to his leading actor. 'When I arrived in Rome,' Burt remembered, 'I had a meeting for three hours with Visconti. He was quite surprised to find that I knew the book backwards, every nuance of it, and quite delighted to know that I was born in a section of New York called Little Italy, that the people I'd lived with were Sicilians, and that I knew a great deal about the background of these people, and the Mafia and these kinds of things. And he confessed to me: "You know, I didn't want you for this part. I wanted to get a man called Cherkasov, a famous Russian actor who has done *Ivan the Terrible*. But I went to Russia to see him and he was too old. Then I engaged Laurence Olivier. But Mr Olivier's programme was such that he could not work when I wanted him to work."'

When straight talking had cleared the air a bit, Visconti got to know Burt and began to see his potential. 'The prince himself was a very complex character – at times autocratic, rude, strong; at times romantic, good, understanding – sometimes even stupid and, above all, mysterious. Burt is all these things too. I sometimes think Burt is the most perfectly mysterious man I ever met in my life.'

Shooting on *The Leopard* began in the broiling June of 1962. The book had been published posthumously so the author's adopted son, Giaocchino Lanza Tomasi, was hired to scour his native island for authentically crumbling ruins and stretches of desolate countryside. As Sicily has a surfeit of both, finding the locations was not the problem, but getting the go-ahead from the Mafia to use them was another matter. The medieval village of Palma di Montechiaro once part of the di Lampedusa estates was the first stumbling block. Visconti wanted to dress it up as Donnafugata, an ancestral home of the Princes of Salina, but there was no road. Plans were drawn up for one, and local contractors hired to build it. Then came the demand for a levy, backed up with threats of force should it be refused.

Instead the unit took the existing, rudimentary dirt track to Ciminna, thirty long and dangerous miles outside Palermo. The name means 'Hospitality' in Arabic, but no one in the cast or crew could think why it should have been applied to this decaying village, and Visconti, at least, had no illusions about what he was up against. 'Official protection is out of the question,' he explained at the time. 'Here this terrible tyranny of the Mafia still rules. Sicily has suffered centuries of servitude and still lives in a kind of torpor. The Mafia persists like some kind of devouring cancer.

'When I insisted on shooting the picture here, I did so because I needed the atmosphere, the toughness, even the very smell of Sicily to tell successfully the real story of the novel. I never realised how close Sicily today is to Sicily of a hundred years ago at the time of the Italian Risorgimento – the days of Garibaldi. Conditions are feudal as they were then. There is the same cruelty, and violence, ignorance and poverty.'

The arrival of 175 aliens, under the banners of the Italian production company Titanus, which flew over limousines, caravans and trucks alike, resembled an invading army and the local peasants watched the interminable preparations, interspersed with sharp bursts of action, with bemused astonishment. Indeed, making *The Leopard* over eleven of the hottest weeks of the year on the budget fixed by Fox (who'd understood the nature of their associates so well that they'd made the Italians responsible for any over-spending) had obvious parallels with running a small local war.

Visconti's intensely precise vision of what he wanted inevitably increased pressure on all concerned in these trying circumstances. If he hadn't the money to extend the schedule, he'd cram more in to the existing one, which meant that dressing began at four a.m., shooting finished at ten p.m. 'Visconti is really a painter,' Lancaster insisted. 'He has the eye of an artist. He thinks that way. He shoots as a director in a way that I have never seen. He will make the camera accommodate itself to what we are, to give a sense of real perspective, not a false one. It puts an enormous demand on the technicians but he gets marvellous results. A visual artist in the best sense of the word.'

As for Burt himself, he was initially rather left out of the process. The crew were Italian and French, as were his fellow actors, headed by Alain Delon and Claudia Cardinale. The language barrier was exacerbated by Visconti's affection for the young French star. 'Luchino idolised Delon,' said Fulco della Verdura, the director's close friend. 'He was the only actor to have a dressing room; poor Burt Lancaster stood around for hours waiting.'

The unit was based in Palermo and many of its members hired villas along the coast of Conca d'Oro. Delon held court nightly in his, surrounded by guests from the Cote d'Azur, plus his regular entourage of Romy Schneider, his agent and two elocution coaches. Burt, however, remained aloof with his family on his enormous yacht which stood out beyond the mole. Conscientiously, he prepared himself for his part by visiting the city's monuments and reading background books on the island's history.

Cynics, who had smiled or raged at his original selection, were quick to knock this transatlantic zeal and dub it affected and arty, but the star continued with his self-immersion unperturbed. Gradually he won the respect of cast and crew for his infinite pains, his professionalism on set and his modesty. They called him the 'anti star', and they meant it as a compliment. Visconti, too, when he saw the potential of the actor being realised in the rushes, warmed to the man, and consulted him more and more, dispelling early rumours of constant friction at the top.

'This man is a master,' said Burt of his mentor. 'I rely on him a great deal – and he's taught me a lot about the Sicilian nobility. All right, he's a difficult man to work with. And I don't like being pushed around by anyone. He'll stalk off into a corner and everybody waits and stews and frets. I did in the beginning, but then I got to know him. Now we sit and talk the scenes over together, and we may chew it about for an hour or more.

'Working on that film was a completely different experience for me.

Visconti took endless pains to get everything right. He was a perfection-
ist. Yet he had this amazing way of trusting you. He wouldn't tell you
how to play a scene. He'd let you do it your own way, once he saw you
knew what you were doing. Once we did have a long talk – about three
hours – on set about the approach to a scene. And the ideas he wanted
me to get across were brilliant. They were far superior to anything I
had in mind.

'I worked on the screenplay with him too. He imparted this tremendous confidence and you couldn't help but share it with him. But
everything had to be exactly as he wanted it in other departments. He
wouldn't work unless it was. We once arrived in a Sicilian village, and
found some of the houses had television aerials on them. He just said,
"I want them down. Every one of them. When they are down we will
shoot. You will find me in my hotel!" They came down okay.'

They made an odd couple, the beak-nosed intellectual in his white
suit and hat giving orders to thousands in the stifling heat and his latest
acolyte, the burly forty-eight-year-old American on his unaccustomed
best behaviour. Lancaster fed on Visconti's brain power, the hard bright
quality of his vision, and envied it, yet he was humble enough to
recognise and learn from it. As a result, his Leopard is a many-shaded
man, a towering physical presence capable of sensitivity, sentimentality,
cruelty, humour and hard nosed common sense.

Lampedusa's Prince was trapped by history. He mourned the passing
of traditional values, yet was pragmatic enough to arrange his nephew
Tancredi's marriage to the daughter of the upstart village mayor who
could give the boy the dowry he would need to establish himself in the
diplomatic hierarchy. Willing to adapt he might be, but there was no
place for him in the new order. The flamboyant sexuality between the
young couple, sparklingly portrayed by the vivaciously handsome
Delon at the start of his career and Cardinale at the brief height of her
voluptuous beauty, depressed the still sensuous – and on occasion
prostitute-seeking – Prince almost as much as the erosion of his way of
life.

At the sumptuous ball, the symbol of the bygone age, that takes up
the last third of the film, he wanders nostalgically through the gilded
throng, with presentiments of his own death that parallel that of his
class. The silly pretty girls, the self-seeking politicians, the bitchy ma-
trons and the bourgeois intruders in their ill-fitting tails who will soon
take over flash before him and ultimately disgust him so that he leaves
abruptly in order to be alone. Rather earlier he joins Cardinale on the

dance floor for what you feel will be his last waltz, the final proof that the old lion, though doomed, has something of value to teach his spellbound audience.

Many of these shades of emotions were quite outside Lancaster's experience. As a self-made millionaire with somewhat unsophisticated tastes, he had much more in common with Lampedusa's nouveau riche than his imminently poor. Just as Sicily's slide into destitution and corruption, still as implacable in 1960 as it had been a century before, contrasted with the effervescent upward mobility of California, so did Don Fabrizio's obsession with a heroic past and a tormented future clash with Burt's irrepressible confidence in himself.

Yet, as he donned the Prince's bushy moustache and period costume, he absorbed himself in his character and portrayed him movingly in all his moods. 'When I go on the set, I know I am the Prince of Salina, even though I may not be sure how I am going to say the lines. With Visconti's long rehearsals you have a chance to come to the right relationships with the objects and people around you – which doesn't often happen in the hectic process of film-making. When I read the book before the part was offered to me, I thought that this story of a prince during the Risorgimento, who only at the last comes to realise that his world, which he has always considered immutable, is actually crumbling away, is the greatest study of a man and his background that has appeared for a century.'

His performance was equal to the task of making the book come alive on film, no mean achievement for a gangster cowboy. As the weeks went by, the imposing figure was accepted into the tiny inner world of Palermo society, some two hundred and fifty privileged people, most of whom were descended from Lampedusa's characters. At the start, they looked on the stranger who'd come to portray the spirit of their ancestors with alarm and suspicion, not unmixed with envy when they compared his yacht with their more modest craft. When he was made a member of the Mondello Yacht Club, he took on a more human form as he lunched at adjacent tables and displayed unexpectedly good manners. Unlike the fifteen-year-old girl from Ohio who greeted him in a restaurant in Rome with, 'If I could shake your hand, Mr Lancaster, it would change my life,' the Sicilian grandees were invariably dignified. However their reserve was imperceptibly broken down until they offered the actor the kind of hospitality they'd previously bestowed on kings and emperors, Wagner and General Patton.

Towards the end of the schedule, Burt took time out to visit the

Venice Film Festival to pick up his Best Actor's prize for *Birdman of Alcatraz*. He stayed at the Gritti and wore his Leopard's moustache with casual distinction. He even answered a trivial question on its future from a reporter, Jean Durkheim of *Cinemonde*. 'Have no fear,' he replied. 'Five minutes after the last shot I'll shave it off. My wife and children never stop mocking my huge moustache. It seems, according to them, to make me look ridiculous.'

Encouraged, Durkheim asked him to talk about the differences between Italian and American film-makers. 'I know only one Italian director: Luchino Visconti, so I can't speak of Italian methods, only of Visconti's. He is very meticulous, knows exactly what he wants and attaches great importance to the tiniest details. He's not quick, but what he does, he does well. In the cinema, only the results count. I have the impression, speaking frankly, that the result will be quite extraordinary.'

How right he was, but sadly only the Europeans reaped the benefits in their cinemas.

The polyglot nature of the cast was always going to be a problem when it came to the sound-track and it had been agreed from the beginning that there should be an Italian and an English version of the film. In the former, Lancaster would be dubbed; in the latter he would speak for himself. For the Italians, it would be the other way round, while Alain Delon, elocution coaches or no, would be dubbed in both. No expense or time was spared in finding actors whose tones were suitable for the characters nor in ensuring that their lips moved in sync with those of the people on the screen.

The Italian film, in which Burt speaks in impeccably cultured and elegant fashion, is excellent. Visconti cut it from the original 205 minutes to 185 and sent it to the Cannes Film Festival where it duly won the Golden Palm in 1963. The same print, in all its glowing Technicolor subtlety, did the rounds in Europe, gathering plaudits and doing good box-office business wherever it went.

The Italians, who invariably dub foreign films for their own markets, have a long history of preferring imitation to sub-titles, and no doubt Visconti and Lombardo assumed that this would be the best method of getting their message across when they made the original agreement with Twentieth Century Fox. Burt, by now in Visconti's inner circle, volunteered his services for weeks on end so that justice might be done for the English language version. But hard though he tried, the end product was brutally American. Twentieth Century Fox compounded the crime by using a cheaper colour process, De Luxe, which made a coarse and garish mess of Visconti's magnificent compositions. As a final nail in the coffin, they hacked a further forty minutes out of the picture to make it more commercial.

Protests from the outraged Visconti echoed around the English-speaking world but he was too late. Fox had what they thought they wanted, and that was the end of it. When the film was due to open in London in December 1963, he wrote to the British Film Institute and asked them to take a subtitled version for England. When they were unable to comply, he threatened to sue Twentieth Century Fox, a move the studio countered with an aggressive statement from Seymour Poe, their executive vice-president. 'If there is ány suing to be done, we may be forced to initiate actions against Visconti,' he said. 'The print we are releasing throughout Britain and the US was prepared under the full and complete supervision of Burt Lancaster, the man delegated by Visconti for this responsibility. At all times, Mr Lancaster had one hundred per cent artistic control and freedom.'

No doubt that was true, but the task of expressing the subtle and characteristically Italian concepts in American accents was doomed from the start. Visconti's last throw was to write to *The Times*, disowning his work in the following terms: 'I am a prisoner. It is not my fault. It is judged that American audiences are simple minded and will understand, but the American version is a terrible disaster and the film is not what I intended it to be.' Sadly he died some years before his judgement was vindicated publicly when the subtitled *The Leopard* was released in London and New York in 1983 as a tribute twenty years after it was made, to great critical acclaim.

Despite all these disadvantages, the American critics were fulsome in their praise of Lancaster. 'Within definite limits, he is superb,' wrote *Time*. 'True his Salina never quite becomes the figure of "leonine aspect, whose fingers could twist a ducal coin as if it were a mere paper". But as the scenes accumulate, the character compiles impressive volume and solidity, and by the film's end, the Sicilian Prince stands in the mind as a man men shall not look upon again: one of culture's noblemen and a very imperfect gentle knight.' *Variety* concurred, though less poetically. 'In the final reels, it is again Lancaster who gives the picture some of its deeply moving moments as he moves, a sad, lonely ageing figure no longer his own.'

In England, John Coleman of the *New Statesman* considered that 'Burt Lancaster's performance is, in many ways, very fine. He has the physical magnificence necessary to accommodate some of the Leopard's wilder moments, as when he plucks from the ground and embraces the vulgar new man whose daughter is to marry his beloved nephew. Unexpectedly, he also has the delicacy of the Leopard.' Dilys Powell of the *Sunday Times* who'd seen the continental version in Paris, was even more enthusiastic. 'Burt Lancaster as the Prince is magnificent: each movement, each gesture has a noble authority, as if it were the product of centuries of ease, wealth and pride. And there is more than formal authority ... The high impatience with the flutterings of his wife, the touch of arrogance towards the family priest, the ironic contempt for the new rich, the rage against a friend who cannot understand the impossibility of social survival without compromise, the sudden awareness of mortality: in everything, his qualities persist.'

However the English-speaking public didn't want to know, and Lancaster returned to his American career a sadder and wiser man. The early sixties had seen his best work in *Elmer Gantry*, *Birdman of Alcatraz* and *The Leopard*, but Hollywood remained Hollywood, its need for sex gods unassuaged, and unassuagable outside the familiar clichéd formulas it lived by. When Burt went to see *The Leopard* in a public cinema, the man behind him kept asking his wife, 'When's Lancaster going to screw Cardinale?' Nor was that lowest-common-denominator spectator alone in seeing that as the film's only acceptable solution. 'Once the public decide what you are, you might as well give up trying to be anything else,' Burt commented ruefully. 'One of the most unusual and valuable experiences in my life was working on *The Leopard* but a lot of my fans couldn't understand why I'd made it. Strangely they all said the same thing – "Burt, I thought you were going to screw the girl, but you never did. What went wrong?" I guess I'm the guy who always screwed the girl, even if it was only after the movie had finished.'

So 'the toughest, most difficult thing' he ever attempted, for the 'best director' he worked for ended in disappointment – and a return to the Hollywood dream factory.

twelve
RETRENCHMENT

Clean-shaven and with a full head of hair for the first time in a couple of years, Lancaster was once again recognisably himself, yet the spirit of experimentation had drained away. It would be nearly a decade before he stretched himself again, years in which he took mature roles and played them with rigid professionalism. Without Hecht's commercial instincts behind him, he went for soft options on tough hombres, a cop-out that was recognised by the public who never restored him to his previous eminence in the Motion Picture Herald-Fame poll, the industry's barometer of popularity.

If he was looking for familiar territory, he certainly found it in *Seven Days in May*, based on Fletcher Knebel and Charles W. Bailey's novel, a project initiated by Kirk Douglas's company and directed by John Frankenheimer. It is a stern relevant drama about a right-wing general (Lancaster) who plans a military takeover from an estimable President who has concluded a nuclear treaty with the Soviet Union against the wishes of the Pentagon. The plot is discovered by his aide (Douglas) who tells all and, after mysterious deaths and a great deal of mayhem, foils his evil deeds.

The film was made in 1963, months before President Kennedy's assassination, with the full blessing of the White House. The Press Secretary, Pierre Salinger, arranged for JFK to go to Hyannisport while a small riot was shot in front of the presidential residence. He also escorted Frankenheimer through the President's office and other rooms so that they could be accurately copied in the studio. The Pentagon, though unhappy about the project, made no attempt to censor it. Lancaster, playing completely against his own political beliefs, contrived to beat down any revulsion he may have felt about the general's totalitarian outlook by being waxily immobile throughout. However, he had no hesitation in using his clout - and his facial muscles - to pressurise Frankenheimer into putting Kirk Douglas in his place, in this, their fifth collaboration.

'I had my problems with Kirk,' the director recalled. 'He was jealous of Burt Lancaster. He felt he was playing a secondary role to him. I told him before he went in, he would be. He wanted to be Burt Lancaster. He's wanted to be Burt Lancaster all his life. In the end it came to sitting down with Douglas, saying, "Look, you prick, if you don't like it, get the hell out."'

Ava Gardner, cast as the general's ex-mistress who betrays him, a part that reunited her with Burt for the first time since *The Killers*, was another thorn in Frankenheimer's flesh, but he was fresh from his triumph in a similar field with *The Manchurian Candidate*, and the picture got made in the end.

However it wasn't supported either by the critics or the public. 'The movie is least successful when it tries to sound significant,' said *Time*, while Judith Crist, writing in the *New York Herald-Tribune*, reserved her kinder words for Lancaster. In her opinion, 'He combines a finely controlled fanaticism with innate conviction.'

For Kirk Douglas, the commercial failure marked the end of the Lancaster line, at least for the foreseeable future. 'I've finally got away from Burt,' he was to say later. 'My luck has changed for the better. I've got nice-looking girls in my films now.'

Frankenheimer, however, came back for more on Lancaster's next film, *The Train*, in which the actor was unwise enough to line up opposite Paul Scofield and Jeanne Moreau. Arthur Penn, the originator of the adaptation of Ross Valland's novel, *Le Front de l'Art*, was the first director to be hired, but he and Burt disagreed so fundamentally about concept and method that Penn was fired after two weeks on the job. The associate producer, Bernard Farrell, filled in for a while, and Burt explained to the press in Paris where *The Train* was being shot that he wasn't the ogre they imagined.

'I know what you have heard about me,' he joked, 'that I am always difficult and grab all the broads. It's not true. I'm difficult only some of the time and grab only some of the broads. You have to make up your mind in this business whether you are going to make every operation a success or not. I don't have trouble with directors because I want to dictate to them. I think the director should have control of his province. But when you are the producer as well as the star and you see things are not working out right, you just have got to do something about it. Of course, a thing like that can bruise a director's ego. Sometimes they sound off a bit about it. But you must expect that.'

What better solution to the temporary embarrassment than to ring John Frankenheimer, in the knowledge that he would see it your way? On this occasion the loyal servant didn't want to answer the clarion call. He was tired after his last brush with super egos on *Seven Days in May*. He did, however, want to visit Europe and he'd never been able to say no to Lancaster. Only on his way across the Atlantic did he read the script, and by the time his plane touched down at Orly Airport, he knew his next ordeal had begun. 'I thought it was almost appalling, neither fish nor fowl,' he commented. 'The damned train didn't leave the station until page 140.'

His first task was to re-write the story of a Nazi general (Scofield) who raids the Jeu de Paume and puts its finest paintings on a train for the Fatherland. The forces for good are headed by a doughty Resistance fighter (Burt) who is also an official of the French railways. Initially he is opposed to stopping the train because of the loss of life it'll cause, but later he changes his mind and prevents the looting.

Although the script makes some simplistic points about the relative values of art and people, it is essentially an action thriller and Frankenheimer used every trick in the book to make it exciting. For the climactic train crash, he put five cameras on or near the track. The sixth he buried beside the rails and installed a remote control. The train was supposed to come off at seven miles per hour, but to his horror the director realised the French engineer had panicked and picked up to something approaching three times that speed. He hauled his technicians out of the way just in time, but five of the cameras were wrecked along with the train and only the buried one produced any usable footage.

The production continued in much the same spirit of delay and alarm. Bad weather in Normandy on what was supposed to be a summer sequence caused a six-month pause until spring came round again, and more hardware was lost in a series of mishaps. However, Frankenheimer remained true to his purpose and produced remarkable authenticity in a grey, grim and tragic picture. Burt contributed to it by doing many of his own stunts with much of his old verve. 'He was in his element, falling from trains, sliding down ladders, climbing walls, yet all the time living his part,' the director said. Others agreed about the action sequences, but were extremely dubious about his credibility as a French patriot, despite the Gauloises that hung continuously from the corner of his mouth. Far from learning from the Anglo-Saxon misfortunes of *The*

Leopard, he again went for a brash American sound-track but later it was Frankenheimer, not he, who admitted the mistake.

'One thing I deeply regret now is that we did not use French speaking actors when we dubbed the French into English. If Burt and I had that film to do over again, we would both do it differently. I came in after it started shooting, but once Burt became involved, he began to live the film so intently that he said to me, "My God, if only we had started this together, I would have played it with a French accent. Then we wouldn't have had to dub the other actors into that hoarse, American-English and the entire film would have been more convincing." '

The mind may boggle at the prospect of his French accent, but he had the right idea. His acting came in for some pretty unfavourable comparisons with Paul Scofield and Jeanne Moreau, cast as a hotel-keeper who assists the honourable railroad official. In any case the French actress had no time for her co-star. 'Burt Lancaster,' she exclaimed in exasperation. 'Before he can pick up an ashtray, he discusses his motivation for an hour or two. You want to say just pick up the ashtray and shut up.'

Of the professional opinion-mongers, *Films in Review* found that, 'Lancaster lacks the grace that derives from true sophistication and his heedless acrobatics have a derailing effect', to which *Time* added, 'Not for a moment does he seem to be a French patriot.'

This debacle was minor compared to his next selection, a 167-minute Western with satirical and racial overtones. On *The Train*, he had answered a question about why he went on working and doing his own stunts with the following remarks: 'Because I just don't want to do anything else. I have all the money I shall ever need. The pleasure is not in making the money, but in doing what you want.' Why on earth he should have wanted to make *The Hallelujah Trail* remains a mystery. Compulsive analyser that he is, he has always recognised that comedy is an essential part of any actor's repertoire and claimed that he could play it, though he has admitted that he's no natural comedian.

This, of course, is his monumental ego speaking and *The Hallelujah Trail* proves that farce, at least, is something he should avoid like the plague. It is one of those merry road japes about a tough no-nonsense army officer (Burt) who is ordered to take a shipment of whisky to Denver in the winter of 1867. Among the hazards he meets are Hollywood Indians who want the liquor, miners, crooks and a band of temperance ladies, led by a rather facetious Lee Remick. At one point, she harangues Lancaster on the perils of alcohol as he lies in his bath tub. 'You'll forgive me if I don't stand up,' he says, in what can be counted among the feeble-minded picture's greatest witticisms. Most of the seemingly endless footage is taken up with heavy-handed humour and routine slapstick with never a hint of originality or panache. No wonder it died.

As for Burt, he was fortunate to be dealt in on *The Professionals*, under Richard Brooks who'd directed him so triumphantly as Elmer Gantry. Brooks scripted the film from the novel, *A Mule for the Marquessa*, by Frank O'Rourke. The picture is a guys' convention with Lancaster, Lee Marvin, Robert Ryan and Woody Strode as a mercenary band. They play respectively a ladies' man and explosives expert; a crude ex-army weapons specialist; an agile breeder of beautiful horses; and a black athletics champion who can throw a mean knife and pull a deadly bow. Between them, they have the qualities required by their employer (Ralph Bellamy) to make their way through the Mexico of the revolution circa 1917 and rescue his wife (Claudia Cardinale). She is being held against her will, her wealthy spouse assumes, by one of Pancho Villa's most resolute henchmen (Jack Palance) but when the soldiers of fortune arrive, it is to find that the pair are lovers. The return journey is even more fraught with violent escapades and ingenious tricks than the outward one until the mercs realise that it is the conveniently absent husband who is the villain, and leave the happy couple to their own devices.

This was the old Lancaster, a rogue, womaniser and resolute fighter who stands by his pals in many a tight corner, and his fans responded to him to the extent that the picture grossed 8.8 million dollars in domestic rentals, and put the star back on the celluloid map. Its pluses include some vivid footage of the Mexican revolution, shot north of the border, mostly in Nevada's Valley of Fire National Park, but it is essentially the four men against the mob element that made it so successful. Judith Crist again gave her unqualified approval: 'A sleek, slam-bang adventure suspense film,' she wrote. 'Burt Lancaster has never been more athletically suave.'

Lancaster saw the film for what it was, and welcomed its box-office success with objectivity: '*The Professionals* sets out to be an entertaining, ribald kind of Western. Let us not overlook the fact that our business is a business industry and we have to make films that make money. There are still a bulk of people who like to go to a pure escapist film, and these films are bread and butter. *The Professionals* is a good film – highly entertaining. People were stimulated and excited by it. People can't live in the darkness of life all the time, saying, "Oh my God, it isn't true." We have to be able to laugh, you know, and have a little fun.'

Considering he was fifty-two, his physical prowess was an indication of the soundness of his training and the quality of his resolution. He looked barely forty, but he worked for it by running a minimum of three miles a day before breakfast no matter where he was and working out for hours in the gym, whenever he could. 'Fitness is a way of life', had always been his motto, and he was assiduous in living up to it.

Mentally though his purpose was becoming blurred. Should he retire and tour the beauty spots of the world? Twin passions for golf and fishing would have given him ample opportunity to find in the gregariousness of the clubhouse and the pause for reflection by the riverside the dualities his nature required, but he never seriously considered a life of leisure. The work habit was too ingrained.

Throughout the late sixties, he made contradictory statements about his future, confirming his rare self-doubt. 'Two years more, then I want to quit acting altogether,' he told William Hall of the *Evening News*. 'Some actors go on for ever into the grave. I don't want to be like that. I've been in the business most of my life, and I'll stay in it – but as a producer. I like being a producer. Reading the scripts, testing the artists, talking to the writers and directors. I do more work that way than when I'm acting. When I get away to do a movie, it's like a paid holiday.'

On other days he took a rather different line: 'It won't be easy to move on and out because an actor lives in a world of adulation, and that's very flattering. As an actor, I know I can still improve. Oh God, yes. We've all got to keep trying to reach new horizons,' he'd say fervently. It was only the parts that lacked and that was the fault of the hacks.

'I suppose I've done everything by now – thrillers, Westerns, swashbucklers, melodramas, dramas, the lot. And if I've learned anything from the whole business, it is this: you cannot do it without the written word. That is more important than almost anything. Generally speaking, stars are not frauds. Gable was Gable and that's it. He brought his credentials with him. But some directors are, and a heck of a lot of writers can be too. You've no idea how poor the average screenplay is, no idea at all. Why do so many writers write so badly?'

The complaint was valid, but he went on trying. It is noticeable that he set his retirement date a year or so ahead, rather than at the end of the picture he was working on. He'd always leave time for one more, just one more...

His next choice was *The Swimmer*, a weird semi-fantasy about Ned

Merrill, a middle-aged, middle-class New Englander whose life has been carefully constructed on quicksand. He has a lot of friends with swimming pools in their gardens around which they sit of a Sunday morning saying 'I drank too much last night.' On one such summer's day, Merrill in a mood of isolation, decides to swim via these pools to his own suburban house, a distance of some eight miles, which gives him time to reflect on his loves, his failures and his subconscious fears in flashbacks. With each visit, his self-delusions and his obsession with staying young become increasingly pitiful, so that the climax, when he reaches his own house to find his family gone and the door locked against him, comes as no surprise. Sobbing, he falls to his knees in the rain in the total realisation of his own failure.

Given our inability to see ourselves as others see us, the theme, based on a short story by John Cheever that had appeared in the *New Yorker*, is interesting, but so convoluted that it needed a genuis to script it into a film. Luckily, it fell into the hands of Eleanor and Frank Perry, who'd scored high critical marks with their first feature, *David and Lisa*, and appeared to be rising on the independent scale of film-makers. Eleanor scripted and Frank directed, but the lack of plot proved to be an insurmountable handicap to its commercial prospects. Lancaster, characteristically attracted by the intellectual fantasy, was as determined as the Perrys to realise the project, despite a well-concealed fear of the water. He took a course of swimming lessons to prepare himself for his ordeal and stripped off frequently, though never frontally, to display his formidable muscles.

Even bared, they were not enough. The solution of the executive producer – Columbia's Sam Spiegel – was to demand a re-make of the scene where Merrill visits his ex-mistress with Janice Rule replacing Barbara Loden in front of the cameras and Sydney Pollack ousting Frank Perry behind them.

This too was not enough, and indeed weakened the picture because of the contrast in directing styles. The reels remained on the shelves for two years while Columbia mulled over the problem, then flopped mightily when it did appear. 'Lacklustre,' said Hollis Alpert (*Saturday Review*) of the star, but the faithful Judith Crist (*New York Magazine*) chipped in with the bolstering, 'perhaps the best acting of his career'.

Unfortunately not enough of her readers believed her to save the film, and even the television companies relegated it from prime time to syndication treatment that was almost unknown for a Lancaster vehicle. History however has proved that Ms Crist had right on her side, and

The Swimmer is now recognised as one of Burt's most underrated films, a victim of Columbia's marketing ineptitude when faced with anything out of the ordinary.

The delay meant that *The Scalphunters*, which Lancaster made two years later, was in the cinemas before *The Swimmer*. It was the first of two successive films with Sydney Pollack in the director's chair, and a very stormy business it turned out to be. The location was the Mex-West town of Durango where heat and tempers run high, and the presence of ex-mistress Shelley Winters in the cast hardly helped.

Burt was a sucker for the film's civil-rights slant, rather simplistically resolved by a white man and a black man fighting in the mud and coming up coffee-coloured. It was a theme on which he felt that his well-established liberal standing entitled him to argue over the concept until the cows came home. And argue he did, forcefully and continuously, day after day. Pollack wasn't a yes-man like Frankenheimer, and he answered back. The fur flew.

That, anyway, was appropriate because Burt plays a frontier trapper during the Civil War who is robbed of his pelts by marauding Kiowa Indians. They leave him with an escaped slave (Ossie Davis), whom he conscripts to help retrieve his livelihood. However Telly Savalas's band of Indian scalphunters get in first, only to be liquidated in their turn by another set of braves who ride off into the sunset with Burt's furs. Resolute to the last, he sets out in pursuit once more. Despite the narrative weakness of a scenario that relies on counter-eliminations, the picture turned out to be brisk and exciting, with elements of humour that were daringly applied to the civil-rights angle, a subject normally treated with sententious gravity. Ms Winters plays Savalas's coarse mistress. At the end, she is captured by the last of the pelt-snatching Indians and borne away into the sunset to a squaw's life. 'A man is a man,' she says, shrugging indifferently, no doubt to Lancaster's amusement.

Between on-set battles, he set about Durango with a culture-vulture's zeal. Every evening he took a Spanish lesson, before attending the nightly performance of the festival of opera that happily coincided with the film-making.

No one in the business expected Sidney Pollack to lock horns again immediately, but he duly signed up for Burt's next film, the ill-conceived *Castle Keep*. Maybe he wanted a trip to Yugoslavia where the war picture, a bizarre mixture of fantasy and bomb-happy realism adapted from William Eastlake's novel, was to be made. Despite *The Swimmer*'s flop, Columbia shelled out big bucks to build a facsimile tenth-century Belgian castle in Novi Sar, only to blow it up in the film's climactic special effect. So magnificent was it that many viewers were outraged at its destruction, believing it to be an irreplaceable ancient monument.

Lancaster, his good looks destroyed by an eye patch, is an American major who discovers the castle in the Ardennes during the thrust for Berlin in the winter of 1944. It is occupied by a count (Jean-Pierre Aumont), who offers it to the liberator as a billet, and throws his beautiful young wife in for good measure because he is impotent and wants an heir. The major obliges, then proves his foolhardy heroism by defending the building against the Nazis with the scant assistance of one captain, one lieutenant and five enlisted men. Only the wife, presumed pregnant, and one black private who acts as narrator, survive.

The problem with *Castle Keep* is that it is never sure whether its woolly anti-war message should be expressed in serious or satirical terms. Flip jokes and convoluted epigrams on the transitory nature of life fight for sound-track space and the result is a fiasco. The major's character, too, is something of a mess, initially logical, but becoming uncharacteristically rash once battle is joined. Burt plays him with subdued intensity in his first R-rated – and very violent – film but the public didn't want to know.

The making of the picture was a fairly unhappy experience for all concerned. Pollack and Lancaster took up their running battle on arrival over interpretation at the Petrovaradin Fortress, now converted into a hotel in which they were staying, and continued it unremittingly. The young actress, Astrid Heeren, who'd been hired to play the count's wife, was so horrified at the verbal fisticuffs that she took a taxi to the airport. She was already waiting for her escape plane before the two men noticed she'd gone and hurried after her to talk her back in. Some years later, however, Lancaster paid Pollack what must have been an unexpected compliment when he said, 'He was the man who worked me hardest and the man I best communicated with.'

There was a further delay to the schedule when Norma, now approaching the tail-end of her patience so far as her husband was concerned, hit him over the head with a bottle and put him in hospital. The incident, which took place in the too public forum of a Belgrade restaurant, earned unwelcome headlines in the world's press and dented his tough-guy image.

The snow piled up to heights of three feet and more and the cold was intense, but Burt, in his faded white tracksuit, found a demanding partner for his daily jog in Bruce Dern, ex-Olympic marathon runner, who had a small part in the film. Burt still weighed in at fourteen stone and toured the countryside at a snappy jog trot, to the amazement of many of his younger colleagues.

It was during the making of *Castle Keep* that Burt flew back to Washington at his own expense to join Martin Luther King's freedom march on the capital. It was a typical gesture by the actor to put a considerable sum of his own money where his mouth was in the cause of civil rights. He was joined in the streets by liberal Hollywood, headed by Paul Newman and his wife, Joanne Woodward.

The fateful day was filmed by producer Ely Landau, with connecting sequences directed by Sidney Lumet, and released two years later as a 182-minute documentary titled *King: A Filmed Record ... Montgomery to Memphis*. An extended five-and-a-half hour version was released to college campuses around America. In November 1968, Burt appeared on a four-hour television marathon on behalf of Hubert Humphrey in his fight for the presidency against Richard Nixon. The show consisted of questions addressed to the two White House candidates, interspersed with comments on their own lives from their supporting stars. Once again Burt was joined by the Newmans, plus Edward G. Robinson, Kirk Douglas and Sonny and Cher.

Between these two political happenings, Lancaster travelled to Witchita in Kansas for a summer sky-diving picture, his fifth, final (to date) and least successful collaboration with the faithful Frankenheimer. Called *The Gipsy Moths*, it reunited him with Deborah Kerr in autumn love sequences that had little of the lust and lustre of their previous close encounters in *From Here To Eternity*. The uncomfortable reminder of the transitory nature of life was entirely appropriate to the film's 'existential pessimism'.

Based on a dense and convoluted, albeit extremely short, novel by James Drought, it follows five tormented characters through one weekend of their hopeless search for a raison d'être. Three of them, Lancaster, Scott Wilson and Gene Hackman, are sky-divers, daring itinerant workers who roam from small town to small town to scratch a living jumping out of planes for the amusement of the gawpers. In Bridgeville they stay with Brandon (William Windom) and his wife (Deborah Kerr). He is a cold, intellectual university professor, overtly contemptuous of men who exist for derring-do; she is lonely, frustrated but trapped by convention and temperament. She and Lancaster, the quietest of the trio, make love, but the next day he fails to pull the cord on his parachute and hurtles to his death. It is a deliberate act of self-destruction, a very public statement on the emptiness of life, whether terrestial or airborne, that drives his two mates out of the sky-diving business. If he has the right to choose death, they have the right to choose life – and they do.

Again it is easy to see why Lancaster was drawn to a man who made his date with his own destiny in such unequivocal terms. Equally, it is not too difficult to imagine why audiences rejected such a downbeat message. *The Gypsy Moths* received high and deserved praise for its brilliant aerial diving sequences, executed by cameraman Carl Boensich who jumped with the stuntmen and filmed their acrobatics on the way down. His photography depicts the three divers as human moths dicing with death in a hypnotic slow-motion ballet, in telling contrast with their rather one-dimensional earthbound personalities. The symbolism is effective but pictures with little dialogue and even less explanation of motivation and background are not the stuff that hits are made of.

Variety's verdict was 'a poor sky-diver yarn' but Richard Shickel showed more sensitivity in *Life* magazine: 'One is uncomfortably reminded of the romance these two (Lancaster and Kerr) enacted in *From Here to Eternity* – and of the passage of time since. As he has grown older, Mr Lancaster had developed a capacity, unique in established stars to "give away" scenes that his status in the movie pecking order entitles him to dominate. He did it in *Castle Keep* and he does it again in *The Gypsy Moths* and he deserves full credit for its shrewd selflessness.'

On the home front, it is unlikely that Norma Lancaster would have commended her husband for selflessness. She'd endured twenty-three years of over-commitment to motion pictures and, allegedly, other women, and she'd reached the end of the line. Although friends and colleagues had a good idea of the state of the Lancaster marriage, it was a subject that very rarely got into the papers, the spectacular Belgrade bottle incident apart. 'The truth is,' Burt had said only a few years earlier while working on *The Train*, 'when I am not working I am just an ordinary family man. My wife and I may have had our disagreements, but nothing like divorce has even been whispered. When I'm at home, I go to the office every day, like anybody else. I find most of my spare time is taken up in driving the kids and their friends around.'

By 1969, however, those kids were approaching adulthood. Bill had been married for three years to Kippie Kovacs, the daughter of comedian, Ernie Kovacs, and even the youngest child, Sighle-Ann, was

131

fifteen. In July, Norma sued for divorce on the grounds of cruelty in the court at Santa Monica, and was duly granted her decree, the custody of the three girls and her share of some two million dollars under Californian law. She respected her husband's paranoia in the matter of publicity by making no public statement on the nature of his cruelty, a silence which he welcomed and shared.

Since his divorce, Burt has lived with ex-hairdresser Jackie Bone whom he had met some years earlier. A woman of strong character who stands up for her rights, she appears to be the perfect mate. 'We have no plans to marry,' Lancaster has said, refuting persistent press rumours of a secret wedding. 'There's no point in matrimony unless a couple plan to have children. And at my age raising another family is not exactly uppermost in my thoughts. The relationship between Jackie and me is great. There is no ownership between us. We aren't possessive.'

Whether the cruelty was mental or physical, Burt reckoned that his violence was well suppressed by this stage in his life, although he doubted whether the toll that the banking of the fires had taken was ultimately good for his character. 'I have been a violent person,' he told Roderick Mann of the *Sunday Express*. 'I am a violent person. But I control it. There's a part of me that doesn't like what goes on inside me; so I work at keeping myself under control. I'm not sure that I'm all that happy that I have conquered that violence; it's not a wise thing to alter your personality. But I had to change. I couldn't go around as I was. In those early days, I was a terror. If someone wasn't doing his job properly and I reprimanded him, if he didn't answer properly, I'd quite likely go at him with, "Now listen, you son of a bitch." My background is black Irish, you see. My mother was a violent woman, though my father was just the opposite.'

It was that rage kept on a tight rein that had given him his star quality, but the last half of the sixties had seen it whittled away by a series of message pictures that satisfied his restless search for meaningful material, but left his fans out in the cold. The studios had stumped up so far but Burt, ever the businessman, knew it couldn't last. A new persona was needed, an older man who could leave his looks behind him and still command attention. Predictably, he was equal to the commercial challenge. Phoenix-like, the seventies Lancaster was about to rise from the ashes.

thirteen
REVITALISATION

The first step in growing old cinematically is casting off the glamour. In Burt's case, that meant a severe curtailment of his japemanship and realisation that he couldn't walk off into the sunset with the girl. 'Filmgoers these days aren't about to accept me winning the girl in movies, although I've been doing it pretty well for more than twenty-five years. For me romance is out. In a couple of years I'll be pushing sixty, so I can't go chasing some young woman. I can still play leading men. But guys with more character than sex appeal.

'I've got to find a way of coping with getting older. I don't mean I'm frightened or impotent or anything like that. But I've got to the stage where I feel I'm a bit outside what's going on in the world. What I need is a new horizon, and that is what I'm looking for now. I don't want to become like Cooper or Gable. They just did the same thing and it became a routine. If Clark met a girl at a dance, he would lower his voice so it would approximate to the sound he made on screen. They were lonely men, although they would probably have denied it, because they were cut off. I think, had they lived, that they would have declined. They didn't know it but they were going along a one-way street with a dead-end at the top.'

It was a cul-de-sac in which Burt had no intention of joining them and he set about re-building his public image by signing up for the blockbuster, *Airport*, based on Arthur Hailey's best-seller. 'It's the big-gest piece of junk ever made,' he stated firmly, pre-empting obvious criticisms of the all-star bonanza, but according to its producer, Ross Hunter, both he and the second lead, Dean Martin, hurried to bite the bullet. 'Both actors accepted their roles even before a script was written, banking on the success of the book and my promises to develop their roles importantly within the framework of a superior production,' he stated, sententiously. 'They were also reassured by the fact that a man like George Seaton (he'd won Oscars for *Miracle on 34th Street* and *Country Girl*) would be both author of the screenplay and director of the film.'

Accordingly the autumn of 1969 found Burt enjoying the novelty of bachelor status, in Minneapolis-St Paul, the mid-western conurbation whose airport was selected for the title role.

The book tells of seven blizzard-plagued hours in just such a complex and the weather obliged with temperatures going down to 43 below zero. The film froze in the cameras making progress impossible and the cast and crew, faces swollen despite masks, shivered in the grim authenticity of the location. The 6,000,000-dollar picture depended heavily on realism for its suspense and Hunter went so far as to hire a Boeing 707 at 18,000 dollars a day, then made it land in a snowstorm, rather than use models. His employees were only too glad to return to Hollywood where another already damaged Boeing was installed at Universal Studios so that the plane's interior scenes could be shot with comparable verisimilitude.

Lancaster plays the airport manager whose job it is to sort out the night's disasters with measured calm. Up in the stormy sky Dean Martin's pilot, with the assistance of Jacqueline Bisset's stewardess, tries to cope with a deranged bomber (Van Heflin) who wants to blow the plane to smithereens.

She is carrying his baby which complicates matters on terra firma because his wife (Barbara Hale) is Lancaster's sister. Nor does Lancaster, despite his resolutions on screen lady-killing, fall short of women to love him. Among the questions set by intransigent trade unionists, fussy administrators and querulous residents, is the key one of whether he should stay with his cold demanding wife (Dana Wynter) or opt for the more obvious charms of a public relations person (Jean Seberg) who clearly adores him. A hero's dilemma, if ever there was one!

As an exercise in soap operatics, *Airport* has everything: a taut, many-stranded plot; an all-star cast that includes Helen Hayes as the gallant wrinklie, Ada Quonsett (the role won her an Academy Award), spectacularly snow-speckled special effects; and performances that are more than adequate for playing second fiddle to an aircraft. How could it fail? The answer was it couldn't – and it didn't. It grossed 45.3 million dollars in the United States, giving Burt's career its much needed shot-in-the-arm in the process. It also set a pattern that he would follow throughout the seventies whenever his appeal seemed to be wearing a little thin. With consummate cunning, he developed a habit of mixing more cherished projects, and particularly those that took him to Europe, with American big-budget soapies for which he demanded – and received – 750,000 dollars a throw, plus a percentage of the gross. In more ways than one, he'd never had it so good.

In 1970, he established the pattern by making two Westerns, *Valdez is Coming* and *Lawman*. In the first, Burt, never one to assume that his WASP physique might make him unsuitable to portray ethnic minorities, is cast as a Mexican-American constable who roams the range on a section of the Rio Grande border that shall be forever Spanish. His race ensures that he is a social outcast in the small community, which is no doubt why Lancaster homed in on him in the first place, and when he accidentally kills a suspected murderer there is no lack of enthusiasm to join a posse to hunt him down. Turning on his pursuers, Valdez initiates a vengeance bloodbath that leaves a dozen dead.

'The film offers little besides its star,' stated *Time* categorically. 'Continual editorials about racism give it contrived relevance. Edwin Sherrin's direction may best be described as functional; the members of the cast do not bump into each other. Call it a Burt Lancaster picture: that says it all.'

From Spain, the actor travelled to Mexico and the by now familiar dust bowl of Durango to work for the young British director, Michael Winner, on *Lawman*, an Englishman's answer to the sombre spaghetti Westerns of Sergio Leone. The inhabitants of the erst-while mining town, some six thousand feet up in the Sierre Madre range, were startled at the audacity of the enfant terrible in making a Western in their midst. Hadn't John Wayne made three there already? Didn't he want to use the place of Rio Lobos, directed by Howard Hawks? Yes he did, but Winner has always contrived to live up to his surname, and he did so this time, beating Hawks to the contract by just one hour, and leaving the legendary American to assemble his horsemen in Tuscon, Arizona.

'I can tell you that smoke came out of his ears,' said Winner proudly to William Hall. 'I always wanted to make a Western ever since I was a kid. And I wanted to be in the real West. This is the only place left where you can find a real Western street.'

Durango also boasted 2,000 scorpion stings a year resulting in 128 deaths, and a round-the-clock scorpion watch at the local hospital, where two doctors were on permanent standby to cope with the stream of cases. For those between twenty-five and forty, however, the major cause of death was 'gunshot wounds' and vultures circled overhead in anticipation of rich pickings. There was no doubt that Michael Winner had found his Western town.

He drew the line at a real Western lifestyle by taking over the house where Wayne normally lived – the only one with a swimming pool. There he installed his cook, Mrs Woodall, who prepared 'the best food in the place', a maid and his girlfriend. Burt and his co-stars, Robert Ryan and Lee J. Cobb, had to make do with second best, but that was still pretty good. When the Lancaster personalised jet touched down on the Durango tarmac, an accountant sped forward with a thirty-thousand-dollar advance to press into his hand. And on set he was treated with deference by the ebulliant cigar-smoking Englishman, who invariably called him sir. 'Partly because I respect him,' said Winner, 'partly because he's one of the few actors who's ever paid for dinner while I've been around.'

That suited the new veteran just fine, if only as a variation on the 'Mr Lancaster' he'd come to expect. 'If people have a preconceived idea about you, they resent it if you turn out to be different,' he commented. 'Nowadays they want me to be Mr Lancaster, so I am Mr Lancaster. In the early days when they called me that, I'd always say, "Call me Burt." I don't do that any more. Now I'm a little older and a little more cranky, I'm beginning to feel like Mr Lancaster.'

The Winner experience was quite new to the star and his fellow performers and they spent much of their time watching the bombastic producer-director in astonishment. He'd spent a year setting up the three-million-dollar project and there was no way Mexican inefficiency was going to prevent him hustling it through on time. Wearing an unseasonable tweed sports jacket in temperatures around 110 degrees in the shade and the shoulder-length hair the fashion of the time dictated, he prowled the dusty main street indefatigably. His cultured accent rang out through a loud hailer with a Union Jack brazenly plastered round it. Its range was four hundred yards and when it said 'cavort', a rather mysterious command to the two hundred roughnecks, cowboys and stuntmen on the set, they cavorted.

His reputation for hubris and humour spread round town and soon he was dubbed, 'Kid Durango, the fastest pun in the West.' 'It's ridiculous that people are surprised to find me here,' he said during a brief pause in the rapid fire proceedings. 'The West is everybody's. Americans come to Britain to film English history. Why shouldn't an Englishman go West?'

Lancaster, for one, agreed: 'He's sharp, bold, without respect for convention. This could be one hell of a Western.' His own part in it is that of Marshal Jered Maddox, an implacable lawman who rides into the town of Sabbath to arrest a rich rancher (Lee J. Cobb) who has shot up his town and accidentally killed an elderly man. Sabbath's sheriff (Robert Ryan) has no stomach for this alien vengeance trail, but is co-opted by the compelling Maddox against the wishes of honest citizens. The only one to get through to him is his old girlfriend (Sheree North), but ironically, her intervention comes too late to prevent the cowman's band trapping the lawman into a bloody showdown.

Maddox is an honourable but unsympathetic character who claims he never draws first. Not that he needs to because he has a remarkable capacity for shooting down adversaries, no matter what the circumstances. He proves to be the sharp-shooting hero with the heart of ice that Lancastrian audiences wanted, and *Lawman* packed them in, despite the conventional plotline.

Back in Los Angeles, the film industry was wearing paper thin. The revitalising influence of *Jaws* and *Star Wars*, Spielberg and Lucas, sharks and comic strips and space, was still four years in the future and meanwhile the business had run out of novelties. Several less than fully employed stars turned to television, among them Shirley MacLaine. Henry Fonda, Glenn Ford, James Stewart, Anthony Quinn, Doris Day and Tony Curtis, but the mediocrity of the American medium made this an infinitely depressing prospect. Apart from a video appearance on the Public Broadcasting Corporation's children's programme, *Sesame Street*, in which he recited the alphabet as part of the educational series, Burt rejected the soft option.

Instead he decided to diversify onto the stage in 1971, as Robert Ryan and Danny Kaye had already done. In Burt's case it was a bizarre choice, both of medium and message. *A Sound of Hunting*, his Broadway debut in 1946, had been his only theatrical experience, wartime revues apart, while his selected vehicle, *Knickerbocker Glory*, was a musical in which he had to sing and dance. Originally written by Kurt Weill and Maxwell Anderson as a topical satire in 1938, it was now dated and strained. The part of Peter Stuyvesant, the military governor of New York, known as New Amsterdam in 1647 when the show was set, is a crusty, one-legged political bully, a colonial dictator whose convictions are a million miles away from Burt's. He had been played in Broadway by Walter Huston (who immortalised Weill's haunting lament on the implacable passage of time, 'September Song') and on screen by Nelson Eddy in 1944. Now the Los Angeles Civic Light Opera Company planned a revival, with seven weeks in San Francisco's Curren Theatre starting on 11 May followed by eight in the enormous Dorothy

Chandler Pavilion in downtown LA. This at least was familiar territory as it was the home of the Academy Award ceremonies. Was Mr Lancaster ready and willing?

Yes, he certainly was. 'I'm no great singer, not that that's any handicap nowadays,' he said confidently. 'I've never sung in public before, but with my vaudeville background, the idea of a musical has always intrigued me. Besides, very few pictures come along now that an actor really wants to make. Most scripts add up to just another film to walk through. And for me, at my age, the result is the same – another Western. I think my last one, *Lawman*, is a good movie, but it's still another Western. There were some Las Vegas people who wanted me to do *The Music Man*. The money was very tempting. But then *Knickerbocker Glory* came along, and it's such a rich, juicy part. So here I am doing this for one-tenth what I could make in Las Vegas.'

The real challenge, however, came not in the singing which he accomplished adequately after a few lessons from Frank Sinatra (who was in temporary retirement at the time), but in the hopalong dancing. For a man as accustomed to athleticism as Lancaster, the restriction of having one leg strapped out of sight beneath a period coat, was almost unendurable. 'Physically and psychologically, it's a brute of a part,' he remarked. 'But if there's anything I do well, it's move. And if I'm not really driving in the part, I get cold. That strap becomes a sack of cement. I simply have to defeat it. Then it isn't there any more. The trick is to get out there and throw caution away.'

In a sense, he'd already done so by taking on the potentially disastrous venture, and his on-stage onslaught was in much the same vein. Ignoring shades of meaning, he rammed his personality, at its most masculine and electrifying, down the throats of the audience, and asked them to laugh along with him. That they did so was a triumph for his flamboyant magnetism, as Dan Sullivan of the *Los Angeles Times* noted: 'Oddly enough, his singing isn't at all bad. It's the acting side of the role that gives him trouble. To begin with, he is no more comfortable in period dress on the stage than he is on screen. Secondly, he has to hop around on a silver peg-leg that gives him much too much to think about. Finally, he is simply not at home in sly, twinkling, mock-ferocious comedy. Lines that ought to come out with deft irony sound like heavy camp, as if the actor were doing a parody guest shot. It's an uphill fight all the way, and the applause at the end is more for effort than achievement.'

Nevertheless the presence of the star in the flesh had novelty value

138

the cinema lacked, and Burt's fans were there to cheer him to the echo when he appeared two-legged to take his bow each night. Ironically he followed his old adversary from *The Rainmaker*, Katherine Hepburn, another non-singer, at the Dorothy Chandler Pavilion. Where Burt declaimed his songs, she croaked hers as Coco Chanel, yet both proved in the process that they knew what survival was all about.

When *Knickerbocker Glory* had run its allotted span and no one had asked it to move to Broadway, Lancaster was quizzed on the possibility of making a musical for the screen. It might have to wait, he warned, but it would happen. He was more prophetic in his response to another question about the retirement he'd forecast for 1971 when he was making *Valdez is Coming* in Spain two years earlier.

'I can't afford to quit,' he responded in light-hearted vein. 'Not because I haven't enough money, but because, over the years, I've acquired too many people whose livelihoods depend on my labours. Let me give you an example. I try to use people whose work I like from one film to another. I'm very fond of them and I know they love me – as long as I keep acting. If I say, one day, I don't want to do another film for six months or a year, to take it easy, they get furious. One by one they come to me and ask, "What about the hell's the matter with you, you no-good bum? Listen, I've just broken ground for a swimming pool in my backyard. How can you think of quitting at a time like this?"

'And God forbid that I should plead poor health as a reason not to work. They couldn't be less sympathetic. "What's wrong – your back? Tape it up and get on with the job," they say callously. "My kids have four more years of college." So I feel obligated – because they've been loyal to me over the years – to go to work, sick or tired. It's a good thing I enjoy acting.'

He recalled the making of *Valdez is Coming* with wry amusement. 'If it was a cold day, I'd try to get into my trailer and there'd be eight guys in there lying on my bed, warming themselves, drinking everything in the icebox, reading my books, playing cards. I'd walk in and they'd all look at me like, "What the hell do you want?" On warm days, when I might be looking for company between scenes, they'd be off playing ball, chatting up the birds and nobody would come near me. I sometimes got a picture of what it will be like when I'm dead and lying in my coffin. All these friends are going to lean over, spit down on me and say: "You bum! Couldn't you have waited another year until I get my Cadillac paid off? Even this you couldn't time right!"'

Certainly he was joking, but not fantasising, as those who knew him well recognised. One of his very best characteristics is his unswerving loyalty to anyone who's ever done him a good turn.

His next exercise in keeping the show on the road was his third Western in a row, *Ulzana's Raid*, which reunited him with his old mid-fifties mate, Robert Aldrich, the director of *Apache* and *Vera Cruz*. 'I'm not kidding,' Burt said of it, 'but during the whole of my career I have only read two first screenplays that I really liked. One was Guy Trosper's for *Birdman* and the other was written for *Ulzana's Raid*. We made the movie in Arizona and it's about the treatment of the Indians, the total inability of any race which controls another to understand the culture and lifestyle of the subject nation.' The writer who earned this high praise was Alan Sharp, who doubled as associate producer.

The fact that the film didn't live up to these glowing expectations commercially was no fault of his, nor of its director and star, but of being the wrong thing at the wrong time. Westerns had been staple fare in the cinema since the earliest days and the public had tired of them, especially since the classic horse opera with its simplistic battle lines of cowboys versus Indians had given way to more sophisticated concepts. *Ulzana's Raid* is just such a many-shaded moralistic essay on race relations, with Burt in the hot seat when it comes to interpreting the behaviour of the natives to his greenhorn associate. 'What bothers you, Lieutenant, is that you don't like to think of white men behaving like Indians,' he tells the impeccable West Point graduate (Bruce Davison) whose first job in his chosen career is to track down the ferocious Ulzana (Jorge Martinez) and his Apache band.

In this he is assisted by Lancaster's grizzled and venerable scout whom he initially despises. On another occasion, the older man tells his inexperienced superior, 'Hating Apaches would be like hating the desert because there ain't no water in it.' Eventually he earns the boy's respect for such staunchly egalitarian homespun wisdom, before electing to die of his wounds alone in the desert, while his conscientious companion returns to the Fort to report the successful conclusion of his mission.

When Burt and Bob Aldrich had worked together on *Apache*, the censor had set very definite limits to the amount of violence that could be shown on screen, but times had changed and *Ulzana's Raid* is a veritable bloodbath, with Apaches and white men reacting to each other with brutal and graphic savagery. Why, the Davison character demands naively after sickening evidence of torture, are the Apaches so barbarous, an enquiry that earns him another Lancastrian homily to the effect that a capacity for cruelty is necessary to survive in such inhospitable surroundings.

The economic failure of this cherished and indeed thought-provoking project convinced Lancaster that the old West had – temporarily at least – had its day, and to date he hasn't donned another marshal's hat. Instead he jumped on the tail-end of the celluloid spy band-wagon when he travelled to London and Vienna in mid-1972 to work for Michael Winner on *Scorpio*. 'I'll be fifty-nine in November. I'm getting on. I don't run up the stairs any more,' he said. But few who saw him in action during the shooting of this fast-paced thriller believed him.

He may be a little paunchier, a little slower and he may pant a bit more on the run, but he pounds through the Viennese construction site selected by Winner for the climactic chase with much of his old verve. Through tunnels, along steel girders, across gangways, up scaffolding and down from high walls, he springs and leaps and bounds in the interests of portraying Cross, a veteran CIA agent, who may be a Russian double.

He is joined in all the activity by a fellow CIA hack played by Alain Delon, whom he already knew well from the long hot Sicilian days on *The Leopard*. The French assassin is blackmailed by their mutual employers into killing his former friend and mentor, a task he accomplishes in the final frames when the American veteran, weary of life on the run and weighed down by a killer's inescapable guilt, urges his protégé to shoot him.

The best scenes take place well away from the action during a Viennese drinking session between Burt and Paul Schofield, as a retired Russian agent with the heart and memories of a Bolshevik revolutionary. The two men reminisce about the old days, in mutual recognition of the realities that they are relics of a past that won't return. Together they agree that there are no more secrets, or anyway none worth stealing.

Michael Winner, who'd directed *Lawman* in the straightforward style he thought suitable for a classic Western, now went for every technical trick in the book in an attempt to make a fashionably oblique thriller of the type that had won friends and influenced people in the Swinging Sixties. This self-indulgence did nothing for a scenario that was already hopelessly muddled as *Variety* noted: 'Despite its anachronistic emulation of mid-1960s cynical spy mellers, *Scorpio* might have been an acceptable action programmer if its narrative were clearer, its dialogue less "cultured" and its visuals more straightforward.'

Burt however came out of it with some kudos. 'Lancaster, always good at playing brashness, was never an actor to show much warmth,' wrote Jay Cocks in *Time*. 'His role in *Scorpio*, a double agent on the run from both East and West, gives him a chance to project the kind of dead-eyed savagery he has nearly patented as his own. He has the proper cunning and just the right kind of careful menace and restrained violence.' The *Sunday Times*'s Dilys Powell described him as 'a far better actor than he is sometimes given credit for', and noted that he'd worn well.

Once again Lancaster and Winner, two men with notorious tempers, worked well together. The director paid the actor a round 750,000 dollars, plus ten per cent of the profits – and was glad to do so. 'You can count the number of stars who rate that kind of money on one hand – and still have a couple of fingers to spare,' he commented. 'I have a respect for a man who knows his own market value.' Burt responded with, 'Why ask for peanuts, when you can get it in almonds?'

Nor, when it came to meal times, did Winner let him down. Everyday, he provided him with an elegant luncheon in his caravan, wheresoever it might be. Delivered by Rolls Royce from Wiltons, an expensive London restaurant, and served by a waiter in line with the director's elitist principles, it was a far cry from the usual egalitarian help-yourself unit catering. Burt appreciated such seasonal English delicacies as fresh salmon and raspberries and cream, accompanied by chilled white wine, while his co-workers queued.

During his time in London, Burt lived in a rented house in Mayfair which he turned into his castle. The few journalists who were granted an audience were directed to a neighbouring hotel where they were met and escorted into the presence. The star showed his customary impatience with trivial questions. 'Madam, I burp in exactly the same way as you do,' he told one of the chosen, who was unwise enough to interrogate him on his diet.

On another occasion, he was more forthcoming about his attitudes towards publicity. 'I have always been secretive,' he admitted. 'I've never been easy with strangers. So it is hard to know what the public has a right to read about me and what they haven't. I've never had a consistent image, so I've had no happy fiction to project. I won't be tolerated though. People either find my opinions interesting, or they do not. But they can't play me along like a tame bear in a zoo. That gets my goat.'

The result of his insistence on his right to privacy was, he considered, reflected in his status in the business. 'I think I may have a respectful following, but not an affectionate one. Anyway, I don't get many fan letters asking for pin-up pictures.' His tone was informative, rather than wounded.

When he wasn't working or answering unwelcome questions, he spent his time in London happily enough. Covent Garden was an irresistable attraction and performances of *Elektra*, *Otello* and *La Traviata*, plus the ballet with Rudolf Nureyev and Margot Fonteyn, were the highlights of his extended visit to the city.

Self-confident as ever, he could see ways in which they might be improved. 'You know what I'd like to do?' he enquired of Roderick Mann. 'Direct opera. That's my great passion. I love it. I'd like to see opera singers trained as actors. As it is, they never seem to know how to behave on stage. When I went to see *Otello* the other night, it was on the verge of being ludicrous. I'd like to change all that.

'When I go to the opera I'm very much like a fan, but I also tend to view it with a very harsh eye. When it's really good for me I glow for the rest of the day. But I'm so used to hearing people yell "bravo" when the guy's a bum. Opera and ballet audiences feel so privileged being there it gives them a sense of superiority, so that everything becomes marvellous.'

Even the great weren't spared the whiplash of Lancaster, the critic. Joan Sutherland, he allowed, has a marvellous voice but becomes 'a strange inhuman person on stage'. Poor Placido Domingo didn't even get an accolade for his singing, though his character came in for praise. 'He's got to belt everything out. He happens to be an absolutely dear sweet man though,' was the verdict.

His affection for London dated back to 1951 when he'd crossed the Atlantic to make *The Crimson Pirate* on his first visit to the city. Comparison with a Hollywood in which McCarthy's reign of red-under-the-bed terror was well into its stride made London into a welcome haven of liberal thinking, as Burt explained.

'When I came here, I walked through Hyde Park and saw people shouting "Down with the King" and so forth and so on, and threatening to shoot people, and nobody paid attention. People sat in their chairs and children played and Bobbies yawned, and I thought to myself how marvellous.

'I still think it's the most civilised city in the world and I still run around Hyde Park. That's one way of getting my heart started in the morning. Other people use masturbation. The first day I was here. I was at Hyde Park Corner and there was an engagement going on between a black man and a white man, who was obviously some kind of minister or someone attached to some religious group, and they were trying to convince each other, at the tops of their voices as to which was the best way of life. And people stood around eating peanuts and talking, and listening, and walking away and I had that same nice feeling.'

In June 1972, the actor was persuaded to give a John Player Lecture at the National Film Theatre during which he declaimed at length on the state of the industry and the changes he'd seen it through. Under the chairmanship of Joan Bakewell, it turned into the kind of public occasion he liked. He had a knowledgeable audience, more concerned with his work than his women, who were obliged to listen to his convoluted analysis, which steam-rollered along, leaving only rare pauses into which questions might be slipped. At one point, however, he was uncharacteristically succinct. 'Directing is the best job in pictures, because when you're the director, you're God.' Perhaps it was Michael Winner, a man who showed no signs of forgetting that particular adage, that gave him such ideas about potential deity. Anyway it was during his time on *Scorpio* that he decided to step behind the cameras again.

'I'm going to make a straightforward whodunnit,' he revealed, 'but with some slight comment on police corruption. But basically it'll be a light film – something for me to get back in stride with. When you reach my sort of age, and have done so much acting-wise, you begin to look around and wonder what to do next. I feel it's about time I made a move towards directing again. I'm always trying to tell my directors what to do, so I really ought to go away and do it myself.'

First however he had *Scorpio* to wrap in Vienna, opera to criticise in Salzburg and the Olympic Games to visit in Munich. Then he returned to Hollywood to submit to the direction of David Miller a project that would arouse a storm of protest throughout America. Called *Executive Action*, it treated the assassination of President Kennedy to the kind of microscopic semi-documentary examination that echoed grimly along the corridors of power. Based on long-term researches and a novel by Mark Lane, and scripted by established Hollywood leftist, Dalton Trumbo, it promoted the right-wing-conspiracy theory that the killing was the work of wealthy Texans in protest against JFK's liberal stance on civil rights and his decision to withdraw troops from Vietnam.

Although the plotters, a financier (Robert Ryan), a senator (Will

Geer) and the ex-CIA spy (Lancaster) whom they hire to organise the Dallas death, are fictitious, theirs and their associates' activities are cut into actual newsreel footage of the assassination which many considered in dubious taste.

Burt, who had been a guest of John F. Kennedy at the White House and a long-term supporter of his policies, waived his usual six-figure fee and accepted the Equity minimum as did all the other actors. His decision to take the role came after months of deliberation. 'After a good deal of private research, I was convinced there had been a conspiracy and the probability that Oswald was set up as a Communist fall-guy,' he insisted. 'Everything we say in *Executive Action* is based on evidence. If I had not been certain this was the case, I would not have made the film. I agreed to do it because I wanted it to serve as a warning against the dangers of powerful men playing God and deciding who should and who should not live.

'I think our dramatisation of events, of a conspiracy by powerful, influential and immensely wealthy men, takes on a new credibility in the light of the Watergate scandal, which show just how conspiracies can operate. Will the film open up a whole new can of beans? I doubt it. Kennedy's death is rather like Watergate. The public would rather draw a veil over it now. They're tired and disgusted.'

He went on to say that Watergate made him ashamed to admit he was American. 'You have to look to a government for some sort of guidance, a set of standards. You accept the disciplines democracy imposes – high taxes, respect for law, standing in line instead of elbowing your way to the front. But for that faith you should get something in return from the men who govern you. People aren't getting anything in return now.'

The title refers to the code name given to an operation which, according to the story-line, was carried out by at least two and probably three, hired gunmen, one firing from the Texas School Book Depository, one from the roof of the County Records building, and the third perhaps from the green banking along the procession route. The multiple-killer hypothesis is fairly old hat, though nonetheless valid for that. The film is more interesting in its angle on Lee Harvey Oswald who is seen being selected as the perfect fall-guy by a computer. His proven track record of distributing left-wing leaflets, living for a year in Moscow and organising support for Cuba, combined with his weak but headstrong personality and the confusion aroused by his possible CIA connection make him a suitable case for mistreatment by the ruthless plotters. Their next step is to steal his rifle and give it to a look-alike to fire, then leave it for the police to find after the crime so that he will be sure to be implicated. Later he is killed in prison by the conspirators' lackeys before his declaration of innocence can be believed.

The timing of *Executive Action* could hardly have been more fortuitous. Eighteen material witnesses had died (six of them by gunshots) in the three years after the Kennedy killing, at odds calculated by an actuary engaged by the *Sunday Times* at one hundred thousand trillion to one. More important still, Watergate had convinced ordinary Americans – as opposed to committed libertarians like Burt – that things they'd imagined couldn't happen went on all the time. If Nixon, Agnew, Erlichman, Haldeman et al could behave like that, why not a bunch of racist militaristic Texans?

Given the burning interest in such matters, it wasn't surprising that the film did well at the box office in areas of the United States that were open to this point of view, and Burt, who was on a percentage, was financially rewarded for his idealism. There were places – mostly Southern places – where it wasn't widely screened, but it was more fortunate than another assassination exposé, *The Second Gun*, which was suppressed after a single run in New York. Certain television stations on both coasts refused to accept the commercials for *Executive Action* on the grounds that they were 'overly violent and violated the standards of taste'. Lancaster protested vigorously, stating publicly, 'I have made many films much more violent than this one and the commercials for them, none of which was ever censored or refused, were more violent than these.'

He also put it on record that it was 'possibly the most important film I've ever been involved with'. Pauline Kael, writing in the *New Yorker*, rated it very much lower: 'It's a dodo bird of a movie, the winner of the 'Tora! Tora! Tora! prize – in miniature – for 1973, with matchlessly dull performances from a cast that includes Burt Lancaster (looking very depressed). It could hardly be called a thriller, and it's so worshipful of Kennedy (while treating him insensitively) as to seem to have no politics.'

Burt's next step was to fulfil the threat he'd made in London the previous year. The vehicle he picked was *The Midnight Man* which he co-wrote, co-produced and co-directed with his old friend Roland Kibbee (whom he'd known even before their first association, *Ten Tall Men* in 1951). Based on a novel by David Anthony, it concerns one Jim Slade (Lancaster), an ex-policeman who has been imprisoned for shooting his wife's lover. When he is released on parole, he goes to live with friends (Cameron Mitchell and Joan Lorring) in a small town and gets a job as a night security officer in a college. A young girl student is murdered and the friendly neighbourhood sheriff tries to pin the crime on a religious nut, only to find that Slade has other ideas. Taking the lid off the hornet's nest involves him in considerable danger as blackmails, beatings, attempted rape and further murders wrestle for screentime before the long and over-complicated drama grinds to a close.

The old friends' reunion finds Nick Cravat in a bit part and Bill Lancaster, Burt's son, as the boyfriend of the first murdered girl. The picture was made on a minimum budget in South Carolina, and Kibbee, an early client of Harold Hecht's who had been dropped when he gave up his agency to go into production with Lancaster, was quick to take the blame. '*The Midnight Man* was a concession to me because I wanted to make some money. It certainly wasn't the kind of project Burt would have picked for himself, and unfortunately it hasn't so far worked out to be very profitable. Burt is one of the most intellectual actors I've known. He loves art and opera and his reading is on a high level. He had no taste for pulp fiction and I had to talk him into reading *The Midnight Man* and *The Mourning Man*, which is pulp. He is – I'm sorry to say, since I owned pieces of some of them – absolutely cavalier about whether his pictures make money or not, and he is quite non-commercial. I know that he has had lucrative offers to do television commercials and he has repeatedly refused – and some of the offers were staggering. Lancaster is the most uncompromising star I know of.'

Kibbee insisted that his colleague's image for toughness was based on mental, rather than physical, activity. 'It seems contradictory, but he actually detests violence and I have never heard of him hitting anyone. He has always been forceful, sure footed and strong in his opinions, although a certain mellowness has come with the years, but he is difficult only in regard to the standards he sets in his works. He has always felt that it was his job as a star to be involved with production, and scripts have always been his primary concern. He is thoroughly honest, his candour can be brutal, but he is critically and constructively valuable at production conferences. He is, to put it as simply as possible, an unusual man. He fits no moulds.'

Despite these sincere tributes, the film flopped. The time for convoluted thrillers had passed and this one was, in any case, incomprehensible and tedious. Directors, Burt learned when he read reviews that harped on words like 'bogged down' and 'needlessly over-complex', were not gods. That slot was reserved for actors, and it was in this capacity that some praise came his way. 'Burt Lancaster is turning into an attractive hard-working actor as superstardom fades,' said *Time*'s Richard Schickel, to which the *New York Times*'s Vincent Canby added somewhat ambivalently, 'Mr Lancaster is an intelligent actor. He thinks about his characterisations. He makes choices. He moves through *The Midnight Man* with studied humility, saying "yes, sir' and "no, sir" more often than is always necessary, listening attentively when spoken to. The mannerisms don't suggest a middle-aged parolee, uncertain of his future, as often as they suggest a reformed alcoholic trying desperately to succeed as a liveried chauffeur.'

Ah well, you can't win 'em all. Since this debacle, Burt has kept his fingers out of the director's business, a wise decision his well-wishers hope he'll stick with. Instead he embraced the television mega-series for the first time – and this time the demi-god slot was for real.

fourteen
GLOBE TROTTER

The stern code of moral practice Mrs Lancaster had instilled in her children some sixty years before in East Harlem had never included orthodox religion. It was probably an advantage to Burt that it hadn't because his social concern, free of the restraints of organised church going, was well ahead of its time during his early years in Hollywood. By the sixties and seventies, the world had caught up with him and his attitudes had become mainstream. 'I'm not at ease with youngsters,' he explained, 'but luckily I believe in all the progressive things that the young support. I'm anti-racialist, anti-pollution, anti-war, pro-the-poor. So none of the things I want will be achieved in my lifetime. But I will keep trim, fighting for them.'

One thing he didn't believe in, however, was the Christian God, so when Lew Grade appeared waving the script for *Moses – The Lawgiver*, six one-hour dramas based on the Book of Exodus, his enthusiasm was definitely muted. Hadn't Charlton Heston, a younger actor forever behind him in the pecking order, played the parter-of-the-waters twenty years before? Hadn't he handed that same Charlton Heston an Oscar on a platter when he turned down *Ben Hur* because he didn't care for its interpretation? Why on earth, after sixty films, should he go Biblical now? It wasn't as if he rated the Ten Commandments: 'I don't live by them. Well, who does? The world is different today. Some of the values which apply now didn't apply then. I am against orthodox religion in any form.'

So what does that make him? 'An atheist,' he replied promptly. 'I don't believe in heaven or hell. If there is a God, then fine. But I don't concern myself. What matters in my life, the set of values I have to live by. What happens, if anything, afterwards, well . . .' he shrugged his shoulders.

Nevertheless, he was persuaded to read a 150-page outline for

Anthony Burgess's script. If it didn't exactly provide him with a divine revelation, it at least threw a hitherto unsuspected light on Moses's historical worth.

'Burgess is a wonderful man, a great novelist. He saw God as a very tough customer with whom Moses was always in conflict. That appealed to me immediately – me fighting God! He provided a valuable insight into the Jewish enigma. It is their vital characteristics which have kept the Jewish race alive through the centuries and if the world allows them to continue for another twenty-five years, the Israelis will show what a truly remarkable people they are!'

Comforted by this contemporary relevance, he took the plane to Rome to head up the huge project, a joint television production by Grade's ATV and Italy's RAI. So began the toughest eight months of his life, much of them spent on location in broiling rocky out-crops in Israel itself and other parts Middle Eastern. That was okay with Burt who embraced the new realism of the Burgess Moses with relish. 'He will be very different from the version put on the screen by Cecil B. DeMille. None of that larger-than-life stuff. My Moses will be a real man. Not a hero, not a leader, but a man who is aware of his own and other people's failings,' he stated firmly.

Once again his son, Bill, went along for the ride, playing the young Moses to his father's 120-year-old grey beard, and bringing a family likeness to the proceedings that pleased the seekers after verisimilitude.

Unfortunately the viewers of CBS television in America, on whose enthusiasm the success of the series depended, discovered their 'off' buttons when it was shown in mid-summer in 1975. Presumably they preferred their Biblical hero to be above the laws they gave, rather than revealed warts and all coming down from the mountain. Then again, granted Lew Grade's somewhat biased attitudes towards the Jewish question, it was not surprising that the end product was historically sanitised for his convenience. 'Makes a stab at realism through location sites, but generally skims over religious-historical aspects as digest of Exodus. Figures lack genuine depth thanks to episodic approach. As drama, film fails to generate dramatic values or, most important, involvement,' wrote *Variety* at its most staccato. Burt certainly did better in the *New York Times*: 'As an actor, Mr Lancaster is not great, but, given favourable circumstances, he can be good. As Moses, he would appear to be extremely good, restrained, intense and, for a man somewhere about age sixty, in superb physical condition. He and most of the other principals are rewardingly, even surprisingly, effective.'

By this time, Rome had become something of a home from home to Lancaster. Not only did he own an apartment there, but he spoke Italian well enough to get by in his favourite trattorias where, on occasion, he would forgo the diet of wheaties and tea that kept him in shape, in favour of more enjoyable eating. Accordingly, he was only too happy to stay on and work for Luchino Visconti on *Conversation Piece*, the veteran director's comeback after a major stroke he'd suffered during his previous film, *Ludwig*. As he was confined to a wheelchair, it had to be planned to accommodate his limited mobility which meant that it was shot almost exclusively in the interior of a Roman house. The screenplay was his own, and it matched both his mood as he approached death and his long-term political commitment. The central character is an American professor (Lancaster), an art historian who lives alone in an echoing mansion with his books and his eighteenth-century oil paintings of English family groups, the conversation pieces of the title.

Crushing out memories of more gregarious times, shown in flashback with guest appearances from Dominque Sanda as his mother and Claudia Cardinale as his long-lost bride, he has become a gentle, intellectual recluse, living out his declining years in sombre isolation. Then his peace is abruptly shattered by the arrival of a queer quartet, an arrogant, chic and neurotic countess (Silvana Magnano) her petulant little lover, Konrad (Helmut Berger) and her adolescent daughter and the girl's boyfriend. Contemptuous of peace and solitude, she persuades the baffled professor to rent her the top floor of the house. Thereafter he is brushed aside, a peripheral factor in the glittering sexual and criminal corruption of their self-indulgent lives.

Unwillingly at first, then with increasing momentum, he becomes fascinated with the alien presence in all its bizarre forms. Konrad, a teasing bi-sexual, teams up with the teenagers à trois as willingly as with his benefactress, and has time to spare to tempt the professor in much the same way as the boy, Tadzio, tempted von Aschenbach in Visconti's earlier film *Death in Venice*. 'One keeps waiting for the professor to make a pass at Konrad,' wrote Pauline Kael in the *New Yorker*, having previously described the film as essentially silly. 'I was profoundly grateful to Visconti that he didn't – the audience might split its sides if Burt Lancaster were to be shown coming out – but part of what makes the film giggly is that it's set up as if he should.'

The situation is further complicated by the conflict, revealed rather hurriedly just before the end, between the countess's support for the politics of her ex-husband, a Fascist tycoon, and Konrad's revolutionary fervour for the cause of Karl Marx. Even if you make allowances for Berger and Magnano's hideous dubbing of themselves into transatlantic English to match Lancaster, it must be said that *Conversation Piece* is no masterpiece, which is a pity because it was to be Visconti's last film. Neither the orgies nor the ideologies seem important in the generally tedious prattlings of these deeply unattractive characters. It may be ironic that Konrad's vices are funded by the contessa's ill-gotten gains, but who cares. Even the dignity of death is denied to the professor for he is recalled to life and forced, as a voyeur, to witness the very things he has scrupulously excised from his daydreams.

'Visconti forsakes the wit of the opening for a kind of tongue-tied general valedictory,' said *Time*. 'He is interested not so much in exposing his characters, as in having the professor embrace all of them, opening his arms to their indulgences and sanctioning their moral impotence.' 'Laid a mighty egg,' added *Variety* after it had been shown on the opening night of the 13th New York Film Festival in September, 1975. The distributors hurriedly hacked the piece to bits in the hope of relieving its tedium, and released it under the title *Violence and Passion* the following year, without persuading even a respectable minority of Americans that they needed to see it.

As for Burt, the antipathetic Pauline Kael had further barbs for him: 'Whose idea can it have been to cast Burt Lancaster as a gentle intellectual? He is as extroverted as an actor can be. His performance made me realise that I've watched him for almost thirty years and I don't know the first thing about him. Whatever goes on inside that man, he doesn't use it as an actor; he doesn't draw from himself. So how can he play a character whose life is all inner? Lancaster simply negates himself in the role, as if by not using any physical energy and by moving slowly with a long face and a demure expression, he would become a thinker.'

Nigel Andrews, writing in London's *Financial Times*, was more positive: 'Lancaster alone lends the film some of the dignity and resonance it may once have had in Visconti's head. Rueful, aristocratic, stoically polite, his performance is a perfect companion piece to the role he played ten years ago for Visconti, as Don Fabrizio in *The Leopard*. But the odds are stacked against him, and even Lancaster can do nothing with dialogue that alternates between stilted would-be profundities and sudden eruptions of banality.'

Burt was always open to the Italian experience, and when Bernardo Bertolucci, trailing clouds of notoriety in the wake of *Last Tango in Paris*, approached him for *1900*, he found a receptive audience. 'He came to see me,' Lancaster recalled, 'and we talked and talked. He was raising the money and there was no way to talk about what my salary might be. So finally I said, "Look, I'll do it for you for nothing." And I did. I wasn't doing anything at the time and it was only two weeks' work. So I went to Palma - right near where Bertolucci was born - and treated the whole thing like it was a vacation. I found the ageing character I play a very rich, exciting part.'

The financial success of *Last Tango in Paris* (it had grossed 50,000,000 dollars) persuaded three studios, Paramount, Twentieth Century Fox and United Artists to back Bertolucci's grandiose project with some 8,000,000 dollars. The overall design of showing the conflict between socialism and fascism from 1900 to 1945 through the eyes and actions of two families, one aristocratic, one peasant, was his own, and he part-wrote the script with his brother, and Guiseppe and Franco Aracalli, then set to work with a will to spawn a seven-hour polemical tour de force.

Lancaster's role, which had first been offered to Orson Welles, is the paternalistic head of the ruling family at the start of the proceedings, and his scenes with Sterling Hayden, the grand old man of the peasantry which works his rolling Emilian acres in conditions akin to benevolent slavery, show the roots the younger generation, represented respectively by Robert de Niro and Gerard Depardieu, have to draw on as the new century gets under way.

The sex, even for the oldsters, is pretty explicit and there was one scene (which was cut by the Italian censors) that had Burt's padrone attempting intimacy with a little girl, and hanging himself afterwards in anger, shame and impotency.

Using the four seasons to represent different periods in an epic class-struggle, Bertolucci tracks the two younger men through youth, war, the growth of the unions, the rise of fascism, the death of Mussolini and finally to the arrival of socialism in the Po valley in 1945. Often the tracking was literal because the director indulged his passion for moving cameras on rails to lyrical effect whenever he could. At a mid-point in the proceedings, a technician calculated that the camera had already travelled two and a half kilometres on tracking rails.

It made for a long, slow schedule in freezing conditions and put Burt in the unusual position of standing around while someone else decided what he should do and when he should do it. 'Bertolucci is brilliant,' he confirmed, 'but extremely difficult to work with because every morning we came on the set, every single thing on the shooting schedule had been changed and we would have to waste about three or four hours so the changes could be made. These were conditions I simply wasn't used to.' Or anyway not in a passive sense.

Bertolucci was astonishingly cool about the endless re-working of the script to accommodate his own improvisations, and the extra cost the delays meant (the budget rose inexorably to nine million dollars before shooting stopped). His star-studded cast was reduced by one when the *Last Tango* lady, Maria Schneider, jealous of another actress, Dominique Sanda, walked off the set after a much publicised bitter row with the director, to be replaced by Stefania Sandrelli. However he found that using the same crew he'd had on *Last Tango*, *The Conformist* and *The Spider's Strategem* kept the pressure at arm's length. 'I feel very alone in the middle of all this machinery,' he commented. 'I've gathered around me a crew who insulate me from the feeling of a grand production. And Grimaldi (the producer) has made a kind of wall between me and the US studios. He protects me.'

It couldn't last, of course. Paramount, the member of the triumvirate of backers who had distribution rights to *1900* in America, had asked for a three-hour film suitable for transatlantic audiences. Eventually they received a five-and-a-half-hour eulogy on the rise of socialism, lyrically beautiful certainly, and with a magnificent Verdi sound-track, but uncomfortably red.

'1900 is the century of a great Utopia which will become a reality,' Bertolucci explained. 'It's the century of the end of the bosses, and the death of the social and moral role of the bosses.' This prediction didn't appeal to the key executives at Paramount, though, as they'd put their money in the hands of a member of the Italian Communist Party and given him the go-ahead to make an overtly political film, the real surprise was that they were surprised. To add insult to what they already saw as injury, the studio supremo was Charles Bludhorn, a declared anti-communist and a member of John Connally's Citizens Alliance for Freedom in the Mediterranean, a group committed to saving Italy from the Marxist menace.

When Burt attended a tribute to his work at the San Francisco International Film Festival in October, 1976, the questions that followed a two-hour screening of clips from his films in the Palace of Fine Arts Theatre, were all about *1900*. 'I think Bertolucci outman-oeuvred them,' he said simply. 'Paramount, Fox and UA all gambled on Bertolucci because of his *Last Tango* success and gave him five million dollars for a three-hour film of *1900*. And all he did was bamboozle them because he knew he wasn't going to give them a three-hour film. The script I saw, which was only the first half, concerned only me and the old peasant, Sterling Hayden. It was one hundred and eighty pages long. Our two sons, Robert de Niro and Gerard Depardieu, were still little boys when it ended, so I knew there was going to be another whole movie there. As Carol Reed might have said, "It was all very naughty." As yet, I haven't seen the movie in any of its versions, but I would be very surprised if it wasn't a marvellous film. The guy is tremendous.'

While the transatlantic rumblings diversified into law-suits and counter-law-suits, Bertolucci stood firm. He would not cut. He quarrelled with his producer, Alberto Grimaldi, who'd arranged the backing originally, then made up the rift, only to quarrel once again. Meanwhile the five-and-a-half-hour version had been shown at a series of private screenings in conjunction with the Venice Film Festival and hailed, in some circles, as a masterpiece. So much so the riot police had to be called in to stop would-be filmgoers storming the cinema.

Left-wing critics, who'd once looked on Bertolucci as their favourite ideological son, were by no means so enthusiastic, accusing the thirty-five-year-old director of selling out to the capitalists by attempting to seduce the public with beautiful images and by making such a lavish film in the first place.

American capital had 'irredeemably polluted' the political content, they decided at a seminar in Venice, and the message was, in any event, 'unrealistically optimistic'. Bertolucci, who always had the stomach for a pitched battle, won no friend on either side by drawing parallels between them. 'The scandalised expressions of the people accusing me [the critics] are identical in intensity to those of the American distributors,' he stated in lordly fashion. 'Therefore I'm caught in the crossfire of two scandalised reactions apparently from opposite sides, but in reality with the same prejudice – moralistic and demagogic in Italy and threatening and authoritarian in the United States.'

In the end, however, he had to compromise on both fronts. Five and a half hours became four, to be shown in two parts by Paramount in America and Fox in England. The surgery was neat; no scenes were cut but the director contrived to pare and trim, producing a tighter, better-paced version that was rated a flawed triumph or, as *Newsweek* put it, 'a "yes, but ..." masterpiece.'

As for his compatriots, he went some way towards admitting they had

155

a point when he called *1900* 'a shameless monument to the contradictions of our system. I have been forced (in order to reach a wider public)
into the absurd contradictions which all directors face, even in socialist
countries – to get money from wherever you can. These contradictions
have exploded in this film.'

So ended Burt's association with the Italian masters with whom he
felt such a bond of sympathy. 'It doesn't matter that Bertolucci was
naughty,' he summed up. 'He made a marvellous movie: his creation.
I remember being with Luchino Visconti on *Conversation Piece* when he
stopped all shooting because he saw three TV antennae in the distance.
I was getting fifty thousand dollars a week overtime and said may be he
should take some of my money back. He didn't approve of that. "I stop
shooting so my producers and crew learn I'm serious when I say no
antennae. At times like this you must be intransigent." '

Shades of those intrusive Sicilian television aerials that had interrupted *The Leopard*. Lancaster liked men who remained true to their
convictions, and he has always insisted that his Italian films were among
his most rewarding. 'These men – Fellini, Visconti, Bertolucci, Anto-
nioni – are extraordinary human beings. We have a whole thing in our
system where people direct only for the sake of saying they are directors.
Where is their background for directing – their education, intellectual-
ity, imagination? You think of Ingmar Bergman. These are informed,
erudite, knowledgeable, creative people. But because ours is a business
of mediocrity, nine out of ten directors are only average craftsmen, but
not imaginative. They are also part of a system where how much money
the picture makes is the criterion for goodness.'

However the time had come to go home, to re-embrace the ego-
tripping world of Hollywood. His Italian projects hadn't added as much
to his reputation as he might have wished so he let it be known that he
was up for financial grabs and waited for the pot-boilers to come his
way. His private life, since his divorce, had undergone major changes.
He and Jackie Bone had no use for a Bel Air mansion, and its opulence
had already begun to pall on Burt before they came together. In the
early seventies, he had considered moving to some outback mid-Western
retreat as proof of his liberalism.

'You can't live by swimming pools alone,' he said at the time. 'Think
of the starving children. It has been a constant source of guilt to me that
I have become so luckily rich. But I haven't yet found a method of
salving my conscience, though I give a lot away to good causes. The
trouble with money, when you have it in bags, is that you don't count

it. Yet I remember my father, who earned forty-eight dollars a week in the Post Office, considered that he was making a fortune.'

It was lucky for him that the wave of ruralism passed before he could act on it. He was a city boy at heart, his interests concentrated on the arts rather than the wide open spaces which he had only seen – and usually despised – during his periodic Westerns. Instead he went to the other extreme and moved into a luxurious high-rise block, the Century Towers Apartments in Century City alongside fellow performers George Raft, Gig Young and David Janssen. He also kept a house at Malibu Beach for the weekends, maintaining that it was too far out of the city to drive in daily.

He maintained close links with his children, and occasional, if rather chilly ones with Norma. So carefully had he screened them from the business that only Bill showed any interest in following in his father's footsteps. After a few attempts at acting, he decided to go into the writing side, with successful results. His screenplay for *The Bad News Bears*, a kiddies' baseball pic with Walter Matthau and Tatum O'Neal, was well constructed and humorous, and Michael Ritchie made it into a very entertaining picture in 1976. Maybe that private ball park at the house in Bel Air had its uses after all. Later Bill proved his versatility with his script for *The Thing*, the John Carpenter re-make of the classic horror science-fiction adventure.

As he grew older, Lancaster senior discovered that his brood wanted to get on with living their own lives, something he found unexpectedly hard to allow them to do. 'When they were young I felt it was reasonable to help them and advise them and I thought as they grew older I'd finish with that. But no. They're still babies to me. I still worry about them. I have to remind myself that I have no right to go on exercising authoritity. "Oh, look dad", they say, when I start on something, and then it sinks in.'

As his daughters married and his clan of grandchildren increased, he carried on going to the office, and it was there that he found people to lean on him, just as he'd always done. The extravaganzas of Hecht-Hill-Lancaster were long gone and his business headquarters were in the same ivory-coloured tower in which he lived. There at a huge glittery desk, surrounded by an eclectic collection of antiques – leather settees, horn chairs, mirrors and books – he sat every day, reading scripts and talking to writers. His appearance was generally as untidy as his cluttered surroundings. He liked to wear track-suit trousers, and jogging shoes topped off by a variety of ethnic drapery, even though his running was severely curtailed when his knee, on which he'd had several operations over the years to cure a persistent injury from his circus days, finally succumbed to arthritis. His hair was longish in the wake of Moses, and he habitually wore spectacles and a battered yachting cap. But then he'd never been vain and his lack of dress sense had never prevented acolytes collecting around him. Nor did it now.

'I suppose I invite it,' he said reflectively. 'It's my role in life. You know, Big Daddy? But that can be dangerous. You've got to be sure you're not doing it for your own neurotic needs, so I have to be careful. Me, I stand on my own. I've nobody to lean on, I can't help thinking it's a sign of weakness, needing someone to turn to. It isn't, I know, but the feeling is there. It's hard, if you've got a name, to have easy relations with others. You tend to get cut off. People don't behave normally with you. When I start a new film, for the first few days I don't talk to anybody. I let them discover what sort of person I am, and then it's usually all right. But it's still difficult.'

One of the first to knock on the new office door was Robert Altman. Riding high after *Nashville*, he had another myth-debunking notion to deliver, and he wanted to offer Burt a week's work as Ned Buntline, a minor luminary of Western history who wrote the dime-novels that fuelled the desire for showmanship of William F. Cody, much better known as Buffalo Bill. Paul Newman, wearing a golden wig and painted wrinkle lines, played the failed scout of the title in the days of his late flowering glory as the hero of a Wild West Show. He may have had an insatiable lust for opera singers and a terror of caged birds but he was, Altman and Alan Rudolph's script insisted, what America is all about: show business.

Lancaster's well-publicised views on the puerile nature of much of that business made him sympathetic to such projects, and he signed up willingly for *Buffalo Bill and the Indians*. He was joined by Geraldine Chaplin's Annie Oakley, a lady whose bullets hit her partner rather more often than her target, Harvey Keitel's dazzled nephew and Will Sampson's articulate attendant to Chief Sitting Bull (who is listed as the show's most 'murderous' and colourful attraction). Despite these promising auguries, the film, a series of loosely related sketches of generally farcical intent, doesn't work.

However, Burt's Buntline, dubbed 'the conscience of Bill' because he won't let the braggart forget who got his act together and put him on the road in the first place, can be listed as a redeeming feature. He appears at odd moments, leaning on bars and reflecting on the nature

158

of his bizarre and fateful creation. 'Only Burt Lancaster's elegantly rueful performance as Ned Buntline manages to give some contours in a flatly conceived role,' wrote Nigel Andrews in the *Financial Times*.

So much for art. The time had now come for commerce as Lancaster himself freely admitted when he agreed to make *The Cassandra Crossing*. 'I needed the money. I kid you not. It's a matter of life style. I have only one dress suit to my name and a few jackets and trousers but it still costs me about three hundred thousand dollars a year to live. I must work.'

Once again the venue was Rome, the eminence grise behind the picture, Lew Grade. 'Wonderful man,' Burt insisted. 'Great business-man. But he does have this occasional wish to interfere.' The film's about a plague. It ends with me ordering a train blown up. So he rings up and says, can't you say something like, "My wife and two children were on that train". He always wants these happy endings.'

Although he was unwilling to jump to Grade's commands, he had no hesitation in getting up to his own improvisatory tricks with the director, a larger-than-life character called George Pan Cosmatos. The film, in the way-over-the-top disaster genre, tells of the misadventures that befall the Trans-European Express on its way from Geneva to Stockholm once it is discovered to have a plague-carrier on board, along with Richard Harris, Sophia Loren, Martin Sheen, Ava Gardner and other stars of stage and screen.

Back in pristine Switzerland, Lancaster's high-ranking Army Intelligence Officer pores over his maps and decides that Poland, rather than Sweden would be a fitting destination for such a can of worms, and orders it to roll towards the Cassandra Crossing, a rickety bridge over an impressive gorge that hasn't been used since 1948. It collapses, of course, leaving Burt's Colonel to congratulate himself on having saved the majority of mankind at the expense of an unconsidered thousand-strong minority.

'Cassandra was broad kitsch, right?' the actor declaimed. 'Not only did I not get to see Poland or the Cassandra bridge, but I never saw the movie. Though I worked with the director, writing scenes for Richard Harris and Sophia Loren, the script was bad. The director would get mad, yell at everyone: "Hell, Lancaster and I worked our asses off to write these lines for you. You don't like them? Well, I'll let you have the the original ones then, see how you like that!" Ha, Ha. Actually, I enjoyed sitting with the marvellous Ingrid Thulin and talking for ten days straight. My best line in that movie was, "Listen, why don't you just take the dog for a walk? Hello? Yes. Yes. The train is approaching." '

The *Observer* television critic, Clive James, was one who did see the movie and has some entertaining comparisons to make between its most venerable star and real life. 'In command of the NATO forces is Burt Lancaster, striding purposefully about in front of lit-up maps of Europe which convey no information at all beyond a rough outline of the Atlantic coast. His hair magically changing from black to grey between shots, he makes the Tough Decision by which the train is sent over the Cassandra Crossing to destruction. Thank God, we laugh, that reality isn't like this.

'Then we turn on the latest instalment of The Defence of the United States and find out that it is. High-ranking American officers preparing for 'nookoola' war in Europe seem to be equipped with the same sort of maps as Burt. They also share his daunting capacity for Tough Decisions, such as the decision to send a plague-stricken train over the Cassandra Crossing, or the decision to start lobbing ten-kiloton war heads in a battle zone where the centres of human habitation are two kilotons apart at the most.'

As if to prove James's point (though he wrote the article much later), Lancaster moved on to Germany to make *Twilight's Last Gleaming*, in which he tampers with the buttons of Titan missiles. It was his fourth film for Robert Aldrich, a director whose ability to put together action footage to a very taut, albeit violent, standard ensured that the actor's physical skills were seen in an advantageous light. The screenplay was based on a novel about four criminals who penetrate a missile base one of them had designed, then hold the United States government up to ransom. Give us ten million dollars or we start World War III is the message. It made a nice tight adventure story until the German producer, Helmut Jedele, decided to make it into a movie, and hired an ex-blacklisted writer to expand the message with a lot of pseudo-liberal claptrap.

Burt is the chief recipient of these unwelcome additions in that he plays General Dell, who is disenchanted with his homeland in the post-Watergate era. While his co-hijackers demand their ransom, his idealistic price is that the President should reveal the contents of a top-secret document declaring American policy on the waging of 'limited' nuclear war in places like Vietnam. Only then, he maintains, can his country be cleansed and its people re-discover their faith in it. The film is directly descended from such early sixties political melodramas as

160

Seven Days in May, Fail Safe and *The Manchurian Candidate*, but unlike them, it spells out its points in relentless detail.

Perhaps the German element had something to do with over-explicitness, but even Lancaster, who was emotionally sympathetic to Dell's actions, was not convinced. 'Bob is a sweetheart and I love him,' he commented, 'but I confess I was disappointed.'

He was not the only one. 'Technically and dramatically, *Twilight's Last Gleaming* is such a lousy film that one suspects unconscious sabotage by its director, among others,' said Clancy Sigal in *The Spectator*. 'The action unfolds with laborious predictability and a number of key players are badly miscast and speak their lines with that utter lack of conviction we have come to associate with message pictures. Lancaster is written and played as a hard-ass zealot who coldly shoots one of his fellow escapees, a black man. This at the start of the caper, and the woodenness of his lines, alienates us from his anti-war rationale.'

Lancaster's militaristic vein was destined to continue from the moment an Air France jet was hijacked by Arab sympathisers in June 1976 and diverted to the Ugandan capital of Entebbe, then the domain of the infamous Idi Amin. The gentile hostages were promptly released but the Jews were held inside the plane. Deliberations by the government in Tel Aviv, led by Prime Minister Rabin and the Defence Minister, Shimon Peres, led to a most daring and dramatic long-haul rescue operation by Israeli forces which freed the captives with the minimum loss of life. No sooner was the job completed, than its inherent dramatic possibilities struck the hawkeyed of Hollywood.

'Why not make a film about it?' they yelled in unison, and an ugly rush of cheque-book producing followed. In the event, three films were dashed off within a year and no 'name' actor had any excuse for being out of work at the time.

Lancaster, along with Kirk Douglas, Elizabeth Taylor, Richard Dreyfuss, Anthony Hopkins, Helmut Berger, Helen Hayes and Linda Blair, signed for the cheapie television production, *Victory at Entebbe*, which won the race to reach the screen, with *Raid on Entebbe* (Charles Bronson and Peter Finch) coming second by a week, leaving the Israeli entry far behind. However it was a case of the first worst, and the rest nowhere as the abysmal exploitation of a heroic story turned to dust under a barrage of lousy dialogue and pitiful direction (by Marvin Chomsky).

'Get everything we have in the files on Uganda,' says Burt's Peres, setting the tone of semi-ridicule which dogged the proceedings throughout. His performance was undeniably authoritative but, in the present context, that was not enough.

Next stop, in a money-making jag that was beginning to read like a travel brochure was the Caribbean island of St Croix for the re-make of *The Island of Dr Moreau*. Lancaster is H.G. Wells's mad visionary who, having partially cracked the genetic code, is trying to turn the beasts of the forest into human beings – and vice versa. The vice versa is played by Michael York who is shipwrecked and captured by the crazed genetic genius and put to sinister misuse. The island is populated entirely by humanoids with animal connections, courtesy of *Planet of the Apes* designers, John Chambers and Dan Striepeke. The more successful results work as servants, while the failures roam the forests in search of their damaged origins.

The science-fiction horror story had been filmed in the thirties, with Charles Laughton as the doctor, but had run into censorship problems on the grounds it suggested bestiality. 'This one is different,' Burt insisted, 'I am playing Dr Moreau as a dedicated scientist who, before he goes mad, feels that what he is doing is a noble thing. I don't think he is a heroic man, but he is unusual, strange. He believes it is the duty of science to investigate all things. But look what happens when it does. God knows what is going on today in the bowels of those government laboratories. Theoretically it is possible for science to create superior people. But who is to determine this superiority? Where shall the seat of that God-like power be?'

Such dislocated musings may be pure Lancaster, but commercial Burt is never far behind, and he leaned on the director, Don Taylor, as and when he thought necessary, which by his own account, was fairly often. 'We had moments that we put into the script like when the boy, Michael York, washes up onto the island half dead. He's running through the jungle. He sees strange things – a cloven hoof, just shadows of a face like an animal. He is thinking he is mad. He falls in this animal trap.

'Well, they were worried that this opening was too slow. They wanted a *Jaws* opening. I blew my top. Now, I don't ask for final cut with anyone, but I was worried about this opening scene. And there my contract protects me from any producer changing the whole concept of the script. It is important the movie reveal slowly the boy's mind. They wanted another man to be in the boat with Michael – almost dead. As Michael goes into the jungle, an animal hand would pull the man into the bush and then you'd see this bloody stump – the man being eaten.

Well, if they use that kind of bloody opening, I can use my right to injunct them if I wish.'

Time and reviews proved Lancaster right in his assessment, because the opening sequence in which the 'humanimals' are heard but not seen, proved to be the only saving grace of the film.

Retirement, it seemed, was further from Burt's mind than ever as he enrolled for yet another gun-toter, *Go Tell the Spartans*. What's more, he invested a hundred and fifty thousand dollars of his own money in it, on the grounds that it was the best part he'd been offered in years. It is a Vietnam Western, set in 1964 when there were only twelve thousand 'American military advisers' in the country, and the influence of the recently departed French hung heavily over the war-torn ex-colony.

Lancaster is Major Asa Baker, a World War II veteran who has failed to rise through the ranks due to some ill-timed humping of a general's lady in a gazebo at a posh reception, proceedings that were watched not only by the cuckolded husband but by the president himself. As a result, this lame, gritty, outspoken character finds himself leading un-fledged white 'advisers' and inexperienced South Vietnamese troops through the jungle to man an abandoned outpost once held by the French. It is a futile mission, but one which allows a lot of scope for Custerish last stands against the malevolent Cong. Eventually a heli-copter comes to the rescue of the survivors, but there is only space for those with white skins, so the veteran major is forced to save his honour at the probable expense of his life by staying behind with his native troops.

Any resemblance to cowboys and Indians is purely uncoincidental. Where once Lancaster played in Westerns that were metaphors for contemporary ills, he now grasped the nettle of American interference in Vietnam. The cynical prophetic message of *Go Tell the Spartans* would have been something of a milestone ten years earlier but by 1977, it was a case of too little and far too late to be anything other than robust and well-acted entertainment. Conscience didn't really come into it, but Lancaster was rather too quick to ascribe its poor reception to the inability of Americans to appreciate a film about a war they'd had to withdraw from. 'It's extremely difficult,' he prevaricated, 'for Ameri-cans to accept the idea that they can be beaten in any way. Nobody else would put any money into our film. It was a struggle for us to bring it out. But what we finally achieved was excellent. I'm very pleased with it. And very proud of it.'

After a pleasure trip to Australia and Bali, Burt turned his attention to South Africa where *Zulu Dawn*, the warriors' answer to the British victory at Rorke's Drift, which had been immortalised as *Zulu* on celluloid fifteen years earlier, was being shot. This time it is the Zulus, all twenty-five thousand of them, who beat the colonial over-lords, represented by one thousand Redcoats, when they surprise and massacre them at Isandhlwana on 22 January, 1879 in what is rated alongside the Charge of the Light Brigade among British military disasters.

The illustrious of the cast matched the poignancy of the occasion with Sir John Mills, Simon Ward, Nigel Davenport, Denholm Elliott, Christopher Cazenove, Bob Hoskins and many other British luminaries lining up behind Peter O'Toole's General Lord Chelmsford. For Lancaster, there was the one-armed veteran, Colonel Anthony Durnford who clashes with the egotistic General at every turn, then leads the troops into the ill-fated battle, there to fall into a gully and be finished off by a spear. Burt was fine until he opened his mouth, when a rigidly determined attempt at an upper-class English accent made for derisive comment.

The actor had already showed artistic, if not commercial, perception in turning down a part in what was to become a smash hit of the year, *The Wild Geese*, because he didn't think it told the truth about Africa. In *Zulu Dawn*, an eight-million-dollar epic, which was destined to sink with barely a ripple, he found no such stumbling blocks. 'This is an honest film, full of action and courage. It is very realistic with an almost documentary approach that follows the course of history accurately. It makes a real change from some of the films being made today. I've turned down a lot of garbage lately.'

And accepted a lot too, it had to be admitted (including his second film for 1979, the abysmal and largely unseen *Cattle Annie and Little Britches*), though he constantly re-iterated his determination to retire. 'I'm at an age where I'm phasing out my work,' he announced in Hollywood in early 1979. 'There are very few pictures that interest me. It's too much personal involvement. I want to take it easy. I've had several offers to do things at considerable money, but they just don't interest me. It's not disinterest caused by more permissive movies. I never had any objection to stripping in a film if I felt there was good reason for it. But to strip to play a love scene doesn't make any sense at all unless it is pertinent to the film.

I have nothing against pornographic films – looking at the beautiful body of a man or woman is a beautiful thing – it depends on what manner they attempt to titillate me. I tend to be permissive because it's in my nature to say to anybody, "Go ahead and do what you want as long as you don't harm me." Sometimes you have to be more positive over what you feel is right. It's a better situation in pictures today. We look back with nostalgia at the films of the past but all of them were not that good. We think of that as the Golden Era – but I think this is the Golden Era. Better movies are being made today.'

As far as his own career was concerned, his words were prophetic because his next film – yes, the phasing-out was still in the future – was the best he'd made since the early sixties, the golden days of *Elmer Gantry*, *The Birdman of Alcatraz* and *The Leopard*. In the early eighties, with his seventieth birthday beginning to loom, Burt Lancaster would rise again and show the world that it had never had him so good.

fifteen
VINDICATION

Growing old gracefully is a problem for everybody, but for actors the problem is growing old at all, and it is accentuated a thousand times for Hollywood superstars. Some, like Cary Grant, duck into premature retirement rather than dent the image. Some, like Kirk Douglas, have their faces lifted and retain their screen toughness through unnaturally stretched skin. Some, like James Stewart, wear hair-pieces, and turn down all villains on principle. Some, like Burt Lancaster, look in the mirror and capitalise on the unacceptable face they see there. By 1981, he had a pot belly unsupported by corsets, a shock of white hair he refused to dye except for work, a patriarchal white beard and the lines time had given him. When he said, 'My romantic leading days are over, I can look at a nineteen-year-old but I'm not allowed to get too close,' he spoke with conviction.

Even so, accepting the part of Lou in *Atlantic City* can't have been easy. Robert Mitchum had already thought the blow to the ego too severe, and refused. Burt may have had the worst dress sense in Hollywood – if anything it had deteriorated from bad to terrible with riches and age – but he was physically vain. A man of normal appetites and intellectual pretention doesn't eat hardboiled eggs and train obsessively far into late middle age for fun. The brain is stimulated by conversation and even for Burt, a fairly natural loner, the self-discipline required to resist conviviality over fine food was severe.

The film industry is peopled by fat technicians working twelve to fourteen hours a day with interruptions for five high-calorie meals provided by the management, and by lean and hungry actors, often with too little to do, anxiously trying to resist them. In the old days, Burt had filled the inevitable gaps while new shots were set up with press-ups rather than pie crusts, but in the late seventies, his knee had given out on him and he started to run to fat.

So too is Lou, the anti-hero of *Atlantic City*. He is a pathetic, sagging-bellied small-time crook, who can't even call himself a has-been because he never was. In his dreams, he is a hot shot, a big-time killer, but in real life he is a kept man, forever at the beck and call of a mobster's widow (Kate Read), who gives him handouts in return for humiliating shopping and poodle-walking chores. He may snarl to himself about it, but he can't afford to refuse, and the insult is only intensified by the circumstances in which they first met: he was her bodyguard when she appeared in a Betty Grable lookalike contest on Atlantic City's famous boardwalk, but even then they were losers – she only came third.

The part gave Lancaster the chance to work with French director Louis Malle, for the first time. The films he'd made in Italy had made him popular with French audiences in a way that was most unusual for an American star, but the great directors like Resnais, Truffaut and Godard, worked exclusively in their own language, then had their films sub-titled for export. This effectively excluded foreigners from appearing in them. Malle, however, had gone American two years earlier with *Pretty Baby*, and enjoyed the experiment sufficiently to continue with it.

Atlantic City is based on a play by John Guare, a typically unstructured piece, full of quirky charm. It is not 'well crafted', but an elusive series of strong images whose loose connections are never fully explained. The Malle version opens with just such an unforgettable cinematic image, when a handsome turn-of-the-century hotel overlooking the famous boardwalk, is dynamited almost silently. With a distant rumble, the wedding-cake façade crumbles from the inside out into millions of fragments until nothing is left but a heap of rubble. Life is like that, says Guare, full of bright hopes and promises that fall apart into wrinkles and disappointments.

And Malle agrees. Throughout the film, he uses the destruction and renewal of Atlantic City as a metaphor for the human condition. It is in the process of losing its gracious relics to the demands of the new concrete and glass brutalism as hotel-casinos spring up to cater for the gambling legalised by the State of New Jersey in 1976. The peripheral characters who inhabit its dusty scaffolded streets are tawdry racketeers, who have moved in to exploit the ordinary man's illusion that the throw of the dice produces dream fulfilment that doesn't have to be worked for.

Lou should know otherwise, but that doesn't prevent him gazing longingly into the night where Sally (Susan Sarandon), a clam-bar waitress whose hopeless ambition is to be the first female dealer at Monte Carlo, kneads her breasts with lemon halves in front of an uncurtained window. To Lou, she is infinitely desirable, unattainable, impossibly remote, yet to herself she is a loser, with a past she probably can't shake off.

Lancaster and Sarandon play beautifully together as they meet, score an unexpected cocaine coup against the Mob and find that dreams can, after all, come true. Though he cowers before any passing thug, Lou becomes a big-timer, a double killer and Sally has money to go to France. For a brief moment, all's right with the world before Malle and Guare resume their elaborate and destructive joke playing.

When shooting was completed, the director paid proper homage to his star: 'It was an act of heroism for Burt to allow himself to be seen so starkly as an old-timer,' he said. 'It is all the more remarkable because he has the reputation of being very difficult and temperamental and a long history of making trouble with his directors. Yet from the start, he was enthusiastic about this project.

'When I first saw Burt I thought: "My God! What great irony if a man, whose image is so much the opposite, should play this silly old man who is a voyeur, watching a girl undress in the opposite apartment?" I did not want to make him completely ridiculous. I wanted to show something moving about him. But because he is Burt Lancaster, an actor who carried around a heroic image all his life, there is that extra sense of humiliation. I am told he saw a copy of the film and reacted very well. I would hate to have an unhappy Burt Lancaster. He can really get mean.'

Had he been tempted, which is unlikely because the mellowing process was very far advanced by this time, the reviews he got for *Atlantic City* would certainly have changed his mind. The once antipathetic Pauline Kael wrote: 'In shallow action roles, he played bloody but unbowed; when he was working with Visconti or Bertolucci, he wasn't afraid to be bloody and bowed. And that's how he is here, but more so, because this time he isn't playing a strong man brought down by age and social change: he's a man who was never anything much – he was always a little too soft inside.'

To which *Time*'s Richard Schickel added, 'The highest pleasure *Atlantic City* has to offer is a little essay on fastidiousness by Burt Lancaster. That is not a quality one automatically associates with a star who was once the most macho of leading men. But in the past decade, he has become a resourceful and wide-ranging character actor. Here he is playing Lou, a small-time crook who seems to feel neatness just might count in the battle to keep his withered dreams intact. You can practically smell the blue rinse in his hair; the pressing of a tie, the caressing of a whisky glass, the sniffing of a wine cork become incantatory gestures. They are supposed to ward off the new tawdriness of the gambling casinos, which is replacing the old salt-water-taffy funk of the boardwalk town. While the wrecking balls swing all around him, Lou complains that even the ocean isn't what it used to be.'

An Oscar nomination followed, Burt's first in nearly twenty years, but the 1981 prize went to Robert de Niro for *Raging Bull*. However there was compensation in London where the British Academy of Film and Television Arts gave him the Best Actor's award for 1982, a ceremony he attended in person when he flew into town coincidentally on just the right day for wardrobe fittings for *Local Hero*, which he was then making for David Puttnam. Turning down kind offers of formal wear from Moss Bros, he wore his blue suit – the only one he owned, by his account – and turned up at the dinner at the last moment, much to the delight of the organisers, who hadn't anticipated such an honour.

The year before had seen him back in Rome, but breaking new ground in the sense that he worked under a woman director. She was the forceful Liliana Cavani whom he considered 'strong and creative' and the film was *La Pelle* (The Skin). Set in Naples in 1943 when the fighting was finished but the aftermath of war dictated behaviour, it tells of victors and vanquished engaging in a new struggle to find pleasure in life again. Naples, the first city to be 'liberated' by the Allies, was a cosmopolitan melting pot for Americans, English, Polish, French, and even Indians, searching for a change of pace.

It will come as no surprise to Cavani followers that her vision, based on the novel by Curzio Malaparte, is of Sodom and Gomorrah, tinged with the last days of Pompeii, an energetic exercise in degradation. The woman who made *The Night Porter* has never pulled her punches as a sop to her sex; indeed, she has often seemed to be even more relentlessly explicit as if in compensation for it. In this instance, she pulls the strings that activate her characters against a background of corruption and prostitution of every possible variety, physical and psychological.

Lancaster again plays a general. For a man who was generally antipathetic to the Pentagon, he certainly infiltrated their higher echelons with astonishing frequency. This one is the representative of the conquerors, in contrast to Malaparte himself (Marcello Mastroianni) who is presented autobiographically as a victim from the losing side

169

intent on the joys of re-birth. His book had been vilified when it first came out by contemporary neo-realist film-makers like Roberto Rossellini. However the Cavani version, which she described as 'hyper realism', was well received at the Cannes Film Festival in 1981, though it was far removed from the mainstream so far as American and British audiences were concerned.

The same cannot be said for *Local Hero*, which brought Burt to Scotland, a land of golf and fishing which he loved, in the spring of 1982. It combined the entrepreneurial talents of David Puttnam, riding high on the triple Oscar success of *Chariots of Fire*, and the writing and directing skills of Bill Forsyth, whose three-hundred-and-fifty-thousand dollar Scottish comedy, *Gregory's Girl*, had proved to be the sleeper of the year. Yet even with their joint track record, the pair were fairly nervous about sending the script of *Local Hero* to the high-rise headquarters of Norlan Productions in distant Century City. For Forsyth, who'd written the character of oil billionaire Felix Happer, with Lancaster in mind, albeit subconsciously at first, the block was that he didn't think the great man would take it. 'In my head I began to hear him saying the dialogue,' he recalled. 'Then I think I started writing it specially for him. Of course it was amazing when he read it and was interested in doing it.'

For David Puttnam the problem was financial. 'I knew we needed a big name, although I don't usually work with stars. Happer has to be a man of power and influence, and there aren't too many sixty-five-year-old American unknowns around who can put that over! However I'd never met Burt Lancaster and had some qualms about approaching him because of the effect his acceptance might have had on the budget. If he were to accept then we would be committed to him. At the same time, we knew his name would help in terms of cable and television rights. We spent some time in Los Angeles looking for people who might play the part if he turned it down.'

Meanwhile enthusiasm was breaking out all over in Lancaster's office. 'Hey Joanna, you gotta read this,' he said to his daughter, who was working with him. 'I've gotta make this movie.' Later he elaborated on what exactly had appealed to him: 'Good scripts are rare and this was the best I'd received since *Atlantic City*. Light and satirical, with no villains, just eccentrics. It was like those lovely old Ealing movies. I don't particularly care if I don't act any more unless I find a piece of work that really excites me. You've no idea the rubbish that's sent to me. Tits and sand. That's what we used to call sex and violence in

170

Hollywood. I had never heard of Forsyth before I received the script. When I arrived in Scotland I was told, though not by him – he is an extremely modest, rather shy man, very strong when he wants but very quiet – that he wrote the part with me in mind.'

That answered Forsyth's question, but Puttnam's remained. Lancaster was too expensive. He had a very heavy business manager who turned out to be one of the toughest the British producer had dealt with. 'He produced a deal we couldn't afford,' he commented, 'and he wouldn't drop the price. I spent four of five weeks shuttling back and forth across the Atlantic to try to arrange it. At home Bill was equally stubborn. He'd written it for Burt Lancaster and he wouldn't budge!' Eventually the star himself got to hear of the problem and broke the deadlock. 'If these guys can't afford it, let it ride,' he told the manager. 'I want to do it.'

Stage one was to fly to Houston for a day and a half's shooting in the 'headquarters' of Knox Oil, the huge Texan company which Happer is head of. Then the party flew on to London and Fort William to meet the rest of the cast. Forsyth's story concerns a young executive called MacIntyre (Peter Riegert) who is sent by Happer to negotiate a deal to buy an idyllic Scottish beach from the natives in order to turn it into a refining complex of unnatural ugliness. There will, he supposes, be problems, and there are – but not of the kind he expects. The natives, far from concerning themselves with environmental matters, only quarrel about how many noughts to add to the asking price while Mac, charmed by the rural tranquillity, the innkeeper's wife and the whisky, wonders if he can ever tear himself away. It is left to Happer, whose normal semi-madness becomes total whenever he looks into the heavens that obsess him, to float out of the night sky in his helicopter and sort things out.

The tycoon's part is not large, but it presented Burt with some odd problems. 'I found it a bit difficult as an acting role because of the characters who are all sort of half-mad in a strange kind of way,' he explained. 'Forsyth is a very perceptive person about human nature, and the frailties of human beings. From his point of view, everybody is a little strange. But he treats it all very gently with a very sweet, light kind of humour.

'It's delightful and when you try to play a character like this you don't know how far to take it – you have to be careful you don't farcicalise it, play it too big which the temptation is to do. Rather you have to let the total effect of what is happening evoke an attitude of charm and mirth in the audience. At first I was not sure what I was doing, but I came to feel pretty comfortable about it after I'd seen some of the rushes.'

During his two weeks at the Scottish location at Morar beach, thirty-seven miles from Fort William, Burt and Jackie stayed with David Puttnam and Bill Forsyth in the exclusive Inverlochy Castle. The amenities included silver candelabra, ancestral portraits and peacocks, a magnificent view of the loch and what is reputedly the best food in Scotland. The manager, Michael Leonard, ensures that his waiters address each guest by name which is not, perhaps, such a problem in a place that attracts Larry Hagman as a regular guest.

Burt didn't confine himself to these palatial quarters, but moved out into the countryside to test the ambiance. When the unseasonal snow and rain that greeted the cast's arrival in the area gave way to an unusually good spring, he was able to fish for trout in the stream near the castle. Saturday night found him in a Glenfinnan pub listening to bagpipes and drinking with the locals. There he discovered, when they discussed *Birdman of Alcatraz* as if 'the whole thing just came out yesterday', that time moves very slowly in Scotland. Other nights were spent in nearby pubs, standing his round with members of the unit and signing autographs for astonished fans, or watching snooker on the television in the billiard-room of the hotel. 'I just eat that guy Alex Higgins at the snooker table. He looks like he survives on booze and nerves – but he sure can put those balls in the pockets,' was his verdict.

On another occasion, he and Jackie went to eat at the Holly Tree Restaurant, the converted railway station at Kentallen, and found a group of forty people from the film already installed. Having won the heart of the owner's wife by agreeing to speak to her mother on the phone (the woman couldn't believe it was really him), he ate and made an unobtrusive exit. Only when the film party asked for the bill did they learn that Mr Lancaster had already paid it.

On the set, his behaviour was equally impeccable, though his long speech on the beach wreaked havoc with his fading memory. He was very encouraging to the inexperienced members of a young cast who were, quite naturally in awe of working with him. When Peter Reigert was playing opposite him, it was suggested he stand on a board to raise him up a bit. The actor obliged, but Lancaster saw him shifting uneasily. 'You comfortable on that thing?' he demanded. Reigert shook his head. 'Then don't agree. That's their problem, not yours. Don't let them hassle you.'

Peter Capaldi, a twenty-three-year-old Glaswegian stand-up comic, who'd never worked on a film before, was treated with equal sympathy. 'The first time I met Burt Lancaster, there he was in a blue tracksuit looking exactly like Burt Lancaster,' he remembers. 'He asked if I wanted to go through the lines and we went into a cafe. I couldn't believe it: me going through lines with Burt Lancaster! I wanted to ask for his autograph but I knew that wouldn't be the right thing to do. Sometimes I had to pinch myself to believe it was really happening.'

'He is very, very good,' Lancaster responded with enthusiasm. 'He is a genuinely funny boy with a comic streak in him. He will go far.'

Denis Lawson, who plays the innkeeper with a finger in every pie, had equally happy memories. 'I only did one scene with Lancaster directly, but I had the opportunity of watching him. It was fascinating to see how he used the camera, how he varied his performance take by take. He was very interesting to watch.'

In his own age group, Burt found a rapport with Fulton Mackay, the star of the television series *Porridge*, whose role as a ragged beachcomber is crucial to Lancaster's. The two men discovered that MacKay had just appeared in the television play, *Going Gently*, the story of two terminal-cancer patients. Ironically, Burt had tried to sell the idea to American television two years before, but failed although he and his proposed co-star, Art Carney, were prepared to do it for nothing. Television, as he'd noted before, was pretty trivial in the States, which was why he'd done so little of it.

Where, the cast and crew were wondering in the face of Burt's relentless good humour, was the ogre of Hollywood, the man whose reputation for arguing made strong men quail? Gone for good they concluded, especially when he agreed to talk to journalists. It fell to Associate Producer, Iain Smith, to bring up this delicate matter before Lancaster left Houston. He'd prepared a list of newspapers which he presented nervously to the star. 'Mr Lancaster,' he said, 'it'd be just wonderful if you could give some interviews.'

'But I never give interviews,' came the succinct response.

Smith pleaded a little, then paused.

'You mean these people will come and write nice things about the picture?' Lancaster enquired. 'It'll be for the good of the picture? Okay, I'll do it.' With which he dropped the list into the wastepaper basket, and never looked at it again. Whenever a journalist was presented, he'd say, 'Was he on the list? Okay then.'

On occasion, he even joked with them. 'I don't try too hard to keep

173

fit,' he told Stanley Shivas, 'I jog for two hours a day but otherwise I prefer to stay home and read or make love. I've jumped through too many windows in the past, and I'm no longer Young Lochinvar sweeping in from the west, but I like stories about an older man with a young woman.'

All too soon Lancaster's part in the film was completed and he moved on to Turnberry, Gleneagles and St Andrews to play golf for a fortnight with friends. His handicap, which in the Hecht-Hill-Lancaster days when he'd practised on the office floor, had been eight, had risen to sixteen, but his enthusiasm for the game is undimmed. First, however, there was the *Local Hero* leaving party to attend.

Finding a present for the man who has everything can be a problem, but it was decided that a kilt would set the right Scottish seal on the proceedings. A hundred and twenty people assembled to watch it being presented, and their eyes opened in amazement as Burt accepted it enthusiastically, then took off his trousers and put it on to wear for the rest of the evening.

'He was a prince,' Iain Smith summed up the whole happy experience. And Bill Forsyth, normally the model of Glaswegian reticence, added, 'He was great. He has the immense power of the billionaire, but there's a soft core inside him. There's a soul crying in there. I usually use young people in my films because I can dominate and short change and manipulate them! I didn't feel I could do that with Burt Lancaster!'

The star had no complaints. 'There's so much gentle ironical humour in *Local Hero*. Bill pokes fun at people gently. He always knew a little bit better than I did what ought to be done. It was very refreshing. He sort of let me alone to do what I thought I should do as the character. Then if it wasn't quite right, he'd come and add to it. Or, if he liked what I was doing, he'd make suggestions to intensify it. He is one of the most original writers I've seen in a long time. He'll go far.'

The film could do no wrong in Britain, but the real test came in America and again, *Local Hero* passed with flying colours. Having noted that Burt Lancaster's choice of films and his work in them 'seem to get better and better with age', Vincent Canby of the *New York Times* went on to say, 'Though he is not on screen as long as one would like, Mr Lancaster is splendidly unpredictable as the oil tycoon, a man so rich and powerful that his psychiatrist comes to him and is told, in no uncertain terms, what the fee will be and what hours will be made available for therapy. In Mr Lancaster's perfectly controlled nuttiness lies the secret of Mr Forsyth's comic method, which is as stylish and original as that of any new director to come along in years.'

Pauline Kael finally put the seal on her conversion to the Lancastrian cause by saying, 'The humour is dry, yet the picture is romantic in spirit, and Burt Lancaster has something to do with that. He is convincing as a sturdy, physically powerful man, and even more convincing as a man of authority whose only intimacy is with the stars above. In this penthouse office apartment in the Knox skyscraper, this tycoon presses the button that opens the sliding dome of his planetarium and he stands under the constellations. Lancaster has an imperial romantic aura; he belongs there, on top of a tower under the stars, and I doubt if there are many actors who could convey so much by just standing there.

Another film, another challenge. Sam Peckinpah hadn't made a picture since *Convoy* in 1978; now he would direct *The Osterman Weekend*, based on Robert Ludlum's best seller. Was Mr Lancaster available to join a distinguished cast on the ten-million-dollar production? Yes, indeed he was.

The story concerns a powerful television journalist (Rutger Hauer) who is told by a CIA agent (John Hurt) and the head of the Agency (Burt) that his three best friends (Dennis Hopper, Chris Sarandon and Craig T. Nelson) are members of the KGB. Not unnaturally, the relevation makes for a suspicion-filled reunion weekend at the journalist's ranch-style home, and few of the cast survive it. Lancaster's part is a cameo, but crucial nonetheless. Peckinpah worked on the script himself to bring it up to standard before shooting started and distributors, Twentieth Century Fox, have high hopes for the picture.

Burt was seventy in 1983, but the year was a difficult one because his health, which had been superb until he was well into his sixties, had begun to deteriorate. In January 1980, he nearly died during an eleven-hour gall-bladder operation in the Cedars Sinai Medical Center, and he remained on the critical list for some time after it. In the summer of 1983, he returned to the Center for further tests and it was discovered that he needed a quadruple by-pass operation to relieve blockages in the coronary arteries. The surgery lasted for five and a half hours, but this time he recovered more rapidly. After three days in intensive care, he was moved into a private room.

The surgery meant that he had to pull out of *Maria's Lover*, in which he planned to share the limelight with Nastassia Kinski, under the direction of a Russian, Andre Konchalovsky. Nor was he able to appear in *Firestarter*, a project based on a Stephen King book about a young girl with pyrokinetic abilities. The first screenplay was written by Bill Lancaster after the author had been paid a handsome one million dollars for the film rights, and Burt was initially eager at the prospect of a family collaboration. Eventually, after a temporary foundering, the hot property went to Dino Laurentis, and both Lancasters withdrew, happily as it turned out, for the film was a critical and commercial failure.

As he moves gracious into old age, there can be no doubt that Burt Lancaster presents a changed face to the world. He is often polite to people he doesn't know, and the dangerous glint in the cold blue eyes is usually masked. The tombstone teeth, the result of the only cosmetic surgery he ever deigned to undergo, still flash but there is merriment in the grin. After *Local Hero*, it is impossible to say, as Willy Newlands once did in the *Daily Mail*, 'His savage fixed smile – thirty-two teeth, all at the front – is the most humourless on film.'

Among his intimates, the massive ego beats as strongly as ever. When asked to write some comments on his trip by the owners of a yacht he'd been a guest on, he simply put 'Burt Lancaster'. Woe betide a secretary who gives his telephone number out of order, even to a friend. Lancaster may take the call, and chat as if he was glad to do so, but once the receiver is down, the strips are torn. Nor has he forgotten how to administer the put-down to those he has no time for. At a gala in New York, Harvey Keitel, who'd always wanted to meet him, watched him approach with a suitably reverential expression. Lancaster looked down at him for a moment, then he snorted, 'Harvey Keitel, Method actor' and, delivering his famous rumbling laugh, he turned on his heel and walked away.

On the positive side, the seventy-two-year-old Lancaster is an actor of repute. Over the years, the habit of underrating him became chronic, and it was only after *Atlantic City* that the blocks were finally eliminated. Going through his own films, he picks out *From Here To Eternity*, *Sweet Smell of Success*, *Birdman of Alcatraz* and *The Leopard* as his favourites, but reserves some affection for the swashbucklers, *The Flame and The Arrow* and *The Crimson Pirate*, that made him rich.

'Not only were they good entertainment and are still shown today, but they were ageless in the sense that they were simple tales of good against bad told with great fun,' he explained. 'I came at a time when boudoirs and drawing rooms were going out of fashion. I was part of a new kind of furniture, tougher, less polished, grainier. I think I realised that at the time, but I have always known that I couldn't settle for the expected. I have always wanted to reach out and I always will. That's why I'm considered such an uncomfortable bastard to be with.

'Before the post-war transition period, if you weren't a character actor like Spencer Tracy, you were a pretty boy leading man such as Robert Taylor or a Gable personality actor. Now you have the Hoffmans, Pacinos, de Niros; we would never have been allowed to play that bloated fighter like de Niro did in *Raging Bull*. Great actors all of them, but these days people seem to want to identify with the actors and the roles they play. They don't look up to them. There's no fantasy and too little romance. They don't want pure escapism. Marriage, for instance, isn't all roses, hearts and flowers and happy endings. There are good times and bad times – terrible tension. Film-makers are more honest than they were.'

In other words, they've caught up with one of the most forward-thinking actors of his generation, a man who battled his way through the morass of Hollywood clichés and type-casting, studio dictates and rigid pecking orders to become his own man. Initially a limited and pitifully inexperienced actor, he barrelled along through gun operas and soap operas and horse operas to find another world out there where people who'd never been to Hollywood made films about people who had no place there. And if he made a lot of enemies in the process, he had sufficient faith in himself not to care. 'People outside Hollywood don't understand how it is here,' he's said. 'It's a battle to maintain a basic integrity, a scrap against bull and baloney. You have to fight all the time.'

So he did, and he won. Unlike his contemporaries who retired because they couldn't buck the system, he has turned it to his own needs as efficiently in the eighties as he did in the forties. Only recently did he come clean about the retirement he'd threatened for some fifteen years. 'As you get older you have to keep your mind open and try new things. When you lose your curiosity, your age begins to show. Some of us finally learn that maturity means consideration for other people. It is the ability to love yourself and consequently others. That is the answer. It's a whole new ball game every day.'

So says the old warrior, and no one who knows him has any problem believing him. For a start, they wouldn't dare.

FILMOGRAPHY

1946

1. *The Killers.* Universal (Mark Hellinger). Director: Robert Siodmak. Screenplay: Anthony Veiller, based on the short story by Ernest Hemingway. Cast also included: Ava Gardner, Edmond O'Brien, Albert Dekker, Sam Levene, Jeff Corey, William Conrad. Remade in 1964 by Universal, with Don Siegel directing and John Cassavetes in Lancaster's role of 'The Swede'.

1947

2. *Desert Fury.* Paramount (Hal Wallis). Lewis Allen. Robert Rossen, based on the novel by Ramona Stewart. Cast: John Hodiak, Lizabeth Scott, Wendell Corey (film debut), Mary Astor. Colour.

3. *Brute Force.* Universal (Mark Hellinger). Jules Dassin. Richard Brooks, based on the story by Robert Patterson. Cast: Hume Cronyn, Charles Bickford, Yvonne De Carlo, Ann Blyth, Ella Raines, Anita Colby, Sam Levene, Howard Duff, Jeff Corey.

4. *Variety Girl.* Paramount. George Marshall. Edmund Hartmann, Frank Tashlin, Robert Welch and Monte Brice. Cast: Olga San Juan, Mary Hatcher, De Forest Kelley, William Demarest and guest stars, including Bing Crosby, Bob Hope, William Holden, Lizabeth Scott, Robert Preston, Veronica Lake, Sterling Hayden, Macdonald Carey.

1948

5. *I Walk Alone.* Paramount (Hal Wallis). Byron Haskin. Charles Schnee, based on the play *Beggers Are Coming to Town*, by Theodore Reeves, adapted by Robert Smith and John Bright. Cast: Lizabeth Scott, Kirk Douglas, Wendell Corey.

6. *All My Sons.* Universal. Irving Reis. Chester Erskine, based on the

play by Arthur Miller. Cast: Edward G. Robinson, Mady Christians, Louisa Horton, Howard Duff, Frank Conroy, Arlene Francis.

7. *Sorry, Wrong Number.* Paramount (Hal Wallis). Anatole Litvak. Lucille Fletcher, based on her own radio play. Cast: Barbara Stanwyck, Ann Richards, Wendell Corey, Ed Begley, Lief Erickson, William Conrad. Stanwyck was nominated for the Best Actress Oscar.

8. *Kiss the Blood Off My Hands.* Universal. Norman Foster. Eric Bercovici, based on the novel by Gerald Butler, adapted by Ben Maddow and Walter Bernstein. Cast: Joan Fontaine, Robert Newton, Lewis Russell. Lancaster's first movie as a producer (with Harold Hecht), under the Norma production company.

1949

9. *Criss Cross.* Universal. Robert Siodmak. Daniel Fuchs, based on the novel by Don Tracy. Cast: Yvonne De Carlo, Dan Duryea, Stephen McNally, Richard Long.

10. *Rope of Sand.* Paramount (Hal Wallis). William Dieterle. Walter Doniger, additional dialogue by John Paxton. Cast: Paul Henreid, Claude Rains, Corinne Calvet, Peter Lorre, Sam Jaffe.

1950

11. *The Flame and the Arrow.* Warner Brothers (Hecht-Norma). Jacques Tourneur. Waldo Salt. Cast: Virginia Mayo, Robert Douglas, Aline MacMahon, Frank Allenby, Nick Cravat. Colour.

12. *Mister 880.* Twentieth Century-Fox. Edmund Goulding. Robert Riskin, based on articles by St. Clair McKelway. Cast: Dorothy McGuire, Edmund Gwenn. Gwenn was nominated for the Best Supporting Actor Academy Award.

1951

13. *Vengeance Valley.* Metro-Goldwyn-Mayer. Richard Thorpe. Irving Ravetch, based on the story by Luke Short. Cast: Robert Walker, Joanne Dru, Sally Forrest, John Ireland, Carleton Carpenter, Ray Collins, Hugh O'Brian. Colour.

14. *Jim Thorpe—All American.* Warner Brothers. Michael Curtiz. Douglas Morrow and Everett Freeman, based on the story by Morrow and Vincent X. Flaherty, and the autobiography by Jim Thorpe and Russell J. Birdwell. Cast: Charles Bickford, Phyllis Thaxter, Steve Cochran, Dick Wesson.

15. *Ten Tall Men*. Columbia (Hecht-Norma). Willis Goldbeck. Roland Kibbee and Frank Davis, based on the story by James Warner Bellah and Goldbeck. Cast: Jody Lawrence, Gilbert Roland, Kieren Moore, George Tobias, Mari Blanchard. Colour.

1952

16. *The Crimson Pirate*. Warner Brothers (Hecht-Norma). Robert Siodmak. Roland Kibbee. Cast: Eva Bartok, Nick Cravat, Margo Grahame, Christopher Lee, Dagmar (later Dana) Wynter, Frank Pettingill. Colour.

17. *Come Back, Little Sheba*. Paramount (Hal Wallis). Daniel Mann. Ketti Frings, based on the play by William Inge. Cast: Shirley Booth, Terry Moore, Richard Jaeckel, Philip Ober. Booth won Oscar as Best Actress. Moore was nominated as Best Supporting Actress.

1953

18. *South Sea Woman*. Warner Brothers. Arthur Lubin. Edwin Blum, based on the play by William M. Rankin, adapted by Earl Baldwin and Stanley Shapiro. Cast: Virginia Mayo, Chuck Connors, Arthur Sheilds, Veola Vonn, Paul Burke.

19. *From Here to Eternity*. Columbia. Fred Zinnemann. Daniel Taradash, based on the novel by James Jones. Cast: Deborah Kerr, Montgomery Clift, Donna Reed, Frank Sinatra, Philip Ober, Ernest Borgnine, Jack Warden. Lancaster won the New York Film Critics Award as Best Actor, and received an Academy Award nomination. Oscars were given to Reed and Sinatra for their supporting roles, to Taradash for his screenplay and to Zinnemann for direction. *From Here to Eternity* was nominated for a total of eleven Academy Awards and won eight.

20. *Three Sailors and a Girl*. Warner Brothers. Roy Del Ruth. Roland Kibbee and Devery Freeman, from a play by George S. Kaufman. Cast: Jane Powell, Gordon MacRae, Gene Nelson, Sam Levene, Jack E. Leonard, Veda Ann Borg. Colour.

1954

21. *His Majesty O'Keefe*. Warner Brothers (Hecht-Norma). Byron Haskin. Borden Chase and James Hill, based on the novel by Lawrence Kingman and Gerald Green. Cast: Joan Rice, Andre Morell, Benson Fong, Tessa Prendergast. Colour.

22. *Apache*. Hecht-Lancaster, released by United Artists. Robert

Aldrich. James R. Webb, based on the novel by Paul I. Wellman. Cast: Jean Peters, John McIntire, Charles Buchinsky (later Bronson). Colour.

23. *Vera Cruz.* Hecht-Lancaster, United Artists. Robert Aldrich. Roland Kibbee and James R. Webb, based on a story by Borden Chase. Cast: Gary Cooper, Denise Darcel, Cesar Romero, Ernest Borgnine, Jack Elam. Colour.

1955

24. *The Kentuckian.* Hecht-Lancaster, United Artists. Burt Lancaster. A. B. Guthrie, Jnr, based on the novel by Felix Holt. Cast: Diana Lynn, Dianne Foster, John McIntire, Una Merkel, John Carradine and introducing Walter Matthau. Colour.

25. *The Rose Tattoo.* Paramount. Daniel Mann. Tennessee Williams, based on his own stage play, with adaptation by Hal Kanter. Cast: Anna Magnani, Marisa Pavan, Ben Cooper, Virginia Grey, Jo Van Fleet. Magnani won Best Actress Oscar, and Oscars went to cinematographer James Wong Howe, and a team of four for best black and white art direction/set decoration. *The Rose Tattoo* was nominated as Best Picture but lost to Hecht and Lancaster's own *Marty.*

1956

26. *Trapeze.* Susan Productions, produced by James Hill, released by United Artists. Carol Reed. James R. Webb, with an adaptation by Liam O'Brien, based on *The Killing Frost* by Max Catto. Cast: Tony Curtis, Gina Lollobrigida, Katy Jurado, John Puleo. Colour. Video available.

27. *The Rainmaker.* Paramount (Hal Wallis). Joseph Anthony. N. Richard Nash, based on his own play. Cast: Katharine Hepburn, Wendell Corey, Lloyd Bridges, Earl Holliman, Cameron Prud'homme. Colour.

1957

28. *Gunfight at the OK Corral.* Paramount (Hal Wallis). John Sturges. Leon Uris, based on the article *The Killer,* by George Scullin. Cast: Kirk Douglas, Rhonda Fleming, Jo Van Fleet, John Ireland, Frank Faylen, Earl Holliman, Lyle Bettger, Dennis Hopper. Colour.

29. *Sweet Smell of Success.* Hecht-Hill-Lancaster, released by United Artists. Alexander MacKendrick. Clifford Odets and Ernest Lehman,

based on the novelette by Lehman. Cast: Tony Curtis, Susan Harrison, Martin Milner, Sam Levene, Barbara Nichols, Jeff Donnell, Lurene Tuttle, Edith Atwater, Queenie Smith.

1958

30. *Run Silent, Run Deep*. Hecht-Hill-Lancaster, released by United Artists. Robert Wise. John Gay, based on the novel by Edward L. Beach. Cast: Clark Gable, Jack Warden, Brad Dexter, Don Rickles, Nick Cravat, Eddie Foy III.

31. *Separate Tables*. Hecht-Hill-Lancaster, released by United Artists. Delbert Mann. Terence Rattigan and John Gay, based on Rattigan's play. Cast: Rita Hayworth, Deborah Kerr, David Niven, Wendy Hiller, Gladys Cooper, Cathleen Nesbitt, Rod Taylor. Best Actor Oscar to Niven, Supporting Actress Oscar to Hiller. Kerr was nominated as Best Actress, and *Separate Tables* for Best Picture.

1959

32. *The Devil's Disciple*. Bryanprod SA and Hecht-Hill-Lancaster (United Artists). Guy Hamilton. John Dighton and Roland Kibbee, based on the play by George Bernard Shaw. Cast: Kirk Douglas, Laurence Olivier, Eva Le Galliene, Harry Andrews, Basil Sydney, George Rose, Janette Scott, Neil McCallum.

1960

33. *The Unforgiven*. Hecht-Hill-Lancaster (United Artists). John Huston. Ben Maddow, based on the novel by Alan LeMay. Cast: Audrey Hepburn, Lillian Gish, Audie Murphy, John Saxon, Charles Bickford, Albert Salmi, Joseph Wiseman. Colour.

34. *Elmer Gantry*. Bernard Smith Production (United Artists). Richard Brooks. Richard Brooks, based on the novel by Sinclair Lewis. Cast: Jean Simmons, Arthur Kennedy, Shirley Jones, Dean Jagger, Patti Page, Edward Andrews, Philip Ober, Rex Ingram. Lancaster won his second New York Film Critics Best Actor Award, and the Oscar. Jones won the Supporting Actress Oscar and Richard Brooks the Oscar for Best Screenplay. Colour.

1961

35. *The Young Savages*. Harold Hecht (United Artists). John Frankenheimer. Edward Anhalt and J. P. Miller, based on the novel by Evan

Hunter. Cast: Dina Merrill, Shelley Winters, Edward Andrews, Tally Savalas, Milton Selzer.

36. *Judgment at Nuremberg.* Stanley Kramer Production (United Artists). Stanley Kramer. Abby Mann, based on his television play. Cast: Spencer Tracy, Richard Widmark, Marlene Dietrich, Maximilian Schell, Judy Garland, Montgomery Clift, Werner Klemperer, William Shatner. Schell won the Best Actor Oscar. Mann won the Oscar for Best Screenplay. Tracy was nominated as Best Actor and Clift and Garland were nominated for supporting awards. Kramer was nominated as Best Director and *Judgment at Nuremberg* was a candidate for Best Picture.

1962

37. *Birdman of Alcatraz.* Hecht-Hill-Lancaster (United Artists). John Frankenheimer. Guy Trosper, based on the book by Thomas E. Gaddis. Cast: Karl Malden, Thelma Ritter, Betty Field, Edmond O'Brien, Telly Savalas, Whit Bissell. Lancaster won his third New York Film Critics Award as Best Actor, and was nominated for an Oscar. Ritter and Savalas were nominated for supporting awards.

1963

38. *A Child Is Waiting.* Stanley Kramer-Philip Langner Production (United Artists). John Cassavetes. Abbey Mann, based on his *Studio One* television play. Cast: Judy Garland, Gena Rowlands, Steven Hill, Elizabeth Wilson.

39. *The List of Adrian Messenger.* Universal. John Huston. Anthony Veiller, based on the novel by Philip MacDonald. Cast: Kirk Douglas, George C. Scott, Tony Curtis, Frank Sinatra, Robert Mitchum, Dana Wynter, Gladys Cooper, Herbert Marshall, John Merivale, John Huston.

40. *(Il Gattapardo) The Leopard.* Titanus/20th Century-Fox. Luchino Visconti. Suso Checchi D'Amico, Pasquale Festa Campanile, Massimo Franciosa, Enrico Medioli and Luchino Visconti, based on the novel by Giuseppe Lampedusa. Cast: Claudia Cardinale, Alain Delon, Rina Morelli, Romolo Valli. Score by Nino Rota. Colour. Re-released in Italian, 1983.

1964

41. *Seven Days in May.* Paramount. John Frankenheimer. Rod Serling, based on the novel by Fletcher Knebel and Charles W. Bailey II.

Cast: Kirk Douglas, Fredric March, Ava Gardner, Edmond O'Brien, Martin Balsam, George Macready, Whit Bissell, Hugh Marlowe, Andrew Duggan, Malcolm Atterbury, John Houseman, Colette Jackson.

1965

42. *The Train.* Jules Bricken Production (United Artists). John Frankenheimer. Franklin Coen and Frank Davis, based on *Le Front d l'Art* by Rose Valland. Cast: Paul Scofield, Jeanne Moreau, Michel Simon, Suzanne Flon, Albert Remy.

43. *The Hallelujah Trail.* Mirisch-Kappa Production (United Artists). John Sturges. John Gay, based on the novel by Bill Gulick. Cast: Lee Remick, Jim Hutton, Pamela Tiffin, Donald Pleasance, Brian Keith, Martin Landau, Dub Taylor, Whit Bissell, Val Avery. Colour.

All remaining movies are in colour

1966

44. *The Professionals.* Columbia. Richard Brooks. Richard Brooks, based on the novel by Frank O'Rourke. Cast: Lee Marvin, Robert Ryan, Claudia Cardinale, Jack Palance, Ralph Bellamy, Woody Strode.

1968

45. *The Scalphunters.* Levy-Gardner-Laven (United Artists). Sidney Pollack. William Norton. Cast: Shelley Winters, Telly Savalas, Ossie Davis, Dabney Coleman, Nick Cravat.

46. *The Swimmer.* Columbia. Frank Perry. Eleanor Perry, based on the *New Yorker* story by John Cheever. Cast: Janet Landgard, Janice Rule, Marge Champion, Cornelia Otis Skinner, Kim Hunter, Diana Muldaur, Joan Rivers, John Garfield Jr., House Jameson, Jan Miner, Dolph Sweet, Louise Troy, Diana Van de Vlis, Rose Gregorio. Score by Marvin Hamlisch.

1969

47. *Castle Keep.* Columbia. Sidney Pollack. Daniel Taradash and David Rayfiel, based on the novel by William Eastlake. Cast: Patrick O'Neal, Jean-Pierre Aumont, Peter Falk, Scott Wilson, Tony Bill, Al Freeman Jr., Bruce Dern, Michael Conrad.

48. *The Gypsy Moths.* MGM. John Frankenheimer. William Hanley,

based on the novel by James Drought. Cast: Deborah Kerr, Gene Hackman, Scott Wilson, Sheree North, William Windom, Bonnie Bedelia.

1970
49. *Airport*. Universal. George Seaton. George Seaton, based on the novel by Arthur Hailey. Cast: Dean Martin, Jacqueline Bissett, Jean Seberg, George Kennedy, Helen Hayes, Van Heflin, Maureen Stapleton, Barry Nelson, Dana Wynter, Barbara Hale, Lloyd Nolan. Hayes won the Supporting Actress Oscar, and Stapleton was nominated for the same award. *Airport* was nominated for Best Picture.

1971
50. *Valdez is Coming*. Ira Steiner Production (United Artists). Edwin Sherin. Roland Kibbee and David Rayfiel, based on the novel by Elmore Leonard. Cast: Susan Clark, Jon Cypher, Barton Heyman, Richard Jordan, Hector Elizondo.
51. *Lawman*. Michael Winner Production (United Artists). Michael Winner. Gerald Wilson. Cast: Robert Ryan, Lee J. Cobb, Sheree North, Joseph Wiseman, Robert Duvall, Albert Salmi, J. D. Cannon, John McGiver, Richard Jordan, John Beck.

1972
52. *Ulzana's Raid*. Universal. Robert Aldrich. Alan Sharp. Cast: Bruce Davison, Jorge Lucke, Richard Jaeckel, Lloyd Bochner.

1973
53. *Scorpio*. Scimitar Films Production (United Artists). Michael Winner. David W. Rintels and Gerald Wilson, based on the story by Rintels. Cast: Alain Delon, Paul Scofield, John Colicos, Gayle Hunnicutt, J. D. Cannon.

1974
54. *Executive Action*. National General. David Miller. Dalton Trumbo, based on the story by Donald Freed. Cast: Robert Ryan, Will Geer.
55. *The Midnight Man*. Universal, 1974. Burt Lancaster and Roland Kibbee. Burt Lancaster and Roland Kibbee, based on the novel by David Anthony. Cast: Susan Clark, Cameron Mitchell, Morgan Woodward, Harris Yulin, Catherine Bach, Ed Lauter.

1975

56. *Moses, the Lawgiver.* Lew Grade, CBC and CBS-TV. Gianfranco di Bosio. Six-part, twelve-hour series for television, later condensed to a two-hour movie. Anthony Burgess *et al.* Cast: Anthony Quayle, Irene Papas, William Lancaster.

57. *Gruppo Di Famiglia in Un Interno (Conversation Piece).* Luchino Visconti. Luchino Visconti. Cast: Silvana Magnano, Helmut Berger, Claudia Cardinale.

1976

58. *The Cassandra Crossing.* Lew Grade/Carlo Ponti—Associated General Films—International Cine Productions (Twentieth Century-Fox). George Pan Cosmatos. Tom Mankiewicz, Robert Pan and George Pan Cosmatos. Cast: Richard Harris, Ava Gardner, Sophia Loren, Martin Sheen, Ingrid Thulin, Lee Strasberg, Ann Turkel, Lionel Stander. Music by Jerry Goldsmith.

59. *Buffalo Bill and the Indians.* Robert Altman. Robert Altman and Alan Rudolph, based on the play *Indians* by Arthur Kopit. Cast: Paul Newman, Joel Grey, Geraldine Chaplin, Kevin McCarthy, Harvey Keitel, Denver Pyle, John Considine, Pat McCormick, Shelley Duvall.

60. *Victory at Entebbe.* Marvin J. Chomsky. Ernest Kinoy. Taped for television, later converted to film. Anthony Hopkins, Elizabeth Taylor, Helen Hayes, Linda Blair, Helmut Berger, Kirk Douglas, Richard Dreyfuss, Theodore Bikel, Jessica Walter, David Groh.

1977

61. *1900 (Novecento).* Bernardo Bertolucci. Bernardo Bertolucci, Franco Arcalli and Giuseppe Bertolucci. Cast: Robert De Niro, Gerard Depardieu, Dominique Sanda, Donald Sutherland, Sterling Hayden, Alida Valli.

62. *The Island of Dr Moreau.* American International. Don Taylor. John Herman Shaner and Al Ramrus, based on the novel by H. G. Wells (Re-make). Cast: Michael York, Barbara Carrera, Nigel Davenport, Richard Baseheart, Nick Cravat.

63. *Twilight's Last Gleaming.* Lorimar. Robert Aldrich. Ronald M. Cohen and Edward Huebsch, from the novel by Walter Wager. Cast: Richard Widmark, Charles Durning, Melvyn Douglas, Paul Winfield, Burt Young, Joseph Cotten.

1978

64. *Go Tell the Spartans.* Mar Vista Productions. Ted Post. Wendell Mayes, based on the novel *Incident at Muc Wa* by Daniel Ford. Cast: Craig Wasson, Jonathan Goldsmith, Joe Unger, Dennis Howard, David Clenner, Evan King, Dolph Sweet.

1979

65. *Zulu Dawn.* A Samarkand Production. Douglas Hickox. Cy Endfield and Anthony Storey. Cast: Peter O'Toole, Simon Ward, Nigel Davenport, Michael Jayston, Peter Vaughn, James Faulkner, Christopher Cazenove, Anna Calder-Marshall, Freddie Jones, Denholm Elliott, John Mills, Bob Hoskins, Ronald Pickup. Music by Elmer Bernstein. Some dialogue was in Zulu with English subtitles.

1980

66. *Cattle Annie and Little Britches.* Lamont Johnson. Robert Ward and David Eyre. Cast: Diane Lane, Amanda Plummer, Rod Steiger, Scott Glenn, John Savage.

1981

67. *Atlantic City.* Paramount. Louis Malle. John Guare. Cast: Susan Sarandon, Kate Reid. Lancaster won his fourth New York Film Critics Best Actor Award, plus Best Actor Awards from the National Society of Film Critics, the Los Angeles Film Critics Association and the British Academy Award, and an Oscar nomination. *Atlantic City* was nominated as Best Picture, Sarandon for Best Actress, Malle for direction and Guare for best screenplay.

68. *La Pelle (The Skin).* Opera Film/Gaumont-Italia. Liliana Cavani. Robert Katz, from the novel by Curzio Malaparte. Cast: Claudia Cardinale, Marcello Mastroianni, Ken Marshall, Alexander King.

1982

69. *Marco Polo.* NBC Television/RAI.

1983

70. *Local Hero.* (David Puttnam) Warner Brothers. Bill Forsyth. Cast: Peter Riegert, Denis Lawson, Fulton MacKay, Peter Capaldi, Christopher Rosycki, Jenny Seagrove, Jennifer Black.

71. *The Osterman Weekend.* 20th Century-Fox. Sam Peckinpah. Alan

Sharp, based on the novel by Robert Ludlum. Cast: Rutger Hauer, John Hurt, Craig T. Nelson, Dennis Hopper, Chris Sarandon, Meg Foster, Helen Shaver.

Hecht-Lancaster films in which he did not appear
1. *The First Time*, Columbia, 1952; Frank Tashlin. Cast: Barbara Hale, Robert Cummings, Jeff Donnell.
2. *Marty*, United Artists, 1955; Delbert Mann. Cast: Ernest Borgnine, Betsy Blair. The film won four Oscars, including Best Picture, Best Actor for Borgnine, Best Director for Mann and Best Screenplay for Paddy Chayefsky.
3. *The Bachelor Party*, United Artists, 1957. Delbert Mann. Cast: Don Murray, Carolyn Jones, E. G. Marshall, Jack Warden, Phillip Abbott, Nancy Marchand. Jones was nominated for the Best Supporting Actress Oscar.
4. *Take a Giant Step*, United Artists, 1959. Philip Leacock. Cast: Johnny Nash, Estelle Hemsley, Ruby Dee, Frederick O'Neal, Beah Richards.

Lancaster stage appearances
1. *Stars and Gripes* (European War Tour, 1942-45).
2. *A Sound of Hunting*, by Harry Brown, on Broadway, 1945.
3. *Knickerbocker Holiday*, Musical by Maxwell Anderson and Kurt Weill, San Francisco and Los Angeles, 1971.
4. *The Boys of Autumn*, by Bernard Sabath, San Francisco, 1981. With Kirk Douglas.

BIBLIOGRAPHY

Bosworth, Patricia. *Montgomery Clift: A Biography.* New York: Bantam, 1979.

Bury, Lee and Thompson, Douglas. (London) *News of the World,* Interview, March 25, 1979.

Cottrell, John. *Laurence Olivier: A Biography.* Englewood, N.J.: Prentice Hall, 1975.

Cutts, John. "Long Shot," *Films and Filming,* December 1971.

Durkheim, Jean. *Cinemonde,* Interview in Venice, September 18, 1962.

Davis, Victor. (London) *Daily Express,* Interview, January 31, 1977.

Dewson, Lisa. "Life, Lancaster and Local Hero," *Photoplay,* April 1983.

Edwards, Sydney. (London) *Evening Standard,* Interview, June 6, 1977.

Garrett, Gerard. "Enter Burt Lancaster with Fireworks," (London) *Evening Standard,* May 1, 1964.

Gow, Gordon. *Films and Filming,* Interview, January 1974.

Ferguson, Ken. "Movies, Money, Religion," *Photoplay,* June 1976.

Graham, Sheilah. *Confessions of a Hollywood Columnist.* New York: William Morrow and Co., 1969.

Haden Guest, Anthony. "How Brooks Brought the Bible to Burt," *Radio Times,* July 1975.

Hall, William. (London) *Evening News,* Interview, February 13, 1968.

———. (London) *Evening News,* Interview, August 6, 1968.

———. *(London) Evening News,* Interview, May 22, 1970.

———. *(London) Evening News,* Interview, January 23, 1974.

Hinxman, Margaret. (London) *Daily Mail.* Interview, May 16, 1982.

Hirschorn, Clive, *Radio Times,* Interview, August 15-21, 1981.

Hunter, Allan and Astaire, Mark. *Local Hero: The Making of the Film.* New York: Frederick Ungar, 1983.

Huston, John. *An Open Book.* New York: Alfred Knopf, 1980.

Lancaster, Burt. "Hollywood Drove Me to a Double Life," *Films and Filming,* January 1962.

_____. *Films Illustrated,* Extracts from National Film Theatre panel appearance, September 1973.

Lewin, David. (London) *Daily Mail,* Interview, July 15, 1970.

Malcolm, Derek. (London) *The Guardian,* Interview, August 4, 1972.

Mann, Roderick. (London) *Sunday Express,* Interview July 2, 1972.

Morgan, James. "Hecht Lancaster Productions," *Sight and Sound,* June 1955.

Mosley, Leonard, (London) *Daily Express,* Interview, September 26, 1952.

Ottaway, Robert. *TV Times,* Interview, March 15, 1973.

Parrish, James Robert. *The Tough Guys.* New Rochelle, N.Y.: Arlington House, 1976.

Pickard, Roy. *The Award Movies: A Complete Guide from A-Z.* New York: Schocken, 1981.

Piller, Jack. (London) *Daily Herald,* Interview, August 7, 1962.

Pratley, Gerald. *The Cinema of John Frankenheimer.* Cranbury, N.J.: A. S. Barnes, 1969.

Prowse, D., "The Leopard," (London) *Sunday Times,* August 1962.

Reed, Rex. *Travolta to Keaton.* New York: Berkley, 1980.

Rogers, Byron. "Burt Lancaster," (London) *Sunday Telegraph,* December 12, 1976.

Robinson, Robert. (London) *Sunday Graphic,* Interview, July 20, 1958.

Salisbury, Lesley. "Sissy Stuff that Led to a Tough-guy Stardom," *TV Times,* January 16-22, 1982.

Schuster, Mel. *Films in Review,* August-September 1969.

Servadio, Gaia. *Luchino Visconti: A Biography.* London: Weidenfeld and Nicholson, 1981.

Thomas, Tony. *Burt Lancaster.* New York: Pyramid, 1975.

Vermilye, Jerry. *Burt Lancaster.* New York: Falcon/Crescent, 1971.

Williams, John. "Between Takes," *Films Illustrated,* October 1972.

Winters, Shelley. *Shelley, Also Known as Shirley.* New York: Ballantine, 1981.

Wiseman, Thomas. (London) *Evening Standard,* Interview, August 1, 1958.

INDEX